CW01673005

ESL ONLINE GAMES

Have fun teaching English

Interactive activities to engage students of all ages and bring the joy of learning into your virtual classroom.

Copyright

ISBN: 978-0-9558645-7-5

Please note that this book is written using British English spelling and punctuation.

Contents

Part One
Detailed Index Key

Long Game — 20 minutes or more

 10 minutes or longer with a class

 5 minutes or longer with a class

 No prep

Low Prep — Preparation under 5 minutes

 Speaking

 Listening

 Spelling
Writing

 Reading

Grammar — Grammar game

Vocab — Vocabulary game

 Conversation

P — Pronunciation

 Annotation tools
Or pen and paper

 Draw or colour

Beg	Beginner
Int	Intermediate student
Adv	Advanced student

Many games have variants and are flexible

Alphabet word game p.59

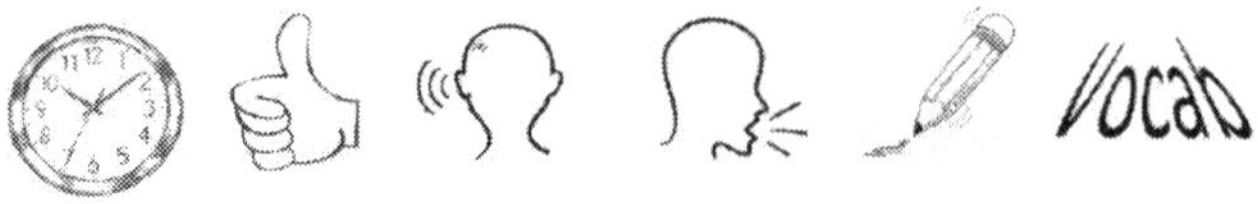

10 to adult All levels Individual or class in groups
Pronunciation, vowels, consonants, alphabet, new vocabulary, spelling

Anagrams p.60

10 to adult All levels Individual or any class
Spelling, vocabulary revision, grammar drill

Battleships p.61

All ages All levels Individual or pairwork for class
Vocabulary revision, grammar, Q&A

Bingo p.65

6 to adult All levels 2 to any class size
Learning or revising vocabulary or grammar

Blind directions p.68

All ages All levels Individual or pairwork for class
Giving directions, commands

Brainstorm p.81

6 to adult High Beg to Adv Individual or teams
Any vocabulary topics, short grammar drills

Buddy reading p.82

All ages All levels Individual, or class in pairs
Multi-level activity, reading, listening, pronunciation, Q&A

Build a sentence p.84

All ages All levels Individual, class in pairs or groups
Vocabulary, grammar, general language, making sentences, parts of speech

Call my bluff p.85

10 to adult All levels Individual, any class size
General language, conversation

Call my bluff definitions p.89

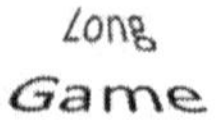

Students prep for homework

12 to adult Low Int to Adv Individual, any class size
Vocabulary definitions, metaphors

Chanting games p.91

Vocab Grammar

All ages   All levels   Individual and Class
Vocabulary, grammar drills. Examples are given for adjectives, adverbs, comparatives, descriptions, pronouns, the past tense of 'to be,' professions, vocabulary, and weather.

Charades p.94

Long Game Low Prep

10 to adult   Intermediate   Individual and classes
General language, film, book, and song titles

Charades race p.96

Vocab Grammar

All ages   All levels   Individual, any class size in pairs
Any vocabulary topics, short grammar drills for any topic

Colour the card p.97

Long Game Vocab Grammar

4 to adult   Beg to Int   Individual, class in pairs
Colours. What colour is? What colour are?

Commands game p.98

Vocab

4 to adult   Beg to Int   Individual, whole-class activity
Great for   Commands, verbs

Drawing race

p.129

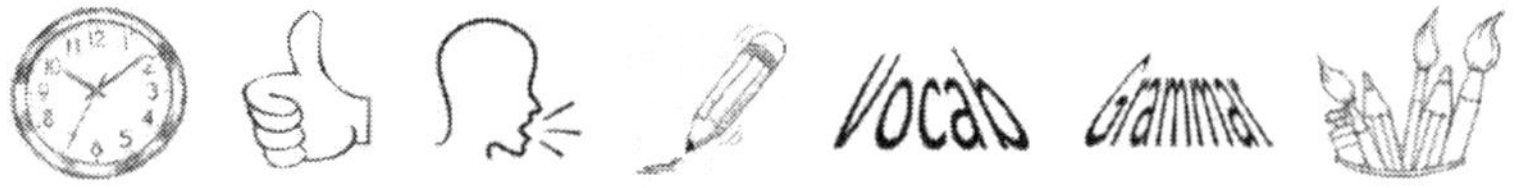

6 to adult   Beg to Int   Individual, pairwork for any class size
Q & A, grammar drill, vocabulary revision

Either-or

p.131

8 to adult   High Beg to Adv   Individual, any class in teams
Conversation, fluency, general English

Fill in drill

p.132

All ages   All levels   Individual, whole-class activity
Grammar and vocabulary drill, general English

Find a friend

p.134

6 to adult   Beg to Int   4 to any number in groups
Q and A, conversation, speaking fluency

Fizz buzz

p.134

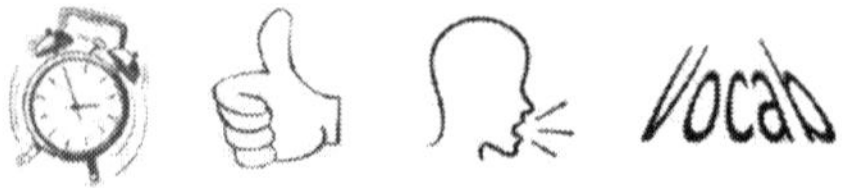

6 to adult   Beg to Int   Individual, any number in groups
Counting, vocabulary

Flip a card p.136

6 to adult All levels Individual, any number in groups
Vocabulary revision, sentence construction, deck of cards needed

Forfeits p.138

Forfeits are silly or sensible things students can do as part of a game

All ages All levels Individual, any class size
Vocabulary revision, grammar, or something fun

Gap-fill game p.139

All ages All levels Individual, classes in pairs or groups
Grammar drills and vocabulary or general English

Getting to know you p.141

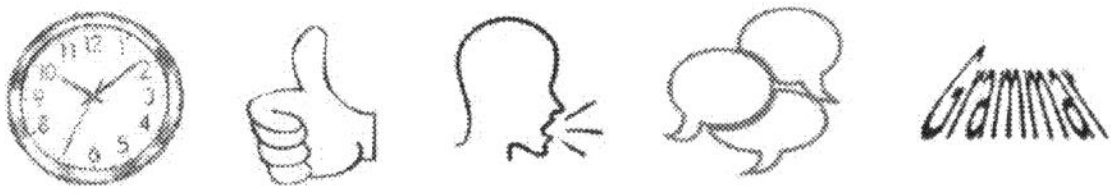

8 to adult Beg to Int Two students minimum to class
Q&A drill, grammar drill, or fluency and conversation game

Grammar auction p.142

8 to adult All levels Two students minimum to class
Grammar drill, grammar revision, general language

Guess the word p.150

6 to adult Beg to Int 2 to 30
Vocabulary brainstorming game

Guess who listening p.151

All ages Beg to Adv Individual, any class size
General language, descriptions

Hand sign stories p.153

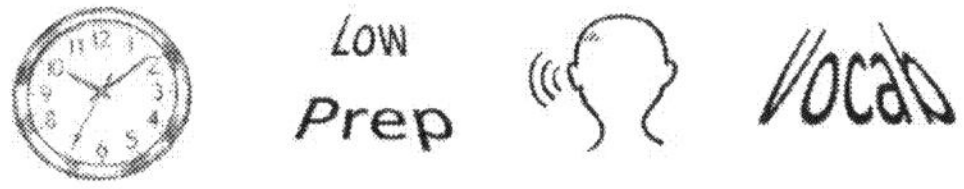

All ages All levels Individual, any class, whole-class activity
Learning new vocabulary, revising, listening skills, TPR

Hangman (Snowman) p.157

6 to adult Beginner Individual, class in pairs
Alphabet, spelling, vocabulary revision

Hangman variant (also known as Rivet) p.159

6 to adult Beginner Individual, any class in groups
Question & answer drill, grammar drill, vocabulary

Interviews p.165

10 to adult Low Int to Adv Individual, any class in pairs
Conversation, Q&A, fluency, general language

I spy p.170

4 to 12 Beginners Individual and small groups
Vocabulary revision, alphabet revision

I took a trip p.171

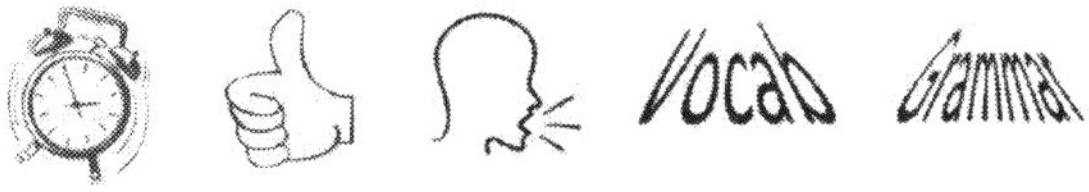

4 to 12 Beginners Individual, any class in groups
Past tense question forms, vocabulary, other tenses

Jigsaw listening p.171

8 to adult All levels Individual, any class size
General listening skills, specific grammar or vocabulary in context

Jigsaw reading find the odd one out p.174

10 to adult Beg to Adv Individual, any class in groups
Reading fluency, reading grammar drill

Jokes p.175

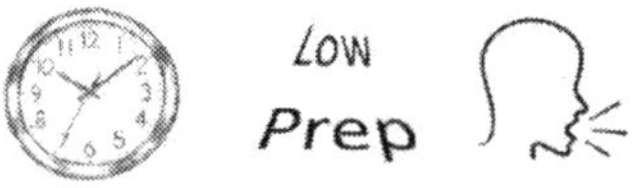

6 to adult Low Int to Adv Individual, any class size
Speaking fluency, intonation, pronunciation, general language

Jump the line p.176

4 to adult Beginner Individual, whole-class activity
Introducing new vocabulary or grammar

Keep a straight face p.177

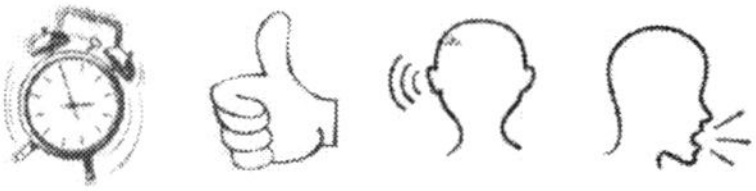

4 to 12 Beg to Int Individual, whole-class activity
Questions

Last word p.178

6 to adult Beg to Int Individual, class in groups
Vocabulary revision, grammar game

Listen and draw p.179

4 to adult Beginner Individual, whole-class activity
Learning the alphabet, learning nouns

Lucky number p.180

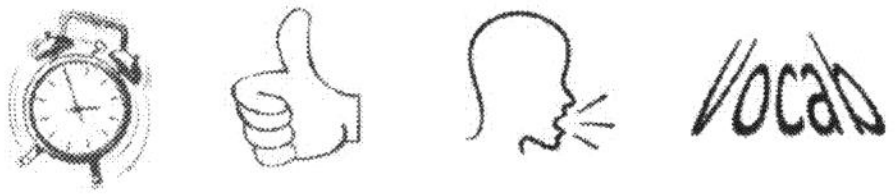

4 to 12 Beginner Any class size in groups of 3 to 6
Counting, alphabet, vocabulary drill

Mad gabs p.180

8 to adult All levels Individual, any class size
Fun, speaking, pronunciation

Mad libs p.181

10 to adult Int to Adv Individual, any class size in groups
Parts of speech review, vocabulary, listening skills

Make a match p.185

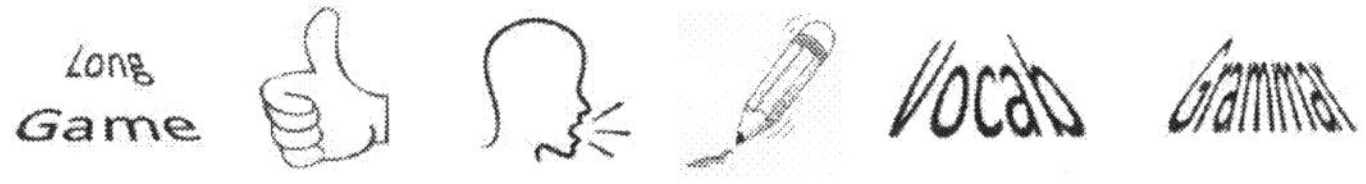

All ages All levels Individual, any class size in pairs
Vocabulary, short grammar drill any topic, parts of speech, comparatives

Make a sentence or a question p.188

6 to adult All levels 2 to 30
Questions, sentences, grammar drill

Making up stories p.189

All ages Int to Adv Individual, any class in groups
General language, storytelling, grammar

Mastermind with words p.192

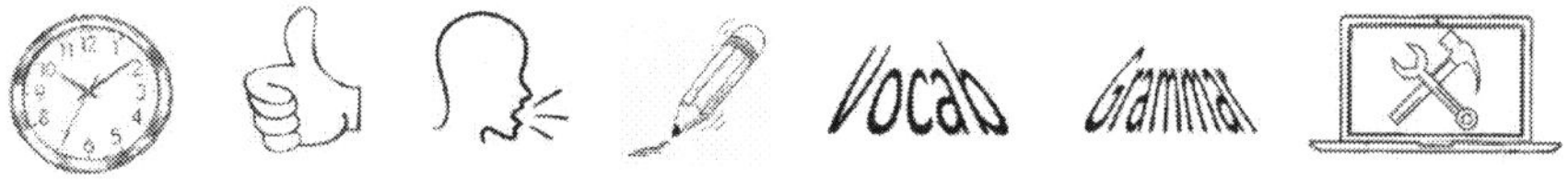

8 to adult All levels Individual, class in pairs
Spelling drill, grammar

Miming game p.194

All ages Beg to Int Individual, class in groups
Vocabulary, grammar, Q&A

Miming vocabulary p.195

All ages Beg to Int Individual, class in groups
Learning new vocabulary, vocabulary revision, alphabet

Movie activity 1 – advertisements p.196

Use my ex. then students prep for homework

10 to adult High Beg to Int Individual, any class size
General language, critical thinking

Movie activity 2 – Film trailers and extracts p.200

10 to adult High Beg to Adv Individual, any class size
Listening, discussion

Movie activity 3 – Extract from a documentary, news, and interviews p.201

Students prep for homework

12 to adult High Beg to Adv Individual, any class size
Listening, discussion

Mystery bag p.204

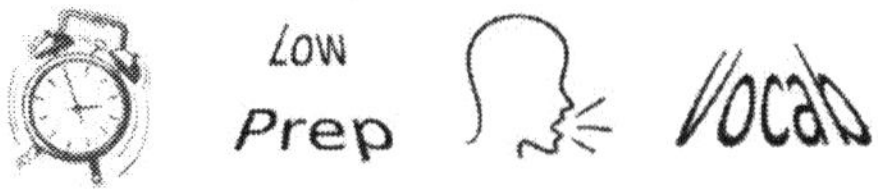

All ages Beg to Int Individual, any class size
Vocabulary

Name the thing p.205

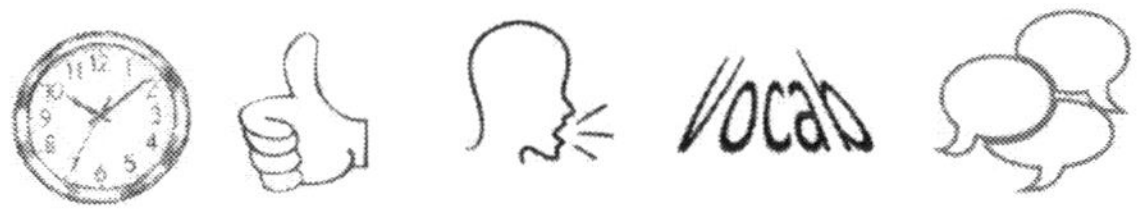

All ages Low Int to Adv Individual, class in pairs or groups
Conversation, questions, comparatives, descriptions

No 'yes' or 'no' p.207

All ages All levels Individual and small classes
Short-form answers, questions, general English, verb tense drill

Noughts and crosses p.208

4 to adult Beg to Low Int Individual, any class in pairs
Vocabulary drill, sentences, questions drill

Odd one out p.210

All ages All levels Individual, any class size
Conversation, speaking fluency, grammar, verb tenses, vocabulary

One lemon p.212

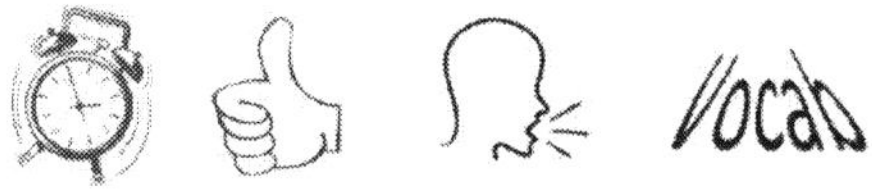

5 to adult Beginner Minimum 3, groups of 8 to 12 students
Warm-up, numbers, singular and plural nouns, vocabulary

Persuasion p.213

12 to adult High Beg to Adv 3 minimum to any class size
Conversation and general English, general and specialist topics

Photo activities p.216

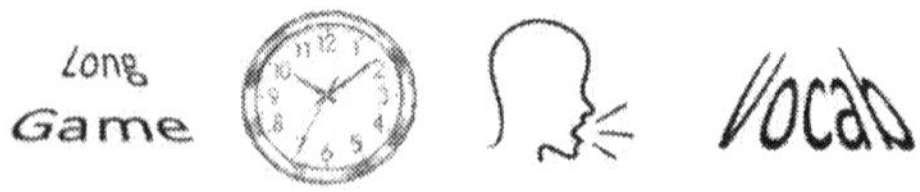

8 to adult All levels Individual, any class in groups
Vocabulary, useful for shy students because participation is anonymous

Pictionary p.218

5 to adult Beg to Int Individual to class up to 40, in teams
Vocabulary revision

Picture flashcards p.219

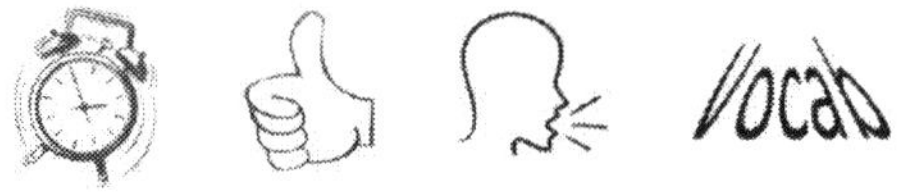

4 to adult Beg to Int Individual, any class size
Learning and revising vocabulary. Flashcards needed.

Picture memory challenge p.220

6 to adult Beg to Int Individual, any class in pairs or teams
Prepositions, vocabulary, Q and A, drilling a verb tense

Ping pang pong p.223

6 to adult Beginner 6 to 30 students
Numbers, vocabulary drill for beginners

Presentations p.224

Long Game *Students prep for homework*

All ages High Beg to Adv Individual, any class size
General English, speaking, listening, skills for life activity

Pronunciation hands up p.225

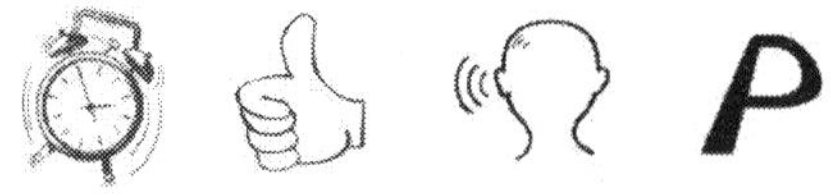

5 to adult All levels Individual, any class size
Phonemes, pronunciation

Question and answer p.226

4 to 12 Beg to Int Small classes in teams
Question and answer drill

Question and answer memory game p.227

4 to 12 Beg to Int Individual, class in pairs or groups
Question and answer drill or fluency

Question and answer lottery match p.228

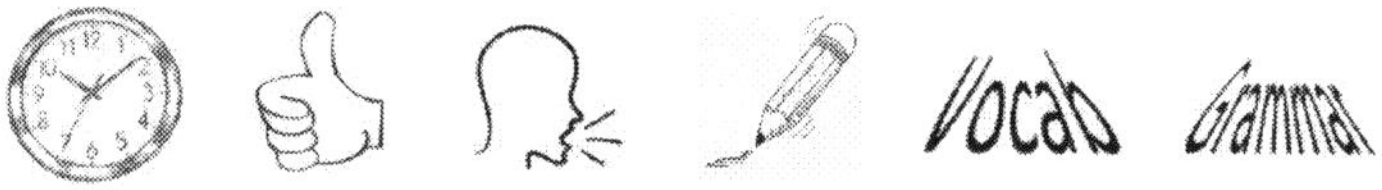

6 to 12 All levels All groups and class sizes
Question and answer revision, fluency

Questionnaires market research project p.229

8 to adult All levels Minimum 4 up to any class size
General language. Individuals prepare beforehand.

Remember and write p.239

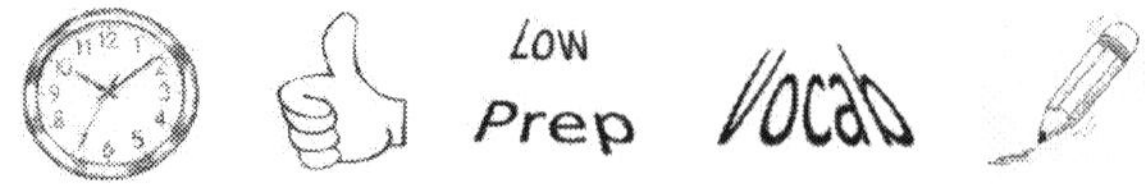

6 to adult Beg to Int Individual, any class, whole-class game
Vocabulary revision, grammar drill

Round-robin p.240

All ages Beg to Int Individual, any class size
Speaking fluency, short conversations, small talk, giving advice

Scissors paper stone p.242

6 to adult Beg to Int Individual, any class in pairs or 3s
Vocabulary revision game

Sentence playoff p.243

All ages Int to Adv Individual, any class in teams
General English

Shopping list memory game p.242

6 to adult Beg to Int Individual, any class in pairs or groups
Vocabulary revision, grammar drill

Spell and act

p.255

6 to 12 | Beg to Int | Individual, class of up to fifteen
Spelling, alphabet, vocabulary, cameras on

Spelling game

p.255

6 to adult | All levels | Pairwork, small groups, teams
Spelling, vocabulary

Spot the Difference

p.256

All ages | Beg to Int | Individual, class in pairs or groups
Contrasting present and past tense, general language, and vocabulary

Stop!

p.257

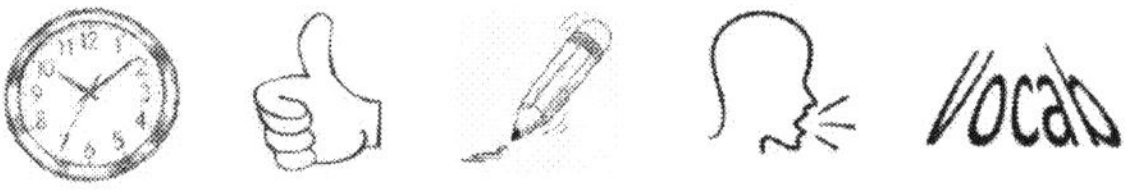

8 to adult | Beg to Int | Individual, any class size
Vocabulary revision, general knowledge

Summaries and expansions

p.259

Teen and adult | Int to Adv | Individual, any class size
General English

Telling stories p.260

8 to adult High Beg to Adv Individual, any class size
Speaking and writing skills for general language fluency

Thirty circles p.263

All ages All levels Individual, any class size
Exploring vocabulary, optional flash-fiction speaking or writing activity

Time bomb p.264

All ages All levels Individual, class up to fifteen
Vocabulary, grammar drill, Q and A

Tongue Twisters p.265

6 to adult Int to Adv Individual, any class in groups
Fluency in speaking, pronunciation focus

TPR p.267

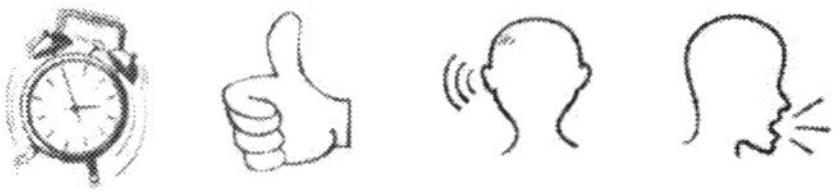

All ages All levels Individual, any class size
Concentration, immersion, participation, energy levels

Triangles talking point p.268

8 to adult High Beg to Adv Minimum 3, any class in groups
Small talk, conversation, comparatives

True or false vocabulary and grammar drill p.269

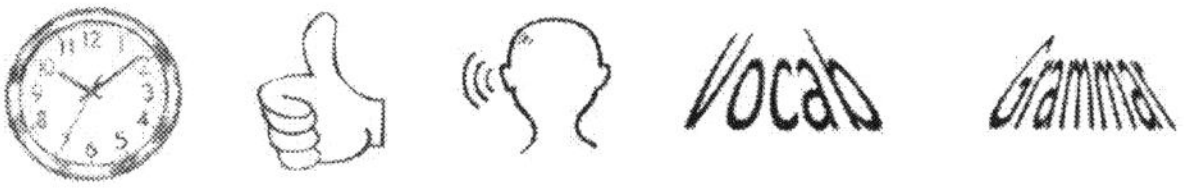

4 to adult Beg to Low Int Individual, any class size
Vocabulary or grammar drill, revision, prepositions, a/an/some, plurals

Twenty seconds p.271

All ages All levels Individual, any class size in groups
Grammar drill and fluency speaking exercise. Timer needed.

Very Large Class Choral Work p.272

4 to 12 Beg to Low Int Any group size and large classes
Question and answer drill, grammar drill

Vocabulary circle game p.273

5 to adult All levels Individual, class in groups
New vocabulary drill, new grammar drill, story invention

Vocabulary memory game — p.274

8 to 12 | Int to Adv | Individual, class in pairs or groups

Learning to spell or revising vocabulary

What am I? — p.275

10 to adult | Int to Adv | Individual, class in pairs or groups

Questions, short-form answers

What's that sound? — p.276

All ages | Beg to Int | Individual, any class size

Vocabulary. Sounds needed. Teens prepare music version.

Which one has gone? — p.277

All ages | Beginner | Individual, class in pairs or groups

Vocabulary drill, Q and A grammar drill. No prep with flashcards.

Who said it? — p.280

All ages | Beg to Low Int | Minimum 5, any class size

Telling the time, Q & A drill, general English

Who wants to be a millionaire? Adaptation p.280

All ages to adult All levels Individual, any class size
General English for fluency, vocabulary drill, grammar drill, Q&A

Why? p.282

6 to adult All levels Individual, any class size in groups
Conversation, general language, imagination

Word association and word chain games p.283

8 to adult High Beg to Adv Individual, any class in groups
Vocabulary, pronunciation, spelling

Word chain around the alphabet p.284

8 to adult High Beg to Adv Individual, class in groups of 3-5
Vocabulary revision, general knowledge

Word flashcards p.285

All ages Beginner Individual, any class size
Vocabulary revision, vocabulary drill game

Word photographs p.287

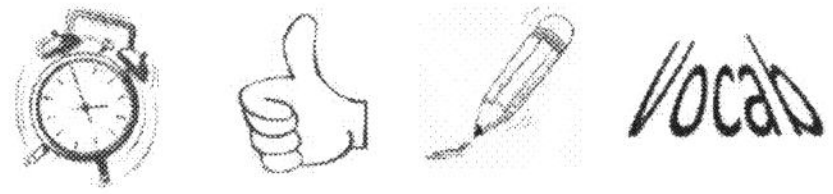

6 to adult All levels Individual, any class size
Spelling, vocabulary revision

Word stress chant and spell or draw p.288

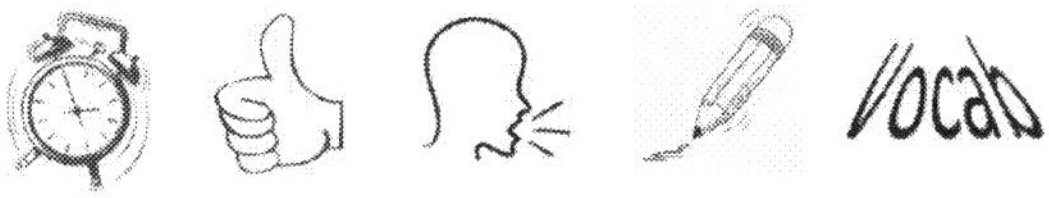

All ages All levels Any class size
Word stress, fluency, vocabulary revision, spelling

Zip zap vocabulary revision p.288

5 to adult Beg to Int Small groups, classes in groups
Vocabulary revision, short phrases

Introduction

Thank you for choosing this book. I hope it will bring smiles and laughter to your online lessons and help your students learn more effectively. I am available to help you make it a success, so feel free to contact me via www.teachingenglishgames.com.

Teaching online can be fun

Teaching languages online has limitations compared to an actual classroom, but lessons can be just as engaging and effective with imaginative activities. Getting to grips with new software or online platforms can be a nightmare for some, but with a willing attitude and some practise, anyone can crack it. Teaching great lessons is so rewarding that it's worth the effort.

This book contains some online dos and don'ts, techie tips, and a host of imaginative and varied activities to help make your online lessons satisfying, successful, and fun!

Get started

Get started with tech

If you are new to online teaching, read the intro and tips and dedicate time to getting set up. Learn how to use your online platform via online tutorials. Practise by giving some lessons to a friend or non-paying customer. Mastering your interface is necessary and will reap its rewards.

Get started with activities

Teachers often want an activity for a topic or grammatical rule. To select one, go to the detailed index and peruse the 'great for' descriptions for every game. The detailed index also specifies the category, group size, level, age, materials, and preparation of every game.

The category tells you if the game is a drill or for general fluency. If it's a drill, use the activity for any grammar point or vocabulary topic. If the category denotes a fluency activity, it is ideal for general English, although the teacher can often orientate students to use a vocabulary theme or grammar topic. The category also refers to the skill solicited, although the four key skills (listening, speaking, reading, and writing) are frequently overlapping. Many games are adaptable to multiple uses.

The group size defines the number of students required, from one to one to a class. The group size also indicates whether the activity is for the class as a whole or whether splitting students into pairs or groups in breakout rooms is required.

The age, level, materials, and preparation are self-explanatory.

The 'Great for' tells you whether the game is suitable for drilling grammar, vocabulary, parts of speech, pronunciation, or anything that fits well, and whether it is for generating conversational.

Just do it

The more you use this book, the easier teaching online will become, so get stuck in and try a game. At worst, you might get tangled in tech, or it might be a flop, but at least that gives you something to improve on. At best, it'll be a hit! Rather than waiting until everything is perfect and reading the whole book, use one game in your next lesson. In fact, do not read the entire book. You will glaze over and may even feel overwhelmed by all the choices.

If you have complete beginners, try One lemon. It's easy, silly, and fun, as well as being an excellent vocabulary drill. It's ideal for beginners to start gaining confidence in saying short phrases in their new language.

For intermediate students, try Battleships or Hand sign stories.

For advanced students, use Call my bluff definitions.

Feel free to contact me at info@teachingenglishgames.com if you are stuck. I am here to help you make using this book a success. If you are enjoying your online lessons, the chances are your students will be too.

Avoid TTT (teacher talking time) and content overdose

If the lesson is a monologue by the teacher, students will soon find distractions. Bored or frustrated children will soon fidget and stop looking at the screen. I have witnessed online language teachers talking relentlessly to fill a void or prevent students from drifting off into their own world. After a quick hello and polite inquiry about the weather, the teacher launches into the lesson, continually chatting and playing one video after the other. The student is bombarded with content. The missing element is active participation. The student can even feel frustrated through lack of opportunity to join in. Students may learn to understand English, but their speaking skills will be close to non-existent. They can take online language lessons till the cows come home, but they won't get any better at speaking if they have no opportunity to do it. This book is about engaging students and help them focus, enjoy, and participate actively in their learning.

Limit passive activities

Some teachers follow an online coursebook, giving the same lesson as if they were all in class. It's useful, but it can be pretty dull. I observed kids being far more interested in the software than in the lesson, fiddling about minimizing windows, moving them around, and clicking on things while the teacher drones on and ploughs through the exercise. This book will help you give more imaginative lessons.

Tips for engaging students

1. Be enthusiastic.
2. Use a lively, engaging tone of voice, smile, look straight at the camera often.

3. Switch off the camera feed of yourself so that students can see you, but you cannot see yourself. Aside from being narcissistic, it's not natural to be watching yourself when you are supposed to be focusing on your students.
4. If you take an interest in your students, they are more likely to take an interest in what you have to say. Ask them how they are and if they had a good weekend. Ask individually with one to four students. With more, suggest an emoji or global thumbs-up response to avoid an endless round-robin that takes a chunk of the lesson. Although cursory, this nonetheless acknowledges your students and shows you care about them.
5. Encourage students to participate and respond physically. Use thumbs-up for yes; as a way for students to interact, vote, respond or check they understand.
6. Have students hold up a number to the camera to score something on a sliding scale or show how many points they won.
7. If your lesson is longer than an hour, include some physical stretching or movement every 50 minutes or so.
8. Make sure students have more talking time than the teacher.
9. Use a variety of tasks and keep the pace moving.
10. Use visuals, such as pictures, diagrams, sketches, illustrations, photos, tangible objects, charts, and short films. This way, students won't have to stare at the teacher for the entire lesson.
11. Use audio other than just your voice—recordings, radio excerpts, and songs, combined with video and stories.
12. With kids, use plenty of actions and physical props like puppets.
13. Use 'breakout' rooms, where students can work in pairs or groups. Zoom has these.
14. Give students control of the annotation tools whenever possible since this makes them more involved in the activity. For example, if playing Connect Four one on one, and using software where only one person can manipulate the controls at a time, let your student fill in the colours for the both of you. This point is valid for kids and adults. Kids often love playing with the software, and either way, it enhances the student's participation. If filling in a Battleships grid as a pre-activity task, let the student do the typing. If the spelling is wrong, type the word into the chat so the student can correct it.

15. Share the load. To allow you more freedom to observe how an activity is going, give some tasks to students. These might be keeping score, keeping time, writing things in screen share or chat, saving screenshots, being team leader, downloading documents for a group task, and so on.
16. Use games from this book, and you'll have fewer students sloping off to use the bathroom mid-lesson or pretending their camera or microphone do not work.

Tips for teaching online

1. Have your lesson plan bullets on your desk, easy to glance at without interrupting the flow of your screen shares or the lesson.
2. It's much better if participants have their cameras on since this encourages participation. Visual contact gives you feedback as to how students are interacting with you and the lesson.
3. Don't be discouraged by blank looks. It does not mean that students are not engaging just because they are staring blankly at their screens. That said, stop talking and get your students to join in.
4. Have students tell you when they are ready, that they understand and when they have finished. Verbal feedback is a form of participation and lets you know students are following the lesson when you have too many to keep track of individually.
5. Have an offline task as a backup in case your network goes down or slows down.
6. You are in charge so call on students to speak one by one. Only one person can speak at a time in the online environment; overlapping dialogue does not work.
7. Don't abandon your students to breakout rooms with no feedback from you for more than 10 minutes.
8. If doing a drill activity, make sure students have all chanted the required language in unison several times before releasing them into breakout rooms to practise. Potentially provide a recording of the drill for students to access if they are stuck.
9. When you put people in groups, pop in and listen without interrupting. Visit all the groups quickly to see how many have understood the task and are on the ball. That is better than going

to one group, discovering that they don't know what to do, and getting bogged down explaining everything again just to them. Then the time is up, and you have no idea what went on in the other rooms!

Making teams

Many games are best played in teams. Teams create a spirit of camaraderie and a friendly way to play for points without individuals being shown up as losers. It's important to make teams quickly. Try these ideas:

1. If your first name starts with A-G, you are on team one, H-N, team two, and O-Z, team three.
2. If your first name has one syllable, you are on team one, two syllables, team two and three or more syllables, team three.
3. If you are fourteen or younger, you are in group one. If you are fifteen or older, you are in group two.
4. If you have light hair, you are on team one, dark hair, team two.
5. If you are wearing anything blue, you are in group one; anything red, you are in group two.
6. Show a numbered list of your students' first names in alphabetical order. Students write down which number is next to their name, and that is their number. Numbers 1-10 are in team one, 11-20 team two, and so on.

Looking good in front of the camera

Do

1. Know your audience, so you choose relevant content and dress appropriately to your relationship with them.
2. Look nice. Wear decent clothes, do your hair and make sure you don't have spinach in your teeth!

3. Sit up straight. Chin up and shoulders back. Keep your chin high all the time; it gives off a positive vibe and makes you look interested. Raise your computer so that your eyes are level with the camera.
4. Look straight into the camera. It takes eye contact to make a relationship. Every student in class will think you are looking right at them.
5. Smile often.
6. Use an open posture, not a power pose (no pyramid hands or crossed arms). You are an approachable guide, not a guru.
7. Keep relatively still but not rigid. If you move around too much, people may get seasick! Keep your eyes on the camera most of the time. 100% camera eye contact can look artificial. It's natural to look up when thinking, so go ahead, but don't swivel your eyes evasively all over the place.
8. Slow down when you state essential points, then repeat the core point slower again, spacing — out — the words.
9. Use repetition. Tell students what you are going to tell them. Tell them. Then tell them what you told them.
10. Avoid distractions. These include kids running about in the background, the dog, however cute, and a load of mess behind you. Turn the volume off on your phone, so you can happily ignore it. If you own a vociferous parrot, take the lesson in another room.
11. If you feel nervous, film yourself and observe what you are doing well and what needs improvement. Work on things you don't like. Do you look natural? Are you blinking and breathing?
12. Record yourself and listen to your voice through headphones. Do you make annoying noises with your lips or saliva when you breathe or pause? Those sounds are irritating, especially if students wear headphones and have your voice right in their

ears. You can avoid them by opening your mouth silently before you start to speak.

13. Prepare. Know what you are going to say for the first minute of the lesson and rehearse it. This way, you'll get off to a great start and feel confident to continue.
14. Practise! You'll get better quickly and become more confident and engaging.

Don't

1. Don't chew gum or eat. It looks unprofessional, and all eyes will be on you. I think drinking water or a cup of something is OK, as long as you don't interrupt the flow. I allow students to chew gum if they wish since multiple studies claim that it helps some people relax and be more focused. So why not. It's a worthwhile trade-off for looking like a cow chewing on cud.
2. Avoid being a stern authority figure. It won't work online. Students may disengage with you as a person and have less motivation to learn from you. Instead, be yourself, relaxed, confident, and enthusiastic. If you are not naturally excited about teaching your topic, you should not be teaching it! If you have confidence issues and a quiet, monotonous voice, work on both. Use activities from this book. Students will warm to you because of your interesting lessons, which will boost your confidence.

Techie Tips

1. Don't be on time, be early! You may take longer to connect than you thought, or there may be a software upgrade pending. Open all documents and online tabs that you plan to share during the lesson.
2. Do keep it simple; limit the number of tabs you have open because it can become confusing in the heat of the moment, especially when you are getting started. There are splendid tools available, such as 'teacher.goguardian,' which lets you view all your student's computers to see if they are on task and allows students to message you. However, having that open

along with your video platform, screen share, annotation tools, documents you need for the lesson, websites you use like Quizlet, or online timers, can be bewildering. You can end up accidentally clicking on the wrong thing and disconnecting from the lesson!

3. Practise; if you are starting out online, thoroughly explore the software and test lessons with friends or family. You will find free online tutorials to learn all about your chosen platform. Play games with volunteer students to find out precisely what is possible with your platform. For example, using Zoom at the time of writing, when I give my student control of the annotation tools, he or she can no longer see my mouse moving, so I can't use it as a pointer. I have to take back the annotation tools, point to what I need, and then return them to the student to continue with the activity.
4. If a game involves using a tool that you have not tried, test it first with a friend or group of volunteers. You should master the technicalities yourself and instruct students how to access and use tools from their side of the screen.
5. You may see things on your screen that the others cannot see on theirs and vice versa. A slow internet connection may cause delays in items showing up on the screen at the other end. It could also be that you need to click the mouse, which tells your software to publish. All these details and functionalities need to be ironed out before you attempt a live lesson. The more you master your platform, the fewer bugs will arise.
6. Always have backup activities in case one is unfeasible due to technical challenges.
7. Make sure you have downloaded any software upgrades and rebooted your computer ahead of time.
8. Connect 15 minutes early to make sure everything is working and open all the files and tabs you will need during the lesson.
9. Shut down anything that you won't need on your computer.
10. Disable automatic backup programmes so they don't kick in mid-lesson and slow your computer right down. Don't let anti-virus software complete a scan of your computer during lesson time.
11. If possible, invest in a backup internet connection in case there is a network problem. If teaching online is critical to your

revenue, then it's worth it. You'll soon lose all your hard-earned customers if they can't hear you properly because the connection is rubbish.

12. If you are teaching at home, get everyone else off the internet to free up the connection for you. You don't want anyone else downloading massive files or playing online games during your class time.
13. Make sure your computer battery is charged just in case there is a power cut. Sometimes there are short power outages where everything goes off and then comes on again a second later, in an online class that can disconnect you.
14. If using a headset, get a comfortable, good-quality one. You might find a bargain second-hand.
15. If you can't see students, or they can't see you, make sure there is no tape over the camera.

What to look for in an online platform

1. You may find one that is free for at least half an hour or forty minutes, which is long enough for an online language lesson.
2. It should be easy for students to connect, from a regular computer, without downloading heavy software. Ideally, you send students a link to click and automatically join the lesson. That said, regular students should download the software too since this often gives them access to more tools.
3. Choose software that lets you split students into pairs and groups. These are known as breakout rooms. The teacher can visit any room to observe or help. Have an English-only rule in the breakout room. A strategy to keep students on track is that if the teacher notices a group is off-task, they are disqualified from the game.
4. A platform that lets students record all or any part of the lesson is best because it saves the teacher from spending valuable free time uploading heavy files.
5. Being able to share your desktop is crucial. You can write, correct, and highlight key points.
6. The platform should easily play audio and video files on your computer and preferably also students' computers.

7. The teacher should be able to mute and unmute students.
8. If you have more than one student at a time, then a platform that detects who is speaking and automatically makes them the focus is helpful. The video of whoever is speaking is enlarged, and those listening are still visible, but in small frames.
9. Annotation tools are essential so students can participate actively.
10. At the time of writing, Zoom is my pick. It's easy, free, and has all the above features.

There may be some privacy issues around using Zoom, but let's face it, if you are online, on your phone, or social media, then big brother is watching you!

Online security

Don't panic; most English learners are not devious hackers bent on ruining a lesson. Think about it, would you deliberately sabotage a meeting at which you were a student? Some geeky kids or weirdos might do this for fun, and there are ways to keep them out, so follow the guidelines below, and you should be fine.

As with any activity online, there are hackers, pranksters, and viruses out there. If you have dozens of students or often teach strangers, it could be worth using a second computer exclusively for lessons. There is a law in Europe now that prevents businesses from throwing their computers away. Associations collect them, and you can pick up second-hand machines for a bargain. Use a unique email account to connect with students and never connect to your apps from this machine. Keep the computer free from all your personal data and sensitive files. Regardless of the computer you use, follow these steps to keep your online meetings safe:

- Make a unique log-in for your online teaching with a dedicated email address, and do not link it to any of your social media accounts or apps.
- Keep your platform software updated with the latest security patches.

- Use a random ID generator, so each meeting has a different name
- Participants log in with a password to join the meeting
- Make students wait in the waiting room and admit them, so you vet who is joining
- If you allow students to share their screens, they will be able to use every game option when in breakout rooms. If, however, you have disruptive students who are likely to show pornography or other unsuitable material, then either do not let them join the meeting in the first place or disallow student screen sharing and allow only yours. Additionally, you may kick people out of a meeting and prevent them from re-joining!
- Avoid file sharing from students during the meeting in case pranksters send a virus. Send any files prior to the lesson and use an external file sharing provider.
- Sharing annotation tools is something I do systematically in individual lessons because the student is more engaged. Sharing tools opens up possibilities for students to play games in breakout rooms together. Do this with groups you know, perhaps not with brand new students or a large class. It's your call, but I choose to trust my students. They are with me to learn English and are usually paying for it to boot. Kids are more likely than adults to mess about with the tools and get distracted. If I want to stop them, I move my mouse, which scrambles theirs. I keep clicking to cancel sharing the controls, and in seconds, I have them back.
- If using the internet during lessons, beware of inadvertently clicking on ads or downloads, especially on free websites.

Bells and Whistles

1. To show the room around you, a physical whiteboard, flashcards, or work on your desk, connect a phone camera up to your computer.
2. To spice up countdowns, use a timer. A hand-held one is quick and easy but means the teacher must keep an eye on it unless you use a timer with an alarm. An online timer frees you from

keeping time yourself. There are clocks, bombs, rockets, and all sorts of free online timers. Choose something relatively calm as it's virtually impossible to think with noisy or busy ones. Since websites change over time, the best thing is to search for 'free online classroom timer,' and you are sure to find one. Be careful what you click. Free websites are full of ads and sometimes dodgy downloads. Familiarize and test the time while using your online platform so you can use it seamlessly, without delays and undue faffing.

3. Annotation tools should include highlighting, colouring, drawing, marking, writing, and so on. Learn your software thoroughly so you know what your options are. Know how to tell students how to access the tools from their side.
4. Colouring tools for the game Colour the card and other activities: In Zoom, you can select various colouring tools and effects. The colouring tool I found to be the best in Zoom is the line-drawing tool; you make it fatter, and then with each mouse click, you get a coloured circle. This setting does a quick, approximate job of colouring and is semi-transparent, so you can still see the picture underneath. These tools are continually evolving, so there is no point in describing here how to select that particular option. Do spend time playing with your chosen platform and learning all about what it can do.
5. For any game where you need dice, use an online dice rolling tool. I found a free one typing roll dice online into the search browser, with no need to download or install anything.
6. Use an online poll maker. Students can choose from multiple-choice answers or vote. You get instant feedback and a pie chart of results.
7. Points and competition; games are about motivating students to learn and making lessons fun, not about winning. Favour team games so you have winning teams, not individuals. Make some games collaborative rather than competitive. Avoid leaving weak students or groups lagging miles behind the rest, it is demoralizing, and these students might decide they hate English because lessons are humiliating. The best students and teams must do twice as well to earn the same number of points as the others. Ask them more challenging questions, as if they had moved up a level in a video game.

Online Games

A day in the life

Category	Speaking drill, speaking fluency, reading
Group size	One to one, any class size in small groups
Level	All levels
Age	All ages
Materials	See Appendix for two boards with card sets plus one blank game ready to fill in; access to screen share and annotation tools; online dice roller or dice.
Preparation	Create your board from scratch or use the example provided in the downloadable Appendix
Great for	100% flexible – vocabulary revision, grammar drill, grammar revision, Q&A, and general conversation

Materials

This activity is based on the Game of Life board game. The board can be made in PowerPoint or a Word document. Three are provided in the Appendix: for adults, teens, and a blank template for you to fill in as per your needs, along with three sets of oh-yeah and oh-no role-plays.

Preparation

Choose from the teen or adult pre-prepared boards or fill in the blank template with your choice of vocabulary, grammar, or general language questions. An excellent way to generate ideas is to have a brainstorming session with your students during a previous lesson.

- To make a beginner's board, use vocabulary pictures. Students name the vocabulary item or make a sentence using the noun.
- To drill grammar, ask all questions in a specific tense or including the target language.
- For general fluency, use a mixture of tenses and scenarios, as shown in the examples provided.

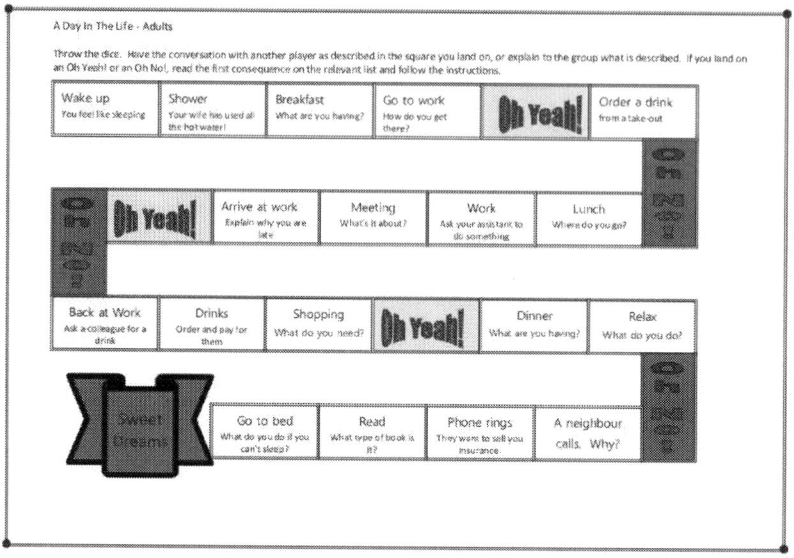

If you or one of your students enjoys design, create your board from scratch. Draw a twisty path with 24 spaces on the board. Remember to leave enough room to write events. Write 'Oh yeah!' in three spaces and 'Oh no!' in three others.

To complete the remaining squares, fill in everyday actions and conversational situations in the order in which they would happen during a day.

Make a list of 15 'Oh yeah!' events, alongside instructions that allow the player to move up the path. For example, 'Win the lottery – tell the person next to you and then skip ahead three spaces.' Make a list of 15 'Oh no!' events that are unlucky. These events could cause the player to move back down the path – for example, 'You've had a car accident. Convince the police officer sitting to your left that it wasn't your fault. Go back two spaces.'

Oh yeah!

1. You win $100 in a raffle; what are you going to spend it on? Go forward one space.
2. Offer to help an old lady across the road, even though you are late. Go forward three spaces.

3. You arrive at work early, and your boss notices. You say '...' Go forward two spaces.
4. Etc.

Oh no!

1. Your daughter tells you she is marrying someone you don't like. What do you say? Go back one space.
2. You get a flat tyre hitting a curb, so you buy a four-wheel drive. Negotiate with the car dealer. Go back three spaces.
3. You get to work still drunk from the night before. Your boss calls you to a meeting. Go back two spaces.
4. Etc.

- The best way to find out what 'good' and 'bad' events would appeal to your students is to ask each class member to write down a few for homework.

Language

For beginners, make the 'Oh yeah!' and 'Oh no!' lists simple – for example, naming vocabulary or making a short sentence including the word. You can indicate whether a player needs to move forwards or backwards by including +2, -1, and so on. For intermediates and up, use scenarios as described above to create the need for conversation.

How to play

With the board in screen share, and the online dice roller page open, players take turns to roll the dice and mark their position on the board via the annotation tools. Students follow the instructions on the space they land and, when relevant, the 'oh yeah' and 'oh no' consequences. They move their highlighter up and down the board according to the dice. The winner is the first player to reach the finish.

If your software allows all players to access the annotation tools simultaneously, this is ideal. The very act of players clicking to roll the dice and marking their spot on the board is a form of participation that involves them more in the game. On the other hand, it can soon become tedious if only one player can access the annotation tools and must pass control to someone else on every turn. It would be better if one person rolled the online dice, or real dice, for all players. A second handled everyone's position on the board, using players' initials or a colour, rubbing them out, and pasting them in the relevant square when the player moves. Zoom has a setting to allow all participants to access the controls. Software features like this will be evolving rapidly, so update your software regularly and explore the novelties.

- The whole board must be visible in screen share at the outset. Do this by reducing the document size to 70% and check players can see the entire game. If you only display half the board, the players' positions will be in the wrong place when you scroll down.

Adjectives memory game

Category	Listening
Group size	One to one, any class size
Level	All levels
Age	6 to adult
Materials	A list of nouns and adjectives
Preparation	5 minutes to make a list of nouns and adjectives
Great for	Vocabulary revision for nouns and adjectives, adverbs, comparatives, Grammar drills

How to play

Read a list of ten nouns with adjectives to the class twice, such as a blue sky, a round table, a tall tree, a big truck, a square window, a pretty lamp, a fat rhino, a thin bookcase, a fast car, a cool bike. The class listen and try to retain the adjective that describes the noun. Next, read only the nouns, giving students time to write down the corresponding adjective.

Once you have read the list of nouns and adjectives, you might put students in breakout rooms with the list of nouns. They work together to remember all the adjectives that went with each noun, which gets them talking. To encourage an English-only rule in the breakout room, say that you will be listening in randomly, and if you hear any communication that is not English, that group can be disqualified.

- Using a multiple-choice format makes it easier for students. A blue sky, a big sky, or a cloudy sky?
- Play with a list of six nouns for younger children. With teens and adults, use at least ten nouns. Experiment, start with less than you think appropriate and if everyone gets over 90% right, use more words next time. The list can be much longer with multiple-choice options.
- If students have too many gaps, read the list a final time after students have been working for a few minutes. They can focus on their missing words.
- Adapt the nouns and adjectives to the level of your students. Note that this is a revision game; it's not meant for learning new vocabulary.
- Play as a team game with students calling out responses rather than writing them down.

List of adjectives for beginners

Some A1 and A2 CEFA level adjectives are: advanced, afraid, aged, amazing, angry, attractive, available, awful, bad, beautiful, best, big, black, blond, blue, boiled, bored, boring, brave, bright, brilliant, broken, brown, busy, careful, cheap, clean, clear, clever, close, closed, cloudy, cold, comfortable, cool, correct, crazy, cream (colour), crowded, daily, dangerous, dark, dead, dear, deep, different, difficult, digital, dirty, double, dressed, dry, early, east, easy, electric, empty, excellent, excited, exciting, expensive, extra, fair, famous, fantastic, fast, fat, favourite, few, final, fine, first, fit, foreign, foggy, free, fresh, fried, friendly, full, fun, funny, further, glad, gold, golden, good, good-looking, great, green, grey, grilled, half-price, happy, hard, healthy, heavy, high, horrible, hot, hungry, ill, important, indoor, interested, interesting, international, kind, large, last, late, latest, lazy, leather, left, less, light, little, long, lost, loud, lovely, low, lucky, mad, married, missing, modern, monthly, more, most, much, musical, national, new, next, nice, noisy, normal, north, old, online, only, open, orange, own, pale, perfect, pink, plastic, pleasant, pleased, polite, poor, popular, possible, pretty, purple, quick, quiet, ready, real, red, rich, right, roast, round, sad, safe, same, second, short, sick, silver, simple, single, slim, slow, small, soft, sorry, south, spare, special, square, straight, strange, strong, sunny, sure, surprised, sweet, tall, terrible, thin, thirsty, tidy, tired, total, true, underground, unfortunate, unusual, upset, useful, usual, various, warm, weekly, welcome, well, well-known, west, wet, white, whole, wide, wild, windy, wonderful, wooden, worried, worse, worst, wrong, yellow, young.

Grammar and short sentences

Multiple-choice example with short sentences using adverbs:

He walked slowly.

a. He walked quickly.
b. He walked suddenly.
c. He walked slowly.

She drank quickly.

a. She drank fast.
d. She drank slowly
e. She drank quickly.

They waited patiently for the bus.

a. They waited impatiently for the bus.
b. They waited patiently for the bus.
c. They waited nervously for the bus.

Multiple-choice example using comparatives:

The fatter rhino was eating.

a. The faster rhino was eating.
b. The fatter rhino was eating.
c. The bigger rhino was eating.

The taller building

a. The bigger building
b. The taller building
c. The narrower building

Multiple-choice example using a grammar drill for the past simple.

We drank milk.

a. We drank water.
b. We drank orange juice.
c. We drank milk.

We ate pizza.

a. We ate pasta.
b. We ate rice.
c. We ate pizza.

They brushed their hair.

a. They brushed their hair.
b. They brushed their dog.
c. They brushed their clothes.

Alibi

Category	Speaking fluency
Group size	Three students to a small class in breakout rooms
Level	Lower intermediate to advanced
Age	12 to adult
Materials	None
Preparation	Optional descriptions of alibis for lower levels
Great for	Q&A, general fluency, and conversation

How to play

Tell the class a crime has been committed and describe someone who was spotted at the scene (one of the class members). That person goes into a breakout room with a few other students to establish an alibi, i.e., to discuss where they were and what they were doing at that time.

While this is happening, the other students prepare questions to ask the suspect and friends. When a few minutes are up, bring the suspect group out of their room and create as many breakout rooms as suspects, with one suspect per room. Divide the questioners up into these rooms. Allow five minutes' question time before bringing everyone back together. The class compare notes, ask additional questions before deciding if the person is guilty or not, depending on how many discrepancies they find in the details of the alibi given.

This game gets better when re-played, as students come up with more questions to snare the suspect. Use it two or three times over a term and make sure different students are chosen for the suspect group.

With lower intermediates – especially the first time you play – you might want to provide pre-prepared alibis and questions.

Examples for suspects:	I was at my friend Dave's house. We went for a pizza and met a friend. I had pepperoni pizza and a Coke.
Examples for questioners:	Where were you? What were you doing at the time? Then what did you do? Did you eat anything? What were you wearing? Was Dave's mother there?

Alphabet game

Category	Listening, speaking, or writing
Group size	2 to 30
Level	Revising and practising the alphabet
Age	6 to adult
Materials	None
Preparation	None or write down the words to spell
Great for	Alphabet pronunciation and spelling

How to play

The teacher or a class member spells a word out loud. The first team has three seconds to name the word spelled. If they cannot do this within three seconds, the rest of the class is free to call out the word to win a point for their teams.

To encourage children to join in, have a rule where the whole team must call out the word within the three-second limit. The quickest children will be first, but the rest of the team must listen and ready to chime in for the team to win its point. If three seconds is too short a time limit, extend to suit your class level.

- To teach the alphabet, use easy words like cat, boy, girl, tree, or book.
- Spell out the names of students in your class.
- Use words that are harder to spell for older children or higher levels.
- Allowing students to write the letters as you dictate is a helpful variant for students learning a new alphabet or learning to write. Writing out the letters also makes it easier to guess the word.

One to One Variant

The student types the letters into the chat while you spell out a word. Swap roles. At first, work on the pronunciation of groups of letters or sounds, not the whole alphabet.

The student listens and names the word after you have finished spelling. To turn this into a game:

1. Spell a word at a steady pace without stopping or repeating any letters.
2. Count five seconds silently. The student must name the word before the five seconds are up.
3. Continue for five to ten words, depending on how long they are and the student's ability.
4. See how many words your learner gets right, then try again.

Use this game regularly and concentrate on words with letters/sounds that your learner finds difficult or has trouble remembering.

Use this as a dictation game, particularly for learners who use a different alphabet. Check the words and see how many are correct. Try this again in another lesson and count correct answers each time. The student will improve and have the pleasure of getting better scores over time.

Alphabet war

Category	Speaking drill
Group size	One to one, any class size in small groups
Level	Beginner
Age	All ages
Materials	Students either need a pen, paper, and scissors, or a printer.
Preparation	5 minutes for students to print or write their alphabet cards
Great for	Learning and revising the alphabet

No prep version

Ask everyone to write a letter of the alphabet and hold it up to the camera. Say a word, and if the students' letter is in that word, they win a point. Continue until someone has five points. Optionally, all those who don't have five points do a forfeit – see the list of forfeits under 'F' in this book for ideas.

Preparation for card game version

Students can print out the Alphabet War cards provided in the Appendix and cut them up, or they can create a set by writing out the alphabet and cutting it up into squares. If students make their own, show them a model to copy, and indicate whether to use upper or lower case.

a	b	c	d	e
f	g	h	i	j
k	l	m	n	o
p	q	r	s	t
u	v	w	x	y
z				

How to play

Pair up the students or play in tiny groups. Students shuffle their decks and place the deck face down. Everyone picks the top card of the pile and shows it to the camera, naming the letter. The player with the letter closest to A wins the point. This game helps students to learn alphabetical order and practise saying the letters. Have another round with the player closest to the letter M winning, and so on.

Alphabet word game

Category	Listening, speaking
Group size	One to one and any class size working in groups
Level	All levels
Age	10 to adult
Materials	None, or screen share
Preparation	None
Great for	Pronunciation, vowels, consonants, alphabet, new vocabulary, spelling

With this activity, students focus on letters and pronunciation but also discover new words. The letters of the alphabet can be introduced early, a few letters at a time, over a series of lessons. While it may seem logical to start a beginners' group by teaching the alphabet, it is more rewarding for students to start with greetings, nouns, and simple sentences, which give them the impression they are getting somewhere fast.

How to play

Let students work individually or in small groups, with a maximum of five groups per class. Name a vowel and give students two minutes to write down as many three-letter words containing that vowel as they can, as long as they know their meaning. Allow dictionaries if you like. Bring everyone back together and see which group has the most words.

Here is a way to score points: Team A gives you one word and a translation or definition for a point. Team B gives you a different word and meaning for a point. Continue around the teams until contributions dry up. See which team has accumulated the most points. It should be very even.

Now add a vowel and put students back into their groups, the same or random new ones, depending on whether you have that option with your software. Students now have two minutes to find as many four-letter words as possible by adding the new vowel to the words they created and maybe finding new ones.

Experiment giving lower-level students one vowel and one consonant; otherwise, they may find fewer words, being lost in endless possibilities. For example, if you give students the vowel i and the consonant t, to make three-letter words, they only need to run through the alphabet to find bit, fit, git, hit, kit, lit, pit, sit, tit, wit, and zit and, with the letter t first, tic, tie, til, Tim, tin, and tip.

Work on four-letter words with all levels too, and for higher levels, try longer ones.

Language

This activity is versatile. Focus on sounds or phonemes, clear pronunciation, diction, or spelling rules, like 'i before e except after c,' compared to e before i. If using dictionaries, the game also allows students to discover new vocabulary.

Anagrams

Category	Spelling
Group size	One to one, any class size
Level	All levels
Age	About 10 to adult
Materials	Screen share
Preparation	Write anagrams for your chosen vocabulary
Great for	Spelling, vocabulary revision

How to play

Screen share word in a jumble, such as 'l e p e h n t a' for 'elephant.' Either use words in the same vocabulary family, such as food words or professions or if using unrelated words, give a clue with every set of letters.

Divide the class into teams and give each one a name. Show the first anagram via screen share to everyone. Team one has 15 seconds to decipher it. If team one has not found the word after 15 seconds, any team may call it out and win the point. Show the second anagram, and this time, team two has priority for 15 seconds. And so on.

- If it is evident that some teams are far quicker than the others, swap the students around, so the talent is evenly spread about the classroom.
- Each student in the team has to take a turn answering as this prevents one person from taking over the game. However, do not leave bright students on the sidelines with nothing to do. Teammates can send answers via private messages to each other, which keeps everyone involved. Otherwise, why would bright students bother to show up for your lessons if you are not teaching them anything or including them?

Gap-fill variation

Write a sentence with a gap. Provide an anagram of the missing word:

Do you _____ (k i e l) butter? Answer: like

Battleships

Category	Speaking drill, speaking fluency
Group size	One to one, pairwork for any class size
Level	All levels
Age	All ages
Materials	Battleships grids (see downloadable Appendix). Coloured pens for players.
Preparation	None if using ready-made games or students prepare grids in or before class
Great for	Vocabulary revision, grammar, Q&A

This game is based on a famous American board game called Battleships. The purposes of this exercise include a review of previously taught vocabulary or grammar and the development of memory, logic, and strategy.

Preparation

Give two Battleship grids to each student. See the downloadable Appendix for blank and ready-made grids.

If not using the ready-made examples in the Appendix, have students prepare their grids, which is a valid vocabulary exercise in itself. Each pair take four grids, two per student, which they fill in together so that all four are identical.

For young beginners, use a simple version and a smaller grid. The example below is included in the Appendix. Green ticks show a hit, and red crosses a miss.

I like	His or her name is...	How old is she?	What's this?	Numbers
	Ann			20
	Sam			13
	Dan			11
	Lucy			12
	Tom			18

- If students are stuck on a square, for example, if they cannot think of an item of clothing beginning with the letter 'G,' they can choose to leave that square blank. However, battleships cannot go in a blank square.
- If students work together to complete a grid for homework, let them use dictionaries and the internet, but specify that they must know what all the words in their grid mean. For example, searching for 'list of countries' will yield a result, allowing students to fill in their grids quickly rather than agonizing over them. Placing students into groups to create grids together will help, as they will pool knowledge and ideas.

In the example below, the vertical axis of the grid has letters of the alphabet. I selected letters that start many words, rather than x or j. On the horizontal axis is a mixture of vocabulary and grammar categories; food, clothes, country, place, adjective, verb, adverb, sport, profession, animal. Then have students fill in the grid. For example, looking at the grid, C–Clothes might have 'coat' or 'cap' written in the box; G–Food might have 'goat's cheese' or 'grapes.'

Each team takes two grids and labels one 'ours' and the other the 'opponent's.' Students do not show their grids to the opposing team. Players now draw their battleships on their own grid, but not their opponent's grid. The ships may be placed horizontally or vertically, but not diagonally. Students should draw ships to take up the following spaces: one covering three spaces, two covering two, and three that cover one. The object of the game is to find and destroy the opponent's ships.

Example of a high beginner-level Battleships grid, included in the Appendix:

	Food	Clothes	Country	Place	Adjective	Verb	Adverb	Sport	Profession	Animal
1	Apple	Shirt	England	Airport	Angry	To eat	Slowly	Football	Actor	Cat
2	Banana	Boots	France	Bank	Big	To drink	Quickly	Rugby	Banker	Dog
3	Pear	Cap	Spain	Cinema	Small	To walk	Badly	Cycling	Doctor	Mouse
4	Potato	Dress	Japan	School	Hot	To die	Well	Skiing	Dentist	Horse
5	Cheese	Gloves	Canada	Garage	Cold	To go	Sadly	Gymnastics	Gardener	Sheep
6	Chicken	Hat	Iceland	Library	Happy	To have	Happily	Walking	Hairdresser	Pig
7	Meat	Skirt	Mexico	Car Park	Sad	To run	Carefully	Running	Nurse	Chicken
8	Rice	Coat	Russia	City	Red	To talk	Rapidly	Hockey	Footballer	Duck
9	Salad	Socks	Malaysia	Shops	Blue	To see	Stupidly	Skating	Secretary	Cow
10	Pizza	Tie	Australia	Town	Tired	To give	Shyly	Tennis	Typist	Lion

Timing

A grid like the one below might take two hours for students to prepare, so this is an excellent activity if you take students all day. For a half-hour activity, provide students with pre-prepared grids.

	Food	Clothes	Country	Place	Adjective	Verb	Adverb	Sport	Profession	Animal
A	Apple	Anorak	America	Airport	Angry	To	Angrily	Archery	Actor	Ant
B	Bread	Boots	Britain	Bank	Big	To beat	Badly	Bowling	Banker	Bat
C	Coconut	Cap	Chad	Cinema	Cold	To count	Creepily	Cycling	Chiropractor	Cat
D	Donut	Dress	Denmark	Dentist	Dark	To die	Doggedly	Darts	Dentist	Dog
G	Goat's cheese	Gloves	Ghana	Garage	Great	To go	Gladly	Gymnastics	Gardener	Goat
H	Hummus	Hat	Haiti	Home	Happy	To have	Happily	Hiking	Hairdresser	Hippo
M	Meat	Mittens	Mexico	Meadow	Mighty	To	Mildly	?	Medic	Monkey
R	Rice	Raincoat	Russia	Room	Red	To risk	Rapidly	Rugby	?	Rat
S	Salad	Socks	Spain	Shop	Silly	To see	Stupidly	Skating	Secretary	Snake
T	Toast	Tie	Trinidad	Town	Tight	To take	Timidly	?	Typist	Tiger

How to play

Once ships are drawn, play begins. The first player attempts to guess the location of the opponent's ships.

- Beginners do this by naming the item and perhaps translating it into the native language.
- Beginners to lower intermediates may drill specific sentences, tenses, or grammar.

For the food column, they drill; I like, I don't like.

For the clothes column, they drill; I'm wearing a, I'm not wearing a.

- Higher level students describe the vocabulary item that is in the square.

Silly: It's an adjective starting with the letter 's' meaning funny or not serious.

If there is a ship in the square guessed, the opponent says 'Hit.' If the ship is completely hit, then the opponent must say 'Hit and sunk.' If there is nothing in the square, then the opponent says 'Miss.'

The player marks his or her grid with the opponent's response. If the player scored a hit, they get another turn; if a miss, the turn goes to the opponent. The game carries on until the one player or team has sunk all the opponent's ships.

- It is easier to keep track of the game by using coloured highlighter pens, yellow for a miss, pink for a hit, and red for a sink.
- When using one on one, if the student is lagging far behind, the teacher can name the column a ship is in and give a clue for the word.
- Save grids you create for future use without preparation time.
- Try the game using a blank school timetable. Use an English battleship of four blocks, two Maths battleships of three blocks, three Science battleships of two blocks, and four History battleships of one block. Students add other activities. In pairs and with their timetables filled in, students find their partner's ships by asking questions like 'What do you do/study at 10 o'clock on Tuesday?'

Bingo

Category	Listening, optionally spelling
Group size	Minimum 2 students, any class size, whole-class
Level	Adaptable to all levels
Age	6 to adult
Materials	Students need pen and paper. List of words.
Preparation	5 minutes in class by students
Great for	Any vocabulary, any grammar topic

Here is an easy vocabulary game to play in your online classrooms. Bingo is perfect for teaching vocabulary to beginners. It's also a useful vocabulary or grammar revision game.

How to Play

Each student draws a grid with eight squares. Students choose eight vocabulary words from a list of twenty and write these into their grid. Next, randomly call out one of the twenty terms. If students have it on their grid, they cross it out. The first student to cross out all the words wins an award; see lower down for prizes.

- For a grammar drill, use short phrases rather than single vocabulary words.
- For listening, use pictures. Students sketch vocabulary pictures onto their grids. If you have kids, make the vocabulary simple to draw, such as the sun, a girl, or a boy. Avoid words like 'supermarket,' or the grid-making will be laborious and take half the lesson!
- For spelling, students write words out onto their grids.
- You might find bingo software to use in the online platform. However, having students participate and create their grids manually assists learning, and being able to draw and write rather than type is currently still considered worthwhile by some dinosaurs, LOL!

Variation for one to one

The teacher writes twenty words, cuts them up, and puts them in a pile face down. Teacher and student each make a grid as described above. The teacher draws each word from the pile and reads it out. Play as above.

An extended variant for children

This long-winded version can be tedious for older players. The teacher turns over a word for the student. If present in the student's grid, it is crossed out. Suppose the teacher has this term on his or her grid as well; too bad! The teacher turns over a second card and crosses it out if present on his or her grid. Continue. If there are no winners when all the cards have been used once, shuffle and use the pile again until someone's grid is complete.

Topics

Use this game for any theme. Topics might be common vocabulary words for beginners to specific business terms such as aviation, customer service, social media, marketing, medicine, and so on.

Easy ideas for prizes

- The student wins a point for his or her team.
- The student wins something tangible but inexpensive and ecological, for when students next meet in the flesh. The prize is just a symbolic gift, like a tangerine when in season.
- The student earns the chance to do an extra homework task that the teacher will mark. Don't laugh; motivated students will be pleased to have this opportunity.
- The student receives a surprise online gift that changes each time, ideas: A sudoku to do in their own time, a recipe to try at home, instructions for an origami, an invitation to find and show a photo to the class, a quiz question, etc.
- Ask everyone to submit five ideas each for simple prizes. Give examples as above. Collect these and use them in the game.

Grammar

Use short phrases or complete sentences rather than single words. Say you are working on a tense; put each vocabulary word into a sentence in that tense. Students hear the word in context in the tense you are drilling or revising.

Alternatively, use single words and have the students use them in a sentence in the correct tense to cross it off the grid.

Blind directions

Category	Listening or speaking
Group size	One to one, pairwork in breakout rooms
Level	All levels
Age	Any
Materials	Breakout room with screen share and annotation tools. Optional scarves or blindfolds
Preparation	None
Great for	Giving directions, commands

Players A and B screen share and open a whiteboard. A selects a pen via the annotation tool and positions it in the center of the board. This step is necessary, or player A might draw the picture offscreen. A can now tie on a scarf, or look down and shield his eyes, so he cannot see the screen. The other hand stays on the mouse. Player B now guides A to draw something, describing exactly where to start drawing, which direction to go in and when to stop. To position the mouse without drawing a line, say to draw two eyes without a line connecting them, or get into the starting position, use 'move.' Here A moves the mouse without clicking. Use 'Draw' when A needs to draw a line or a shape. For example, 'Move the mouse down, down, stop. Draw a line to the left, stop. Draw a line down. Stop. Draw a line to the right. Stop. Draw a line upwards. Stop.' A has just drawn a square or a rectangle.

To create mystery and anticipation, A should not know what the picture is.

Keep pictures simple! Favour pictures with straight lines or rectangular things like buildings, trucks, furniture. It is hard enough to get a decent picture without trying a complicated one. The black and white drawings included in my flashcard sets are suitable, as are stick figures.

Language These words are the minimum needed: Move the mouse up, down, across, draw, a line, a circle, go, stop, start, left, right, up, down, diagonal, slow down, short line, long line, up or down a bit.

Blind drawing

Category	Listening or speaking
Group size	One to one, pairwork in breakout rooms
Level	Beginners
Age	Any, though childish
Materials	Breakout room, screen share, and annotation tools Optional scarves or blindfolds
Preparation	None
Great for	Body parts or any vocabulary

Set up as for Blind Directions above with Player A on the mouse. Player B gives instructions; draw a face, draw the eyes, draw the nose, and the mouth. Draw a body, the neck, the left leg, etc. Draw a zebra. Draw a house, the door, the windows, and the garden. Draw a supermarket. Draw three flowers in a pot. And so on. Younger children usually find the results extremely funny. Younger students will also enjoy attempting to draw the tail on a donkey's body while blindfolded, or the nose on a snowman, windows in a house, and so on.

Blind painter

Category	Listening or speaking
Group size	One to one, pairwork in breakout rooms
Level	Beginners
Age	Any
Materials	Breakout rooms, screen share, annotation tools Optional scarves or blindfolds
Preparation	Find two black and white pictures
Great for	Giving directions, commands

How to play

Play as for Blind Directions described above. This time provide a black and white picture to player A. Player B must not see the picture and wears a blindfold or scarf throughout. Player A guides B to select a drawing tool and a colour as described in Blind Directions. Select a fat pen to cover a greater area with each click. To pick a colour A might say, 'up, stop, click once.' Next, A moves B into position, hovering over the picture. With each click, a coloured circle will appear. Semi-transparent colouring tools are the best because you can see the image underneath. The Techie Tips in the introduction include a paragraph on colouring techniques.

Any of my black and white flashcards or story scenes would be suitable for this activity, like this one where the robots buy fruit and vegetables for study at their spaceship. Using Zoom drawing and colouring tools, we got all the vegetables coloured in using simple commands: 'up, click, up, click, up, click, left, click, left, click, down, click' and so on.

Blow your house down

Category	Speaking
Group	One to one, any class size in groups
Level	Beginner to lower intermediate
Age	All ages
Materials	Pen and paper plus cameras, or screen share and annotation tools
Preparation	Five minutes to write grammar or vocab questions General knowledge questions tailored to your students might take longer
Great for	Vocabulary revision, grammar drill, fluency

How to play

Divide students into two teams of a maximum of 10 students each, or the game will become boring. If you have more than 20 students, play a demo game first, then run two games simultaneously in breakout rooms.

Show a picture flashcard to Team 1. A student names the item and draws the first line of a house on the board if successful. (Provide a model to copy like a simple sketch you can finish in six strokes.) If incorrect, the student cannot contribute to the team's drawing. Team 2 decides if the word is correct. If Team 2 is wrong, their house is blown down. Involving Team 2 in Team 1's question keeps everyone engaged all the time. Now it's Team 2's turn to name a word and Team 1's to say if it is correct. If a team member makes a mistake, their house is blown down. The winner is the team that 'builds' their six-line house first.

Language

- For a vocabulary drill, students name pictures or translate written words.
- For a grammar drill, students make a specific sentence or question using the word. Consider using verbs or other parts of speech, not just nouns.
- For general English, students make up any question or sentence using the target word.

- Ideally, use screen share, so both team's houses are visible, and a student from each team uses the annotation tools to draw or erase the sketches. If your students do not have access to annotation controls, they can draw their houses on paper at desks and show them via the camera when they are complete.
- Blow your house down can also be a collaborative game, where team members correct their sentences to save having the team house blown down. This variant empowers the whole team and keeps all students involved.
- Show teams their next card while the other team is still drawing to keep the pace flowing, so they can think about possible sentences ahead of their turn. Team B's student can be thinking about his or her sentence while team A's is writing/saying his or hers and drawing the house. Get help from teammates to prevent students from sitting around waiting while someone tries to come up with an answer. It also takes the pressure off the student whose turn it is, which may be appreciated. If a student does not like being put on the spot, they can get help from a teammate.
- For mixed-ability classes, let the stronger students arbitrate a group, referring to the teacher if in doubt over a particular sentence.

One to one

I give my adult students three attempts to build the house using different sets of six questions. One does not have to do this, but I personalize the students' categories, starting with things they are sure to know and making the last question harder. It takes time, but the lesson is more interesting because it makes the student think, and practise listening and speaking skills and discover new words.

Here is an example I prepared for an English student living in France using geography, history, and grammar categories:

Geography

1. What is the capital of the Cheque Republic? (Easy question, any educated adult living in Europe knows the answer to this.)
2. What is the second-largest city in France?

3. Which ski resort has the most pistes? Espace Killy, Paradis Ski, or Les Trois Vallées? (This student lives in Espace Killy and is a skier, so he will enjoy this question and is likely to know the answer.)
4. Which river flows through Paris? (Again, this question should be a no-brainer for my student.)
5. Which is the biggest country in the world, China, Russia, or Canada?
6. What is the population of China, 1,4 billion, 900 million, or 450 million? (Using multiple-choice makes this easier.)

History

1. Who built the Eiffel tower? (An essential piece of general knowledge for my Brit living in France.)
2. Which bland prime minister followed the Iron Lady? (A straightforward question for my student, who was about 25 when Margaret Thatcher was in power.)
3. Six wives, divorced, beheaded, died, divorced, beheaded, survived. Which king was their husband? (Henry VIII is one of Britain's most famous kings.)
4. In 1940, which leader said, 'We shall fight on the beaches, we shall fight in the streets, we shall fight in the hills. We shall never surrender.'
5. In what year did Harold, the last Anglo-Saxon king, lose the battle of Hastings? (1066 is THE date every English person knows when William the Conqueror invaded, and we became subjects of a French man.)
6. In which year was the French revolution, 1789,1879, or 1786? (1789 is the one date every French person knows!)

Grammar – focusing on things covered in previous lessons

1. I have a __________ (adjective) car.
2. I went _____ plane.
3. They went _____ foot.
4. Have ______ seen my glasses?
5. _____ he seen my glasses?
6. Where _______ my glasses?

Board games

Category	Speaking drill, revision
Group size	One to one, any class size in groups
Level	All levels
Age	All ages
Materials	Screen share and annotation tools See the Appendix for ready-made board and question suggestions
Preparation	None once you have the board and questions
Great for	Vocabulary or grammar drill, general language, conversation, speaking fluency

Board games work well online with one to four students; with more, they are a drag. There are plenty of fancy themed games to download online, type “free online board game” to find them. That said using squares, with a start and a finish is sufficient. Optionally use different colours for the squares, each corresponding to a language category or type of question.

Beginners could name picture cards. Higher levels could define meanings or find synonyms. The possibilities are endless for grammar; students can put a verb into a specified tense, convert a dialogue to reported speech, or make one sentence from two using an appropriate conjunction.

Display the board in screen share and use the annotation tools to mark each students’ position. Students roll one dice, real or online, and when they land on a square, they complete a task from the relevant category. Use the online rubber to delete a student’s previous position when they move further along.

It is preferable if one person handles the positions and someone else rolls the dice. If the teacher does everything, learners will not be physically involved and will not be so engrossed in the activity.

Students call on the teacher to verify an answer if no one in the group is sure.

There is a pirate-themed board game, in colour, with example questions and a master to edit with your topics. In the game sample provided, purple numbers are for naming vocabulary, red is for doing an action, and blue is for answering the present continuous question, 'What are you wearing?' This sample game is complete, meaning all questions and the board are visible at once, so learners could play it independently from the teacher in break-out rooms. If the teacher or an advanced student animates the game, then they can make up questions on the cuff.

Boggle

Category	Spelling
Group size	One to one, any class in groups, whole-class
Level	Lower intermediate to advanced
Age	10 to adult
Materials	Create grids, optional online timer Optionally use free online Boggle websites
Preparation	2-5 minutes
Great for	Any vocabulary, spelling

This picture shows the official Boggle game, which has strict rules but for ESL learners, relax these. You do not need a Boggle since a teacher can make a grid in a trice; the bigger the grid, the easier the game. I recommend grids with twenty-five letters for lower levels and 9 or 12 letters for more advanced students. Make them up with letters of the vocabulary or grammar you are teaching. You might include as many superlatives as possible in one grid and the months of the year in another. In the example shown, the first grid contains the superlatives biggest, fattest, longest, tallest, shortest, smallest, and thinnest. The second grid has the months January to July. Both grids contain all sorts of other random words. In the third grid, made from the letters from 'adventure,' I found fifty-two words, and there are doubtless more.

B I G G E	J A N U	A	U	E
S T F A T	A R Y F	D	V	T
L O N G L	E B M C	N	R	E
S H R M N	H P I L			

You'll find free online Boggle websites with handy integrated timers. Still, I don't use them because frequently, the rule is that letters should be adjacent, making the game too difficult for students learning English as a foreign language. Making your grids is the best solution. Get students to prepare them for homework using words from your current teaching unit.

How to play

Write the chosen letters in rows. Include at least four vowels and various consonants, which is often the case when you insert vocabulary into the grid. Students race to create as many words as possible without duplicating any letters. If there are two 'o's in the

Boggle, then words like 'boot' are allowed. If there is only one 'o,' then 'boot' is not permitted. My rule is that the letters do not have to be adjacent because it is much easier to find words.

Speaking version

Put students in teams. Students race to call out the words they spot while the teacher or team leader quickly write them down. Vocabulary that has already been found cannot be called again. The same student cannot call out more than one word in a row, which prevents one student from stealing all the action and helps the others have a chance to join in.

Writing version

Allow two minutes for players to write all the words they can find. When you say 'Stop,' have students copy and paste their lists in the chat or online area. If that is technically impossible, then have students take it in turns to share one word on their list verbally.

Scoring

Students award the same number of points as there are letters—for example, two points for a two-letter word, three for a three-letter term, and so on. If this points system is too complicated, give 1 point per word regardless. Students total up their points. To avoid drawing attention to the best and the worst students, ask all those who have more than 30 points to raise their hands and congratulate them. Repeat with all those who have over 20.

Grammar

To use this game for grammar, have students make a phrase or sentence for each word they find. Define the criteria, such as which tense to use. The teacher could also do this to give students the chance to hear the words in context, in the required tense.

Brainstorm

Category	Listening, speaking, writing option
Group size	One to one, any class size in teams
Level	Lower intermediate to advanced
Age	6 to adult
Materials	None, optional online timer to spice up the game
Preparation	None
Great for	Any vocabulary topics, short grammar drills

How to play

Give each team 20 seconds to call out as many words as possible in a category until the time is up. Count the number of words. To prevent one student from taking over the whole game, have a quota of words per team member.

Once the 20 seconds are up, the other teams have a chance to earn bonus points if they can name additional vocabulary in the category in the 10 seconds following. Then give the next group a new theme for a 20-second brainstorm. Lengthen the time limits if more appropriate to students' ability, but always err on the side of giving too little time to keep up the element of adrenalin and fun.

Categories for nouns include; animals, body parts, clothing, colours, food, fruit and vegetables, family and people, hobbies, sports, school, the house and furniture, days, months, seasons, telling the time, directions, places, transport, musical instruments, toys, jobs, countries, favourite characters, and the weather. Categories could also be parts of speech like pronouns, prepositions, adjectives, and verbs.

To make the game harder, consider brainstorming nouns beginning with the letter 't' or antonyms such as hot-cold, near-far, big-small. The teacher may call out a word for which the class race to suggest an antonym.

To make the game easier, brainstorm with any English noun without the limitations of a topic. To keep top students challenged while preventing them from invading a game, they could be required to name terms from a theme while the rest of the class have carte blanche to contribute any vocabulary. Even the weakest students can contribute easy words they know. Display a list of topics as a prompt.

- Picture prompts and mimes help elicit vocabulary from a team that is lagging.
- Recruit a class member to be on the online timer for you. (This can be a constructive way to deal with a disruptive child or discreetly remove someone who always answers first.)
- When students contribute a word, they write it in the online area for the team, so it is easy to count the total and make sure there are no repeats. Visualizing written words as well as hearing them reinforces learning. Therefore, fear not; even quiet pupils will listen to and see the vocabulary even if they are not contributing, which is still helpful.

Variation for one to one

The teacher and student take it in turns to name vocabulary. The teacher should hold off calling the easy choices, so for an animal theme, the teacher could say, 'boa constrictor' rather than 'snake' or 'cat.' Play with the same topic several times in a row and watch the student become more confident and fluent. Give students the theme for the next lesson in advance so they can prepare. For younger children, I like to display my small-sized flashcards for a topic as prompts. I name other related words, leaving the student to name the pictures.

Here are ideas to even out the score between teacher and student:

- The teacher contributes words from the theme only while the student may contribute any vocabulary. The student earns 2 points for every theme word and 1 point for any other English term. When the student is ten points ahead, the game is over. Adapt this as required. If the teacher is stumped for another word, the game is over.

- The student gets 2 points for every contribution while the teacher only earns 1.

- The student has a longer time window to name words; for example, instead of alternating turns, give the student a 30-second window to say as many words as possible. The teacher then has 10 seconds to attempt to name more. Experiment and adapt these timings to make the game close enough to be interesting.

- Use an online timer to prevent players from spending too long thinking.

Writing option

Give a time limit for students to write as many words as possible for a given theme. Each student has a list. When the time is up, put students into teams. Students take it in turns to call out a word. The opposite team must hit back with a different term until the teams run out of ideas. The winning team is the one that speaks last.

Drill categories of words such as sports or food, or play with short sentences like 'I'm French,' 'I'm Spanish,' 'I'm British,' and so on. Drill sentences and grammar as well as vocabulary items.

To make three teams easily, all students whose first name starts with A to H are in group one. Those whose name starts with I to P are in group two, and the rest are in three. Give students the format to speak, for example, Anne, team one, I'm wearing a shirt. Pedro, team two, I'm wearing a hat. Sylvain, team 3, I'm wearing a scarf.

One to one

Set a timer for two minutes. The one speaking when the timer goes off does a forfeit. See the forfeits section for ideas.

- Scoring option: Jot the words used under each team as the game plays but do it fast. I write them down at my desk because I'm quicker at handwriting than messing with three columns onscreen. Have a rule where each team may only use a word once, so if team one says scarf, teams two and three may also say scarf, but only once each, and not immediately after team one has said it!

- Teens and adults may keep track of words used by keeping notes during the game since this gives them spelling practise. Avoid this with kids since it will slow the game down.
- Play a rhyming brainstorm variant for advanced students. For example, all the words that rhyme with the sound 'a' as in 'lay.' Intermediates might produce day, say, play, clay, pay, tray, bay, Fay, gay, hay, May or may, way, pray. Advanced players might think of weigh, daily, neigh, neighbourly, fray, playful, delay, jay, nay, and flay.

Buddy reading

Category	Reading out loud and listening
Group size	One to one, any class size in pairs
Level	All levels
Age	All ages
Materials	Texts, poems, articles
Preparation	None if you have texts already
Great for	Multi-level activity, reading, listening, pronunciation, Q&A

Buddy reading involves one student reading, while the 'buddy' helps the reader with pronunciation. The buddy also asks questions about the text to check comprehension.

Model buddy reading for the group first. Higher-level students monitor lower-level students. It is worth pointing out that by taking a teacher's role, they will still learn and be challenged. Interestingly, having lower-level students helping higher-level learners also often works, as the latter become more aware of embedded errors that they are making.

After the activity, ask the more advanced students to share what they learned from monitoring lower-level learners. Everyone should benefit from a lesson, regardless of an individual's level of English.

Build a sentence

Category	Reading, writing
Group size	One to one, any class size in pairs or threes
Level	All levels
Age	All ages
Materials	A choice of nouns, verbs, adjectives, and adverbs
Preparation	Prepare four lists of five of the following: nouns, verbs, adjectives, and adverbs
Great for	Vocabulary, grammar, general language, sentences, parts of speech

Prepare four lists: five nouns, five verbs, five adjectives, and five adverbs. For example:

Nouns	Verbs	Adjectives	Adverbs
Cat	drink	big	slowly
Jacket	jump	beautiful	away
Carrot	eat	delicious	greedily
Chair	stand up	hard	quickly
Sun	shine	hot	strongly

Play for 10–30 minutes, or for as long as there is interest.

How to play

Build a sentence is a co-operative activity. Play a demonstration game before breaking your class up into teams (ideally of three) and give each one a set of lists. Each teammate chooses a task: writing the sentence down, timekeeping, reading, and keeping score.

- The reader reads the first noun aloud: cat.
- The timekeeper starts the clock, and the team has one minute to decide on a sentence such as I like cats.
- The recorder writes it down.
- The group now has two minutes to continue building their sentence, to contain each noun, verb, adjective, and adverb in the list. The reader reads each card aloud, and the team

decides where to put it in the sentence. So, for example, the second word might be the verb: drink.

- Students think up and write down the sentence: I like cats that drink.
- The third word drawn is: big. Students write down: I like big cats that drink.
- The fourth word is the adverb: slowly. Students produce a grammatically correct sentence: I like big cats that drink slowly.

> Another example is: bottle, had eaten, heavy, dutifully.
>
> These words might form sentences like:
> We bought a bottle of beer.
> We had eaten dinner before we bought a bottle of beer.
> We had eaten a heavy dinner before we bought a bottle of beer.
> We had eaten a heavy dinner before we dutifully bought a bottle of beer.

If players cannot use a word, it is discarded. Students win a point for every card they use correctly and lose a point for every card they do not use.

Players cannot add any nouns, verbs, adjectives, or adverbs other than those specified, but any other parts of speech are allowed – there are no points for using them, but students do not need to draw a card for them either.

- You do not have to keep score unless you are playing teams against each other.
- Sentences do not have to make perfect sense – sometimes they will be funny and surreal – but they must be grammatically correct.
- This game works well with one student, who places the nouns and adjectives while the teacher inserts the verbs and adverbs.

Call my bluff

Category	Speaking fluency
Group size	One on one, any class size
Level	All levels
Age	10 to adult
Materials	None
Preparation	Prepare a description with false elements about yourself to use as a demo
Great for	General language, conversation

Demonstrate this task first and then allow a few minutes in class for students to consider what they will say about themselves. Then have someone make three statements about him or herself, two true and one false. The class decides which fact is untrue. Do this a couple of times together and then split into small groups to continue the activity.

To practise the simple past, students prepare a description of what they did at the weekend and include three untrue facts. The other students try to guess what these false facts are, either by pure guesswork (easier) or by asking additional questions about the weekend to the student (a more advanced activity).

Set your scenario according to the language you are teaching or revising. Describing anything that has happened, such as a previous holiday or job, elicits the past tense—describing planned events, such as what students intend to do after school or during an upcoming holiday period, drills the future. To work on the conditional tense, students imagine what they would do if they could do anything; or say to the country's president. The same scenarios work for modals.

It is best if beginners submit their descriptions for homework before the lesson, and you correct the grammar. Students will be more confident, and the activity will run more fluently. Higher levels can perform off the cuff for more of a challenge.

Example with adult learners, A2 level, working on simple past:

A. Yesterday I went to Tignes Le Lac.
B. What did you do there?
A. I went to the supermarket.
B. How much did you spend?
A. (laughs) 3 pounds ninety-two.
B. False. I don't think you went to Tignes yesterday to do your shopping.
A. You are right; I didn't go.

One point for B. Now it's A's turn to ask B questions.

B. Yesterday I didn't drink any alcohol.
A. Were you alone last night?
B. Yes, I was.
A. Are there any bottles of wine open in your flat?
B. Yes, there are two, one red and one white.
A. Did you watch a film last night?
B. No.
A. I think that you DID drink alcohol last night. Is that true?
B. No, it's false. I did not drink any alcohol last night.

Zero points for A.
Have two turns each.

Call my bluff definitions

Category	Writing, reading
Group size	One to one, any class size
Level	Lower intermediate to advanced
Age	12 to adult
Materials	Optionally cameras
Preparation	Students prepare definitions for homework
Great for	Vocabulary definitions to enriching knowledge of English through metaphors

Vocabulary version

Students prepare three definitions of a word that they look up in the dictionary, one true and two false. The class listen to these and decide which are false. Once students have heard all three, have them listen as these are read out again. This time, students do thumbs down to the camera if they think a definition is false and nothing if they believe it is true. This way, it is easy to see who is correct. Tell those students who were right to award themselves a point. Ideally, give the preparation task as homework so as not to use class time for research.

Metaphors, idioms, or sayings version

Idioms are phrases or expressions that cannot be translated literally—in other words, when used in everyday language, they have a meaning other than the basic one you would find in the dictionary. Every language has its idioms. Learning them makes understanding and using a language more fun! They are best tackled with higher-level learners.

For example, 'break a leg' is a common English idiom. The literal meaning is 'I command you to break a bone in your leg.' The idiomatic meaning is 'Do your best.' Often, actors tell each other to 'break a leg' before they go out on stage to perform.

Students choose a metaphor or expression and give three possible meanings, two false and one accurate. This exercise is enriching for vocabulary and taxing the imagination. Alternatively, distribute metaphors or idioms, one or two per student, and let them research the meanings for homework. More advanced students could be given free rein to find metaphors or expressions.

Here are some metaphors, with one true and two false definitions to try with this game:

Albatross

- Someone who is overweight or clumsy
- A white-haired person
- A handicap or burden

Songbird

- A female vocalist
- A person who tells secrets
- A boasting person with a big ego

Chicken and egg
- When you don't know what to do
- When you can't decide what comes first
- Productivity

Beating a dead horse
- Wasting time on a project that will never succeed
- Behaving like a weird sadist
- Getting upset over things that happened a long time ago

A white elephant
- Useless and irrelevant
- Magnificent and powerful
- Miraculous

Jumping the gun
- Fire off all the bullets in one go
- Do something before the time is right
- Dodge a bullet

Cold turkey
- When a drug addict has withdrawal symptoms
- The favourite Christmas dish in Britain
- When you feel too scared to do something

Couch potato
- A slob who spends all day watching TV
- A dish made of layers of cheese and potato
- A potato with a long flat shape

Cold feet
- When you are scared to do something
- When you have holes in your shoes
- When you are homeless

Melting pot
- A mix of ideas or peoples
- A deep pan often used for making a sauce
- A British dish often served in the North

Rosetta stone
- A jewel
- A clue to understanding something challenging
- A paperweight

Cherry-picking

- Choosing the best, sometimes in a way that can seem unfair
- Working as an immigrant in Australia
- Looking for soulmates

Greek to me

- When you consider something or someone to be out of date, as if from Ancient Greece
- When you do not understand
- When you do understand

Green shoots

- Indications of a recovery, often the economy
- Learning to use a gun and missing the target
- When someone starts getting better from an illness

In a nutshell

- To be concise
- To be stubborn and inflexible
- A well-rounded and balanced view

Pear-shaped

- When things go wrong
- When fruits are ready for picking
- When things are an undefined shape

The roof of the world

- High Asia, including Tibet
- The mountains
- To be successful

Salad days

- A period of youth and inexperience
- The early days of summer
- Days when the harvests are ripe for picking

Son of a gun

- A rascal or dishonest person
- An incredible shot
- Someone who loves hunting

Tunnel vision

- A narrow viewpoint, not looking at all the arguments
- A telescope for night vision
- Side-lighting in tunnels

Catch-22
- A fishing term
- A baseball term
- An impossible situation

To spit it out
- To say something
- To find an idea immoral or disgusting
- To spit over a great distance

Warm reception
- When someone is welcoming
- A party in a warm room
- A wedding reception with a lot of guests

Weighty subject
- An important matter
- An overweight person
- A scale to weigh ingredients

Chants

Category	Speaking fluency
Group size	One to one, any class size in groups
Level	Beginner to intermediate
Age	All ages
Materials	Sentences
Preparation	Practise the sentences in a rhythm while clapping
Great for	Speaking fluency, confidence builder, grammar drill

Give students a few sentences containing useful vocabulary or grammar. Students are to read out their text in a rhythm. Clap the beat with a partner. Students are free to fit the sentence into the rhythm as best they can. Musical students will naturally do this well, while for others, it will be more challenging. If you try this yourself, you will see that it is excellent for encouraging fluency, as one is frequently obliged to run several words together quickly to fit into a beat.

The rhythm should be slow and steady. One beat per second is a good pace for beginners. Here are some examples of how to fit a regular sentence into a rhythm.

The first example is one syllable per beat; this is easy, boring, and there is no point to it unless you are working with young children who need to learn to coordinate clapping and speaking at the same time.

She—went—to—town—to—buy—a—tooth—brush

The next rhythm is better, and students have to say 'a toothbrush' quite quickly to fit it into the beat.

She **went**—to **town**—to **buy**—a **tooth**brush
Clap clap clap clap

Here is a jazzier rhythm where we fit all the words into three beats. Hold 'she' for longer. For musicians, the rhythm for 'She went to' is a crotchet followed by two quavers.

She went to—**town** to buy a—**tooth**brush
Clap clap clap

Vary rhythms by using pauses.

Clap	Clap	Clap	Clap
(silence)	She went to **town**	(silence)	to buy a **tooth**brush

Here is an extended example for those of you who may still be unsure. Clap on, and stress all syllables in bold. The other syllables fit rhythmically into the space between claps. Keep in time. Even the teacher has to practise this a few times!

She went to **town** to buy a **tooth**brush but there **were** none at the **chem**ist. (Breath) She **walk**ed to the **sup**ermarket and **bought** a toothbrush **there**.

Or start on an upbeat:
She **went** to town to **buy** a toothbrush but **there** were none at the **chem**ist. She **walked** to the super**mar**ket and **bought** a toothbrush **there**.

If you are not musical and do not know what an upbeat is, don't worry – you do not need to know these things. Experiment beforehand, saying some text in different rhythms to a beat so that your demonstration is convincing. Everyone benefits from this activity, whether musical or not!

Be patient. Students may have to try many times before succeeding; once they do, ask them to read the sentence normally, and they will be amazed at how it effortlessly trips off their tongue.

Chanting games

Category	Speaking drill and fluency
Group size	2 players to a class
Level	All levels
Age	All ages
Materials	None
Preparation	None
Great for	Any vocabulary topics and short grammar drills. Examples are given for adjectives, adverbs, comparatives, descriptions, pronouns, past tense of 'to be,' professions, vocabulary, and weather.

Chanting aids fluency, is relaxing, non-threatening, and gets everyone participating. It's easy and boosts confidence among shy students, who are more likely to join in than if asked to speak alone in the spotlight. A chant can be anything; it does not have to be a known nursery rhyme. Poetry is a good source of chants. I love the Puffin Book of Children's Poetry for finding fun chants for all ages, but you may chant literally anything.

- To make the chant more meaningful, add actions that reflect nouns, verbs, or what is happening.
- Chant tongue twisters, getting slightly faster each time.
- Chant and do something at the end.
- Chant and guess something at the end.

Chant and do something at the end.

Together chant this extract from James Reeves:

The sea is a hungry dog, giant and grey; he rolls on the beach all day.

At the end of the sentence, students mime an animal, holding the position; or write down their chosen animal. The teacher picks a fact like 'it eats grass.' All those miming an animal that eats grass win a point. Animal facts might be; bigger than a human, heavier than a horse, lives in the mountains, it's a pet, and so on.

Alternatively, at the end of the chant, students hold a mime, the teacher picks someone. If your platform does this, the person miming should say something so that his or her video is enlarged. The other students watch and guess what this person is doing. Students could be in teams and earn points for correct guesses.

Chant and guess something at the end.

Everyone chants together, and at the end, students guess an item from a theme. The teacher thinks of an item, say a chair, if using a furniture theme. Make up a chant, for example:

Class chant: A big bookcase, a round table, a large bed
Teacher: A wide...

The class call out furniture items that could fit with 'wide' until someone guesses the word chair. That person or their team wins a point. Students repeat the chant while the teacher quickly thinks of something different, like a blue lamp.

Class: A big bookcase, a round table, a large bed
Teacher: A blue...

Try with adjectives as in the above example.

Try with comparatives:
Chant: Smaller than a mouse, stronger than a horse, bigger than a house
Teacher: Faster than a...

Try with adverbs:

Chant: slowly slowly ticked the clock, quickly quickly did we pop
Teacher: To… (the shops, the chemist, the supermarket, school, the pool, the gym)

Adverbs:

Chant: He walked quickly, she drank thirstily, they went home and
Teacher: We read…slowly. We played music…loudly. We jumped up…suddenly.

Descriptions:

Chant: She's got brown eyes, he's got blue eyes, and they've got red hair.
Teacher: She's got…short hair.

Pronouns:

Chant: I know you, you know me, we know him, and they know
Teacher: Who? (Students guess between me, you, her, him, us, them.)

Past tense to be:

Chant: Was it a bus, was it a plane, was it a car?
Teacher: It was a… (Students call out different types of transport till they guess which one the teacher is thinking.)

Vocabulary:

Chant: Are you a bird? Are you a horse? Are you a cat?
Students: All mime one of the three animals.
Teacher: The teacher, or a selected student, names one of the three, and anyone miming that animal wins a point.

Professions:

Chant: Are you a painter? Are you a cleaner? Are you a writer?

Weather:

Chant: Sometimes it's sunny, sometimes it's hot, sometimes it's cold, but today it's NOT.
Teacher: It's... (Students guess the weather the teacher is thinking.)

Charades

Category	Speaking fluency but probably no good for mixed nationality classes.
Group size	Groups and classes
Level	Intermediate
Age	10 to adult
Materials	Cameras on
Preparation	Film and book titles relevant to your students
Great for	General language.

How to play

One person mimes a book, a song, or a film by acting out each word of the title or miming something specific that others could recognise to identify what it is. Those watching guess the book, song, or film.

- This game is possible if students stand further back from their cameras so you can see more of them.
- It can be tricky with movies because film titles are often poorly translated and even renamed. Disney's 'Frozen' is 'La Reine des Neiges in French,' which could be translated as 'The Snow Queen.' So, if you have French kids, then mime a queen and snow, rather than someone frozen!
- To save yourself time and guarantee titles are relevant to your students, have them think of books, songs, or films they could mime before the lesson.

The player miming is not allowed to speak at all and starts by indicating if he or she is miming a book (pretend to open a book), a song (pretend to sing), or a film (pretend to hold a movie camera). The other players respond to the mime by calling out the answer, for example:

It's a film

The player miming then specifies how many words are in the title by holding up the relevant number of fingers, and the other players respond, for example:

Two words

The player miming can then either act out the full title or choose to act out one of the words; for example, he or she might hold up two fingers, and the audience responds with:

Second word

The actor mimes a donkey or mule until someone guesses:

Mule

Next, he or she might hold up one finger for the first word and indicate that this is a little word by holding the thumb and forefinger close as if holding a small object between them. The audience responds with 'a,' 'it,' 'an,' and so on. Eventually, someone says 'the,' which is the correct word in this mime. So now we have 'the' and 'mule' – in this case, the film is Clint Eastwood's:

The Mule

Mime syllables: You may also mime syllables of words. For example, hold up two fingers for 'second word,' and then place one finger on your forearm to indicate the first syllable. To elicit the syllable 'pot,' as a clue for a Harry Potter film or book, mime making a pot on a wheel.

It sounds like: You can also mime things that sound like the word to be guessed. Indicate this by holding a hand up to your ear. The others respond with 'it sounds like.' Now mime 'carry,' which sounds like Harry, for Harry Potter.

Charades race

Category	Speaking
Group size	One to one, any class size in pairs in breakout rooms
Level	All levels
Age	All ages
Materials	None, optionally use an online timer
Preparation	None
Great for	Any vocabulary, short grammar drills for any topic

How to play

Player A acts as many words as possible in the timeframe, and B guesses them and writes them down. Swap. The total of the pair is their final score. Repeat and try to do better or compare totals with the rest of the class.

- This game comes as a welcome break, especially in a one to one class, where your student's brain may be fried from intense concentration.
- It works even better if students prepare mimes for a given vocabulary theme in advance.
- Don't be shy; try this with your adult students. You may be surprised how much they enjoy it and how it can help them to relax.
- Scoring the totals of each pair makes it a collaboration as opposed to a competition. A team effort means students will do their best to mime well and guess. When competing, players could pretend they cannot work out what the mime is. You might be surprised just how much some people will cheat to win!

Colour the card

Category	Speaking
Group size	One to one, pairwork for any class size
Level	Beginner to intermediate
Age	4 to adult
Materials	Black and white pictures, or pairs, one coloured and one black and white
Preparation	Finding pictures in black and white
Great for	Colours. What colour is? What colour are?

How to play

Divide your group into pairs. Give player A a coloured picture and player B the same image but in black and white. Player A must not show the coloured picture to player B. Player B asks what colour the items are in the picture and colours them in. For example, if the image is a lady in a dress, player B could ask:

What colour is her dress?
What colour are her shoes?
What colour is her hair?
What colour is her belt?

Player A replies:

Her dress is red. Her shoes are white.

Player B takes the relevant colour and puts a dash of it on the picture but does not colour the whole thing in at this stage. Once player B has made a note of all the colours, the players swap roles with a different picture. Colouring can be done manually with images shown via the camera or via the screen share. I recommend manual colouring for children unless printing the pictures is onerous. For adults, I recommend an onscreen colouring tool since it's quicker. The game Blind Painter mentions more on colouring with annotation tools.

Materials

One way to make these pictures is to print a coloured clip art picture and then save the image in greyscale or black and white. Alternatively, take a photo with your phone and make a copy in black and white. My flashcard sets are a handy resource (see other resources section) as they all contain B&W and coloured pictures.

A way around finding or creating pairs of pictures is to give out black and white images to both children. The children themselves then decide what colours to use.

Have students show their coloured pictures to you or classmates to acknowledge task completion.

In my lessons, I noticed that boys tended to prefer to colour knights and cars rather than girls in dresses, so always give players a choice.

Commands game

Category	Listening
Group size	One to one, any class size, whole-class activity
Level	Beginner to intermediate
Age	4 to adult
Materials	None
Preparation	None
Great for	Commands, verbs

Divide the class into teams. Children are seated at their desks. Give a command, such as run, jump, hop, or skip. All children stand up, carry out the action, and sit down as fast as possible. The team finishing last has a forfeit. Potentially, give forfeits for pathetic mimes or misbehaviour.

This game helps introduce vocabulary if the teacher mimes the action for students to copy. As the class become familiar with the language, stop miming and only give the commands. It's is also perfect for quick revision before a game such as Simon Says. Here are some examples (assuming the lesson is in a classroom and not in a playground, where there are more active possibilities). Add freely to them!

Dance / jump / run on the spot / touch your nose / touch your knee, ankle, ear … / touch anything red, blue, green … / touch a shoe, sock or another item of clothing / touch a friend's leg, arm, etc. / open a book / pick up a pen / fold a piece of paper / pass the paper to a neighbour / screw up the paper / throw it on the floor / pick it up / unfold it / write you name on it / throw it in the bin / be silent / crouch down / mime a chicken / write the number seven / sing do re mi / tap your feet / clap your hands once / clap your hands five times / stand up / sit down / stand up if you're wearing a skirt / sit down if you are wearing black shoes / stand up if you like tennis / sit down if you like chocolate / be a Jedi knight / be a princess / be a prince / fly a plane / drive a car / eat a melon / eat a sticky toffee pudding / hop on one foot / make the letter t with your hands / make the letter d with another child / be happy / look up / look down / look around / look out of the window / look under your desk / and so on.

Concentration

Category	Speaking
Group size	One to one, any class size in pairs or small groups in breakout rooms
Level	Beginner to intermediate
Age	5 to adult
Materials	Pictures, PowerPoint or similar, students need screen share and tools
Preparation	Ten minutes if you already have flashcards but re-useable for future lessons
Great for	Highly versatile, any vocabulary, grammar, Q and A

Preparation

Copy and paste pictures into a blank PowerPoint sheet, which takes five minutes if you already have flashcards. Here is an example for types of transport, using my flashcard set. There must be two of each picture.

Next, make one coloured box big enough to hide a picture. (insert > shape > choose rectangle > fill with any colour). Copy and paste this over the first line of pictures. Then highlight the row of boxes and copy and paste as a second row and a third row. I used two colours to make it easier, but they can all be the same colour. Make a spare copy of the game, so you always have one intact. Re-use your boxes and replace the vocabulary pictures to play with a different theme.

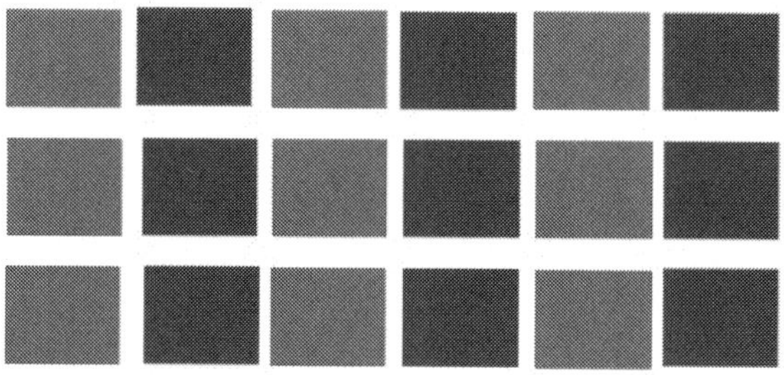

How to play

Player A drags two boxes to the side to reveal two pictures. If these form a pair, player A wins a point and keeps the boxes stacked on one side of the game. If the images do not match, player A drags the boxes back over them, re-hiding them. Player B now has a turn. The game continues until all the pairs have been found.

The younger the players, the fewer pictures you use initially.

Language ideas

Language possibilities with this game are endless. Keep an eye, as always, on the complexity so that the game does not drag.

Vocabulary: Each player names the items on the cards he or she turns over.

Phrases: Each player forms a short phrase, using the item on the card. With pictures of people or with places, you might add an adjective, such as:

a pretty girl, a tall boy
a big city, a small village, a clean beach, a deep pond

Sentences: Each player forms a sentence using one or both of the items. For example, transport is good with prepositions:

I go to school by bus.

Transport goes with any verb tense:

We flew to Spain by plane.

I say a place, and my private students make up a sentence using the means of transport. So, if it's a plane, I'll name a foreign country. If it's a bicycle, I'll mention somewhere local, like the pub or the supermarket.

If using pictures of food, players could say:
I like butter and milk, or I like butter, but I don't like milk.

If using pictures of people, players could say:

Her name is Claudia. She is a dentist. She is from Spain. She is wearing trousers. Etc.

One can also work on comparatives, such as:

The girl is taller than the boy. The girl is older than the baby.

Intermediate students can practise structures of greater complexity. For example:

I was going to buy some milk, but I bought some cheese instead.
I have never been to London, but I have been to Paris.

Questions: Players ask questions related to each picture they turn over. For example, with sets of people, ask:

What's her name? Where does she live? How old is she?

If playing with pictures of countries or places, team 1 asks:

Where did you go last summer?

A player from team 2 turns over two cards and replies:

I went to London and Paris.

- In the classic game, when players find a matching pair, they have another go. However, as the goal is to have the group master language rather than find a winner, it is preferable to let each person have only one turn. Therefore, it is less likely that the ablest students will win all the pairs, leaving the others with nothing.
- An excellent way to keep everyone interested, even when it is someone else's turn (aside from the fact that they are supposed to be memorizing the cards), is to split each group into two teams. Each person has a go as usual, but team-mates can help with vocabulary if need be. When counting all the pairs at the end, have a winning team rather than a winning individual.

- When learning vocabulary, pictures produce better results than written words. If a bit dry and visually harder to remember, word cards are good for spelling or to practise making sentences. With children, pictures are necessary since they are vivid, and words might seem boring. Alternatively, play with one image and one written word, which is good for spelling and vocabulary. There are themed sets of vocabulary pictures included with my flashcards set on TeachingEnglishGames.com. Just copy and paste the small-sized flashcards into a PowerPoint to make a Concentration game.
- If you are not sharing controls with your students, add letters and numbers to your concentration game so people can call 'A-7' rather than 'top left, top line, 5th one along.'

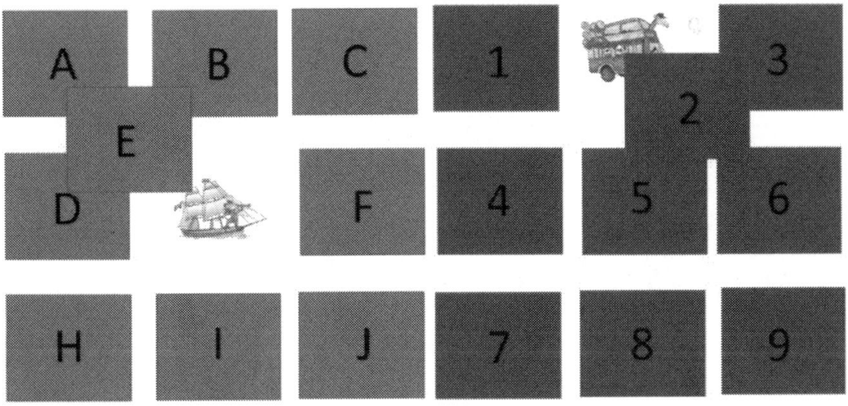

Concentration spelling and pronunciation

Category	Reading, speaking
Group size	One to one, any class in small groups
Level	High beginner to advanced
Age	10 to adult
Materials	Contrasting or matching words
Preparation	Use the example provided or fill in the blank (Concentration-pronunciation.pptx)
Great for	Spelling drill, pronunciation

Play as described in Concentration above but using words that rhyme. Easy vocabulary like floor and door suit beginners, whereas words with silent letters or homophone pairs, like 'nose' and 'knows' – that sound the same but have different spellings – may be used for advanced students,

Two example games are provided in the Appendix; see concentration-pronunciation.pptx

Here are examples of rhyming words with different spelling:

- light, might, kite, site, sight, slight
- bridge, fridge
- carriage, marriage
- few, dew, do, to, threw, you, through
- sew, mow, go, though, dough, toe, show
- buy, cry, die, fly, sigh, my, tie, lie
- leek, tweak, peak, peek
- eat, sheet, meet, meat, tweet
- some, dumb, thumb, mum, plum
- cake, bake, break, shake, make
- we, see, tea, me, fee
- hair, flare, snare, glare, air, pear, fair, fare, tear (to rip)
- saw, bore, gnaw, floor, tore
- learn, turn, fern
- sent, cent, percent %, meant
- whether, weather, together, forever
- rose, rows, goes, shows
- loud, rowed, cloud, allowed, now, plough
- wood, would, could, good, should
- there, their, they're.

Connect four

Category	Speaking
Group size	One to one, any class in pairs in breakout rooms
Level	Beginner to intermediate
Age	6 to adult
Materials	Blank charts provided in the Appendix A list of exercises or questions

	Students need access to annotation tools
Preparation	Decide on the themes or questions
Great for	Alphabet, phonemes, numbers, vocabulary, grammar drill

Connect Four is a well-known game where players have to make a line of four counters to win. Put players in pairs and give each one a blank copy of the chart below (Connect-Four.pdf in the Appendix) or display a six-down by a seven-across grid in screen share while students copy it down. Players decide who is X and who is 0 and who is to play first, and they should alternate for each round. Each pair has a list of questions, which may be a vocabulary flashcard question such as ‘What’s this?’, a grammar question such as converting a sentence into a question or a different tense, or even a general knowledge question. What you choose depends on the level of your class and what you want to drill.

If player A can answer a question, A can place an X anywhere on the bottom line. Player B answers the next question, putting a 0 on the bottom line or just above player A’s X. Each X or 0 must either rest on the lowest row available or on top of another X or 0. An X or 0 cannot hang in the air, so to speak. Each line of four made horizontally, vertically, or diagonally earns a point, and the game continues until there are no spaces left. Students enjoy

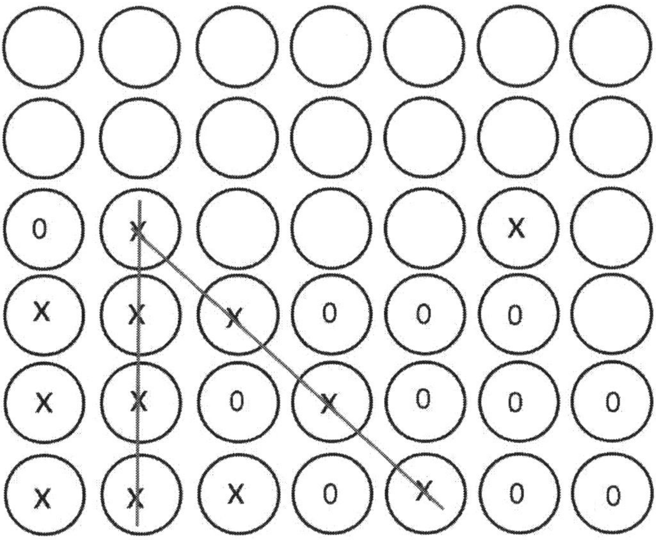

the challenge of trying to make four in a row while working on their English.

Play also using annotation tools. Each student names a circle and colours it. Write the alphabet or numbers inside the circles for beginners. Any words or pictures could go inside the circles.

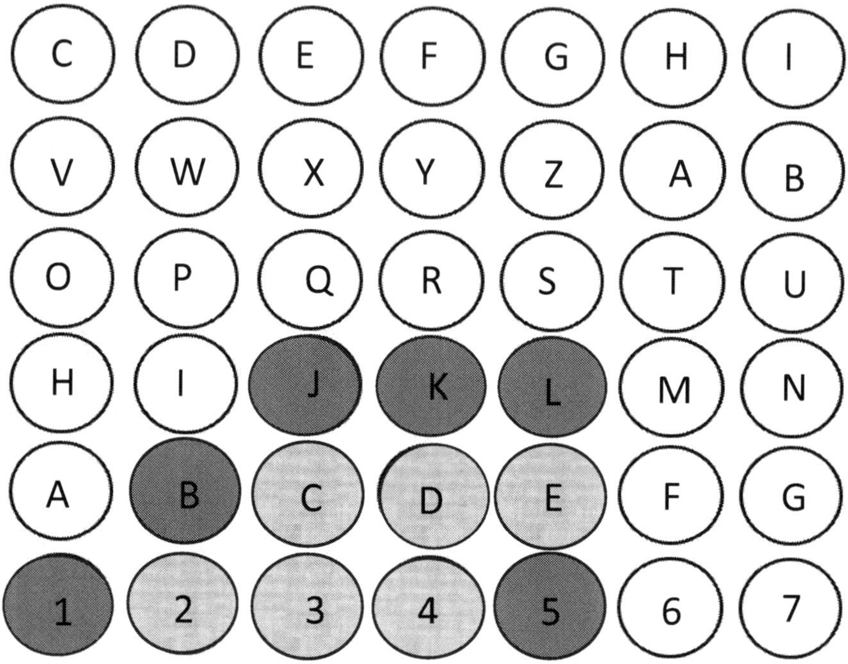

Connect-Four.pdf

Multi-level classes

Give a different task to higher-level students, such as making questions using words in the circles rather than naming vocabulary.

Counting and number game 1: Add up the dice

Category	Speaking
Group size	One to one, any class in groups in breakout rooms
Level	Beginner

Age	6 to adult
Materials	Online dice rolling website or app
Preparation	None
Great for	Adding up, revising numbers

At the time of writing, typing 'roll dice online' leads to a free website (https://turboluck.com/en/roll-dice-online/). Select four rolls to get four digits. Students race (or not) to add these up. Beware of advertising and links to gambling websites.

How to play

Demonstrate first before putting students into pairs or small groups in breakout rooms. Roll two dice and have players add up the total. For older kids and adults, roll three or more. One student rolls the dice, and the others race to add them. Players take it in turns, though it may be more practical to have one person roll all the dice while the others take it in turns to do the maths.

To practise higher numbers, say that each number on the dice is x10 or x100 its face value, so 6 would become 60 or 600. 6 could equally become 66 and 5 become 55, and so on.

- Wherever possible, have students play in small teams to avoid some poor person being shown up as the slowest to add up every time. This game does not have to be a race.
- Pairs of students can have a time limit to add up as many sets of dice as they can in two-minutes, taking turns to add up, which avoids the same person doing all the work. The pair then play again and see if they can beat their score.

Counting and number game 2: Clap and count

Category	Speaking
Group size	One to one, any class size in pairs in breakout rooms
Level	Beginner
Age	Any
Materials	None

Preparation	None
Great for	Counting

How to play

Clap or several times and have pupils call out how many claps they hear. Clap slowly for younger children so they have time to follow. Clap slowly and then accelerate with older ones to make it quite tricky. Pupils may play this in pairs.

Have teens and adults count while you clap. Start at any number, say twenty-seven. Clap and count up to 33, then ask, how many numbers is that? Answer: seven. (33-27=7)

Counting and number game 3: Guess the price

Category	Speaking
Group size	One to one, small groups in breakout rooms for bigger classes
Level	Flexible
Age	10 to adult
Materials	None
Preparation	A list of items and their price
Great for	Numbers, prices, currencies

Preparation

Go to an online store and copy and paste pictures into a PowerPoint or document; It's quick to invent fair prices for the products though nothing stops you from using the ones from the store. Choose objects likely to appeal to your audience. Your ten-year-old pupils might not be interested in a range of cookware. Visually appealing, colourful products are also fun.

How to play

Players are to guess the price of an item you show via the camera or screen share. Each player writes down a price, preferably onscreen, to see how much everyone guessed. The winner is the one who either correctly estimates the cost of the item or is closest to it.

Ask any player for his or her estimate. Respond by saying whether the actual amount is higher or lower. If it is higher, all those with lower guesses know they are 'out' for the moment. Continue asking players for their prices until the winner is identified.

The prices can be simple for beginners, such as $1, £2, or a round figure. For advanced players, price objects at $1.98 or $358.43, and so on. Introduce currencies to teach dollars, euros, pounds, yen, etc.

Use items that are of interest to your students. Kids might like to guess the price of familiar sweets, burgers, and food they enjoy, toys, bikes, skateboards, and so on. Adults might enjoy guessing the cost of holiday packages, works of art, antiques, or property. If you are teaching refugees; or think luxury items are not appropriate, stick to useful things people buy in their daily lives.

Counting and number game 4: How many?

Category	Speaking
Group size	One to one, small groups in breakout rooms
Level	Beginner
Age	7 to adult
Materials	Pictures of things or tangible items to count
Preparation	One to ten minutes
Great for	Numbers, counting, how many

How to play

Find a packet of biscuits, a page of words, a bag of pasta, a pile of paper, a pot of pens and pencils, a roll of toilet paper, cotton buds in a jar, nails in a toolbox, or a bowl of fruit. Fill a glass jar with random items. These could be sweets, coins, or small toys. Either use the real thing from home and show it via the camera or find pictures online. To figure out how much pasta there is in a bag without counting every piece, weigh ten pieces, and do the maths.

Show your items while students write down their guesses. Give a tight time limit to keep everyone focused and prevent too much lingering from counting all the objects.

Play as for Guess the Price above.

Creative story modification

Category	Speaking fluency
Group size	One to one, any class size in groups
Level	Intermediate to advanced
Age	6 to adult
Materials	None
Preparation	Decide which well-known story titles you will use
Great for	General English, fluency

Share three or four well-known story titles, like Little Red Riding Hood, or a famous film title, the kind of movie on TV every year at Christmas. Short stories that are not too complicated work best. Try and pick a tale everybody knows, but if in doubt, ask your pupils to give you titles. Next, ask a student to recount the gist of one of the stories as briefly as possible. Ask a different student to do the same with the next one, and so on.

Now divide the class into small groups of two to four students per group and give them ten minutes to invent a new version of the story. Students create a different genre altogether, using the same characters and primary events. Thus, a James Bond movie' becomes a comedy, 'Little Red Riding Hood' turn into a horror story, 'The Princess and the pea' becomes a romance, and 'The Emperor's New Clothes' transforms into an adrenalin adventure. Students can add new characters, change the ending, and have creative leeway. Finally, students listen to each other's stories and judge them for entertainment value, creativity, and dramatic delivery.

Creative writing

Category	Creative writing
Group size	One to one, any class size
Level	All levels
Age	10 to adult
Materials	None
Preparation	Decide which words are to be included in the story
Great for	Writing skills, general English

Include four words or grammar

Students make up sentences or paragraphs about anything they like as long as they include four words you specify. Give students a model of what you are expecting so they know how long the tale should be. There is no need to agonize over choosing four words. Relax, your students have imagination! Any four words will do. To focus on grammar, say if the story is to be in the past, present, or future, or include specific phrases. Here are some examples with 'doctor,' 'carrot,' 'door,' and 'jacket.'

Beginner: I am a doctor. I eat carrots. My door is yellow, and so is my jacket.

A higher-level student:

I caught my jacket in the door while eating a carrot, fell over, and had to go to the doctor.

An advanced student:

A few months ago, I went to the doctor's, and she told me to get a blood test, so I did. It turned out that I was deficient in vitamin D, so I decided to eat a ton of carrots. I had them delivered by a local farmer, who tipped them into my garage. The pile spread out, and I couldn't get the garage door shut. I had to park my car in the street for the rest of the month. So anyway, I started munching through the carrots and soon was absolutely sick of them. However, I kept at it, working my way through the pile. I had carrot soup, carrot purée, carrot salad, carpaccio of carrot, baked carrot, roast carrot, and so on. After a while, my skin started turning orange. At first, people asked me if I'd been on holiday. Then they started joking with me that I had overdone the fake tan. Eventually, they started asking me if I was feeling alright, until one day, I just passed out, and when I woke up, I found myself back at the doctor's.

Luckily, unluckily

Students start with an opening sentence: I was on my way to the shop when I saw my sister in her boyfriend's car. Students make up the following sentence, which must start with 'unluckily.' The third sentence must begin with 'luckily.' Continue alternating and creating lines of the story, and see how far you get!

Giving a topic

Generally, it's best if students choose their topics because they are more likely to be motivated to express themselves and have something to say. That said, a fun way to encourage creativity is to have students pick silly ideas for each other. Here's an idea: students think of the most boring topic possible. These ideas are collected, shuffled, and handed out again randomly. The challenge is to write a super-interesting paragraph on the allegedly dull subject, which is an opportunity to invent and be imaginative. Sometimes other students will learn something, as something void of interest for one person might be another's passion. Students read out their creations in small groups, and the group picks the best one to read to the class. (It could prove long-winded to listen to every single story, hence the selection process in groups!)

Creative story group project

Category	Speaking
Group size	One to one, any class size
Level	All levels
Age	12 to adult
Materials	None
Preparation	None
Great for	Speaking, creative writing, general language

Small group version focusing on speaking skills

Put everyone into teams to encourage participation. Have a student start a story with one sentence. For example, Yesterday I decided to change my life. The teacher quickly jots this down on screen share. Other students ask the narrator questions relating to the story. Questions might be:

Where were you? What were you doing? Why?

Someone else takes over the narration, answering one of the questions. The teacher writes the answer, and the teams call out further queries relating to the new element. And so it continues until a story emerges. Optionally, put students in groups for five minutes to finish it off in an interesting way. Listen to the alternative versions.

As a motivator, each question asked earns a point for the team. A shy student might be given the task of keeping score. You can keep score if students call out their team number before the question; 'Team one, What time was it?'

Big class

For a big class, play as above but without teams or points for questions. Do a demonstration for five minutes. Then put create groups with a narrator, recorder, and others to ask the questions. After five minutes, bring everyone back and listen to the various tales.

Creative story re-write

Category	Reading and writing
Group size	One to one, any class size
Level	Intermediate to advanced
Age	Teen to adult
Materials	Text from a coursebook or any written text
Preparation	5 minutes to copy an extract from your coursebook
Great for	Vocabulary development

Copy an extract from your coursebook, a novel for children, or a travel guidebook.

An example for higher-levels, from a guide to New York:

> If you like wandering the galleries at the Metropolitan Museum of Art, we think you'll enjoy the Asia Society and Museum. Founded in 1956 by John D Rockerfeller, this cultural center's museum has rare treasures from across Asia, such as Jain sculptures from India, Buddhist paintings from Nepal, and jade from China.

Students have a mission to render this text exciting or exotic by making, say, four to six changes. Allow dictionaries and let students work in pairs or groups. Hear the different versions and vote on the most poetic, the funniest, the most ridiculous, and the most intelligent.

Exaggeration:

> If you like wandering the enormous galleries at the Metropolitan Museum of Art, we think you'll enjoy the Asia Society and Museum. Founded in 1956 by John D Rockerfeller, this gigantic cultural center's museum has priceless treasures from across Asia, such as gargantuan sculptures from India, microscopic paintings from Nepal, and an interminable jade collection from China.

Crazy:

> If you like wandering the cheese-filled galleries at the Metropolitan Museum of Art, we think you'll enjoy the Asia Society and Museum. Founded in 1956 by a lunatic, this cult center's museum has mysterious treasures from across Asia, such as prehistoric eyeballs from India, blank paintings from Nepal, and three-eyed invisible ghosts from China.

Silly:

> If you like jogging in the galleries at the Metropolitan Museum of Art, we think you'll enjoy the Asia Society and Museum. Founded in 1956 by John D Rockerfeller, this sporting center's museum has rare tracksuits from across Asia, such as sacred tracksuits from India, yak wool tracksuits from Nepal, and luminous tracksuits from China.

Try another layer of editing for higher-levels, adding four clauses starting with who, which, because, and when.

If you like jogging in the galleries at the Metropolitan Museum of Art, we think you'll enjoy the Asia Society and Museum **when** you have nothing else to do. Founded in 1956 by John D Rockerfeller, **who** was unhappy **because** he was bored, this sporting center's museum has rare tracksuits from across Asia; sacred tracksuits from India; yak wool tracksuits from Nepal; and luminous tracksuits from China, **which** are visible from space.

Cryptic clues

Category	Writing
Group size	One to one, any class size
Level	All levels
Age	6 to adult
Materials	Optional picture flashcards or objects
Preparation	None when you play with the examples here Students prepare for subsequent games
Great for	Vocabulary revision game

Preparation

Prepare sets of picture cards or words, each to represent a theme. For example:

- School: book, pencil, desk, chair, table, whiteboard
- Beach: sea, sand, shells, towel, sunglasses, suntan lotion
- Airport: plane, runway, terminal, ticket, check-in
- Restaurant: waiter, tables, chairs, food, plates, kitchen, bill
- Cinderella: a glass slipper, pumpkin, ugly sisters, a princess, a prince
- Cinema: Film, popcorn, ticket, armchair, big screen

For older students, be a little more cryptic, for example:

- Chocolate cake: chocolate, flour, butter, cake decoration, candles
- Police station: policeman, handcuffs, key, parking ticket
- Hairdressers: hairbrush, scissors, money, mirror

- Supermarket: food, products, trolleys, bags aisles, cashiers, shelves
- Bicycle: wheel, handlebars, seat, bell, pedals, chain

How to play

Display the clues or sets of pictures and give a short time limit for the task. Students guess the themes and write down their answers. Pupils can work individually or in pairs or groups. Allow a couple of minutes to go through the answers.

- Once students have played this once in class, they can think up clues for others to guess in the next lesson for homework. Keep their ideas in your library of resources.
- Use themes relevant to your students. Kids from a tribal school in Africa might have difficulty identifying a skiing holiday.

More cryptic clue ideas

Divide the class into teams. For 5 points, display a clue, like:

You watch it

Wait for a few suggestions. If no one guesses, add the second clue for 4 points.

A tool for communication

If there are still no correct guesses, add the third clue for 3 points.

A rectangular device used for entertainment

Finally, for 2 points, the last clue: Most people have one of these in their sitting room, and they watch it.' If no one has guessed, then it's zero all round, and you can tell the class that the item is a television.

Try these objects and clues for size, and once you have played with the class, students can work in small groups to develop series of clues for another team to guess, which could also be a homework assignment.

Telephone	Most people never leave home without it A small electronic device that people are constantly typing into A portable device you use to talk to people
GPS	A small electronic device that helps you find where you are going It tells you to go left, right, and straight on Global Positioning System
Stiletto	You could probably kill someone with this item of clothing Often worn by women and models Perfect for spraining your ankle and having sore feet
Glass	Usually transparent and breakable Contains liquid, but not often taken on picnics You drink out of it
Porc	A animal that loves to dig up fields with its nose Not eaten by vegetarians Some people do not eat it for religious reasons
Nose	Useful to breathe through Block it if it bleeds! It's on your face
Dog	They love being taken for walks They keep you company They are a man's best friend
Sheet	Sleep on it, but it's not a bed You fold it up to put it away Comes in single or double size for beds
Books	Something you often take on a journey Contains words Often best-sellers
Music	Small black dots and lines on a page called a manuscript You can learn to read this, but it's not letters You use an instrument to play it or your voice to sing it
Wheel	Man's most useful invention? A round object with many uses

	ALL cars have these to get around on
Pill	Small edible item meant to be a cure
	Prescribed by the doctor
	Medicine is often taken in this form
New York	A big apple
	A place where concrete and sky meet
	Famous multi-cultural city on the East Coast of America
Chocolate	Irresistible to many people
	You can melt it and mix it with cream to make a sauce
	Dark brown treat that often comes in squares or boxes
Credit Card	The worst possible way to borrow money
	Often the numbers are used fraudulently
	Money
Paper	Made from trees & is newsworthy
	You can recycle it though it burns well
	You can write and draw on it
Recipe	A combination of ingredients makes one of these
	You can buy whole books just with these in them
	For people who love to cook
Love	The most beautiful thing in the world
	It makes you feel warm and happy inside
	The best kind is unconditional

Debates

Category	Speaking fluency
Group size	One to one, any class size
Level	High beginner to advanced
Age	12 to adult
Materials	None
Preparation	None
Great for	General language and speaking

Debates are already dangerous territory in a regular classroom. As society advised in Jane Austen's 18th century England, it is safer to stick to talking about the state of the roads and the weather. The traffic and the weather are still hot topics in England today! Debating 'hot topics' can be divisive and even traumatizing, especially when students are from diverse backgrounds and cultures. Stay away from marriage, adoption, abortion, assisted pregnancies, sex changes, politics, vegetarianism, family values, euthanasia, immigration, and anything where your students are likely to clash. In all likelihood, there will not be a lively discussion but a monologue from someone who feels passionately and bullies everyone else into silence. You may end up with students who dislike each other and a gloomy atmosphere.

Conversation in an online environment can be trickier than in the classroom as the internet may be slow, and students are more reluctant to take center stage.

To steer clear of problems:

Use frivolous topics suggested in 'Either-Or' and 'Triangles Talking Points.' Keep it light, but relevant: What food should be served in the school canteen? Is fast food a good idea? It's better to be an electrician than a rap artist.

- Put students in pairs and have them argue with each other regardless of their personal point of view. Tell them to defend their point of view with whatever ideas they have, even if they are unreasonable or crazy - it's just a game! Rotate students so that they have a chance to repeat their arguments to others and hear different retorts.
- Share a topic and ask students to vote whether they are for or against and note those numbers down. Next, put students in small groups and quickly come up with as many points to argue their views with as they can. After five minutes, bring everyone back together and have students vote again; notice if there has been a change in the viewpoints thanks to the debate.

Describe and draw the picture

Category	Speaking fluency
Group size	One to one, any class size
Level	Beginner to lower intermediate
Age	Fun for kids but use with any age
Materials	Pictures
Preparation	Find three suitable pictures
Great for	Describing things, there is, there are, prepositions, present continuous

« Did you sleep well? »

Students work in pairs or small groups. One student describes a picture without showing it to the others, who listen and try to draw the picture. Family groups, rooms in the house, a classroom, a beach scene, a park, a garden, a town, or a farm are all good for basic vocabulary. It's easy to find suitable pictures. Type 'classroom scene' into your browser, and boom, a whole bunch come up, which you can copy and paste into a document. If you want something more original, type 'joke park scene,' scroll past the ads to the images, and click for more suggestions. You'll find a host of funny photos, cartoons, and weird stuff. Funky pictures will be more enjoyable for higher-level students to describe.

You need one picture to use for the demonstration and then two different ones for the pairwork. Once students have played this game in class, they could find a photo or cartoon to use in the next lesson.

- Pre-taught phrases such as 'in the foreground,' 'in the background,' and 'to the side' will be useful.
- Drawing is not a requirement – the student listening can imagine the picture being described and see how the real thing compares afterwards.

Describe the word

Category	Speaking
Group size	One to one, any class size
Level	Intermediate to advanced
Age	10 to adult
Materials	None
Preparation	None or a list of things for students to describe
Great for	General speaking fluency, adjectives, vocabulary

The purpose of the game is to describe words allowing students to use a wide range of language and work on speaking fluency. This activity is also useful because, in real life, one can sometimes be at a loss for a word and need to describe what one is trying to say.

Miming is not allowed!

Give students a minute to write down objects they could describe. To be on the safe side, have lists of words ready to use with children who might be slower to think of them. Divide students into teams and the team leader describes as many as possible to their team members within a two-minute timeframe. This game is fun to watch but if you have more than twelve pupils, use breakout rooms once everyone knows how to play.

If students cannot guess a word, players can move on to avoid getting stuck. Descriptions often include adjectives or actions, such as, 'you write with it,' for a pen.

As a variant for more advanced students, teams could have only one guess, so the person describing the object should be as detailed as possible to have the best chance of gaining the team point. For example:

It is a large animal with big ears and a trunk, and it is usually grey.
It is a small, flat, rectangular piece of plastic that you use to pay for things.

To challenge advanced students, they could describe concepts or emotions, such as timid, feeling blue, insurance, assurance, and vitality.

Once students know this game, you may set them the homework task of preparing words and descriptions for the next class. Students should be motivated to prepare difficult words for opposite teams to guess.

With a multi-level class, let the higher levels describe the words while the lower levels guess.

Decoding

Category	Listening and spelling
Group size	One to one, pairwork, whole-class activity
Level	Beginner to intermediate
Age	6 to adult
Materials	Code for alphabet, see below, or pictures
Preparation	Five minutes
Great for	Numbers, or vocabulary, alphabet

How to play

Display a code where numbers are equal to letters, for example 348 = a, 468 = b, 708 = c. The teacher reads out a number. Students write down the corresponding letter until a word is formed.

For vocabulary, use words instead of numbers. For example, display the following in screen share or chat:

pig = a	chicken = i	duck = l
sheep = m	cow = n	frog = s

The teacher or a selected student reads out the words, 'pig, cow, chicken, sheep, pig, duck, frog.' The class write down the corresponding letters and find that they have spelled the word 'animals.' In this task, students learn to spell while reviewing familiar vocabulary. To revise meanings rather than spellings, place animal flashcards next to the letters instead of the written words.

Have students create a complete alphabet and play again in pairs in breakout rooms.

An example alphabet might be:

apple = a	bottle = b	car = c	d = dog
e = ear	f = football	g = garden	h = hair
i = ice cream	j = juice	k = kite	l = lake
m = man	n = nose	o = orange	p = paper
q = queen	r = rabbit	s= school	t = table
u = umbrella	v = vegetable	w = water	x = xylophone
y = year	z = zero		

Detective game

Category	Speaking fluency
Group size	Small groups, as a class or in breakout rooms
Level	Beginner to intermediate
Age	4 to 12
Materials	None
Preparation	None
Great for	Q&A revision game, conversation skills game

How to play

One student is chosen to be the detective, and another, but secretly via a private message, the thief. As a class, the detective has three chances to find the thief. To find the thief, the detective chooses three people and asks each of them a question, such as:

What is your name? Where do you live? What were you doing last night?

If the person answering the question is the thief, they must give themselves up for arrest after replying. If the detective has not found the thief after asking three people a question, someone else takes over as the detective. Continue until the thief is found. Choose a new thief and a new detective for the next round.

The above setup works well for a small group of up to ten children. Increase the numbers of thieves and detectives to ask and answer questions simultaneously so that more children are involved in speaking.

Variation

Reverse the procedure with a different scenario for variety. For example, have a wicked witch who turns people to stone if they speak to her. The questioner could play an imaginary character and must ask three people a question. If one of those three is the wicked witch, then the questioner is turned to stone and has to be released by the whole class chanting a spell.

Dictation

Category	Listening and writing. Drill or general language.
Group size	One to one, any class size
Level	Beginner to intermediate
Age	All ages
Materials	Pen and paper or an online writing tool
Preparation	Decide on the text – no prep if you make it up spontaneously or read from a coursebook
Great for	Specific grammar or general language

Although this is an old-fashioned way to teach, call me a geek, but I enjoyed it as a student! Once in a while, it can be utilized as a listening and writing exercise.

If you decide to use this activity, do not dictate slowly, one word at a time, but read out whole sentences at average speaking speeds and repeat them several times. This method is much more challenging than writing down detached individual words and makes for a more meaningful experience for students, who have to listen more intently and also hear the language being used in context.

Grammar drill; dictation is useful as a listening activity when introducing new grammar. After using the rapid-dictation method just described, share the correct sentences onscreen, and let students check their work quickly at the end.

Draw, chant, and guess

Category	Speaking drill and fluency
Group size	One to one, small groups
Level	Beginner to Intermediate
Age	6 to adult
Materials	Drawing tool in the breakout room, or pen and paper
Preparation	None
Great for	Chanting for speaking fluency, vocabulary

All children draw an object from a choice of three. If you are doing professions, have children choose between three, such as a doctor, a farmer, and a builder.

Make up a chant for the group. Name a pupil who is to guess someone's picture. Everyone says the chant, and clapping along can help keep the rhythm.

For professions, this might be:

What does he do? Buzz, buzz, buzz.
I want to know what he does!
What does she do? Fizz, fizz, fizz.

I want to know what she is!

Ask one of the pupils now to guess the profession that someone else has drawn. If the pupil guesses correctly, the other one shows the drawing. If not, everyone chants the rhyme again, and it's someone else's turn to guess. Carry on until everyone has shown their picture. If you teach one to one, then take it in turns to guess each other's drawings. If kids don't want to draw, then writing the item down is an option.

Drill any language with the chants. Chants can be nonsense though it's best if the phrases are grammatically correct.

Chant ideas

Alphabet:

What's your letter, ABC, what's your letter, EFG. Your letter is A!

Colours:

Colours of the rainbow, red, green, and yellow, colours of the traffic lights, ready, steady, go! Your colour is blue!

Weather:

It's raining, it's pouring, the old man is snoring. The weather is sunny!

Numbers:

1,2,3, I climbed up a tree, 8,9,10, I climbed down again. Your number is 14!

Food:

I like coffee, I like tea, I like my friends and my friends like me. You like milk!

Clothing:

I'm wearing two shoes, red shoes and blue shoes, two are the shoes I'm wearing. You are wearing a hat!

Transport:

We're on a bus, we're in a car, we're on a plane, we always go far! You are on a bike!

Drawing dictation

Category	Listening, speaking fluency
Group size	One to one to any class size
Level	All levels
Age	All ages
Materials	Pen and paper or prepared pictures
Preparation	None or find scenes for students to draw.
Great for	Listening skills if the teacher dictates. Speaking fluency skills of students dictate. Prepositions, shapes, positions like left, right, middle, and top

How to play

Describe a scene for the group to draw.

Beginners

Use simple language; draw a bucket, a stick figure, and a fish. Where are you? Draw a flower, a sun, an insect, and a child. Where are you? In the park or garden. Draw a river, some fish, and a person with a stick. What are they doing? Fishing. Draw a person, some teeth, and a chair. Where are you? At the dentist.

Intermediate-levels

For example, tell students to draw a stick figure in the middle of the paper, then five others around it. Add a big rectangle around them. Draw a box in the middle of the rectangle's left-hand line and a ball next to one of the stick figures. What have you got? A football pitch! Have students share their pictures via the camera or screen share.

Example two; draw a big square, a triangle on top of the square, a small rectangle on top of the triangle, and a door in the square. What have you got? A house!

Example three; draw two lines across the paper. Draw a bird and sun in the top third, a bucket in the bottom third, and some fish in the middle. What have you got? A beach and the sea. Add a sandcastle on the beach and some stick figures.

Example four; draw an oval, a circle on top of the oval, two triangles on top of the circle, and two small eyes inside the circle. What have you got? A cat! Add a tail and a nose.

Students can also work in pairs, with one telling the other what to draw. Put mixed-ability students in groups and let the better students describe a picture to the others.

Higher-levels

Tell a long joke or shaggy dog story, which is an endless story that usually has no point to it! Students attempt to sketch and note elements of the story with the aim to re-tell it in groups, using their pictures as prompts. If you type 'shaggy dog story' into your browser, you will find some. Please check they are suitable for your age group and do not offend. Here is an example:

A man is driving down the road to a special event. As he listens to music on the radio, he hears a loud bang under his car. He pulls over and finds he has broken down outside a monastery.

He goes to the monastery, knocks on the door, and says, "My car has broken down. Do you think I could stay the night?" The monks graciously accept him, feed him dinner, and even fix his car. As the man tries to fall asleep, he hears a strange sound, a beautiful, haunting sound, like nothing he has ever heard before. He can't sleep, so he gets up and softly creeps around, trying to get closer to the sound, but to no avail.

The next morning, he asks the monks what the sound was, but they say, "We can't tell you. You're not a monk." Deeply disappointed, the man thanks them and goes on his way to attend the special event.

Years pass, and the man never forgets the sounds, so one day, he goes back to the monastery and pleads with the monks to tell him what the sound is. The monks reply, "We can't tell you. You're not a monk." "OK," says the man, "if the only way I can know that sound is to become a monk, make me one."

The monks reply, "You must travel the earth and tell us how many blades of grass there are and the exact number of grains of sand. When you find these numbers,
you will have become a true monk."

The man sets about his task. Some forty-five years later, he returns and knocks on the door of the monastery. He says, "I have travelled the earth and have found out what you asked. There are 145,236,284,232 billion blades of grass and 231,281,219,999,129,382 billion grains of sand on the earth."

The monks reply, "Welcome. You are now a monk. We shall now show you the way to the sound." The monks lead the man to a twisted old wooden door, where the head monk says, "The sound is behind that door." The man reaches for the knob, but the door is locked. He says, "Master, give me the key." The monks give him the key, and he opens the door. Behind the wooden door is another door made of sculpted stone. The man demands the key to the stone door. The monks give it to him, and he opens it, only to find a door made of gleaming ruby. He demands another key from the monks, who provide it. Behind that door is another door, this one made of sparkling sapphire. And so it continued until the man had gone through doors of emerald, silver, topaz, and amethyst. At last, they reach the final door, made of solid gold.

The monks say, "This is the last key to the last door." The man is apprehensive. With trembling hands, he unlocks the gold door and turns the knob. Behind that door, he is amazed to find the source of that strange sound.

But I can't tell you what it is because you're not a monk.

Drawing race

Category	Speaking or writing
Group size	One to one, class in pairs in breakout rooms
Level	Beginner to Intermediate
Age	6 to adult
Materials	Drawing tool in the breakout room, or pen and paper
Preparation	None
Great for	Q & A, grammar drill, vocabulary revision

How to play

Students play in pairs. Student A names an object for student B to draw, and vice versa. On "Go," both race to finish drawing first.

A speaking variant is for one pupil to draw while the other completes a task, and they race to finish. Scenarios are, student A draws an object while:

- A asks B a question, potentially from a list of questions the teacher provides, and then immediately starts drawing. Questions that have more than a one-word answer are what you need:

What jobs have you done during your life? How do you make pancakes? What are your five favourite foods? Tell me about your weekend.

- B attempts to answer the question before A's drawing is complete.

Or:

- B attempts to name five vocabulary items before A has finished.

Or:

- B attempts to do a grammar task, like a fill in the blanks, before A's picture is finished.

Language

- The Q&A might be to drill one specific question and answer form or a selection. For conversation skills, students think of random personal questions.
- A grammar task might be to; fill in some blanks in a sentence, transform a sentence from present to past, or from 'I' to 'he,' or put a sentence into reported speech or the passive tense. It might be to form a sentence that uses specific words or to turn a question into a sentence, or vice versa. Etc.

Materials

Students use pen and paper and show their pictures by holding them up to the camera. Alternatively, if your software allows, students may screen share and draw onscreen using annotation tools.

Either-or

Category	Speaking fluency
Group size	One to one, any class size in teams
Level	Intermediate to advanced
Age	8 to adult
Materials	None
Preparation	Decide on some either/or juxtapositions
Great for	General language, conversation, fluency, comparatives

See also Debates and Triangles talking point activities. A student comes up with an either/or phrase such as ‘love or hate.’ The next student proposes another choice, such as:

earth or sky	trick or treat	big or small
valley or mountain	fat or thin	tea or coffee
near or far	bigger or smaller	little or large
more or less	now or later	true or false

Take any either/or idea and let students take turns, in one sentence, discussing which is better: trick or treat, big or small, valley or mountain, and so on. Students argue for either big or little and define the context of their argument:

‘Little’ is better because if you eat a big plate of food, you get fat.
‘Little’ is better because the smaller shoe sizes are always in the sales with big discounts.
‘Little’ is better because little rooms cost less to heat.
‘Big’ is better because there is more room in a big car.
‘Big’ is better because a big plate of food is better than a small one.
‘Near’ is better because it takes no time to get there.
‘Far’ is better because it is exciting and exotic.
‘Near’ is better because you get there quicker.

- If this is too difficult and students cannot think of arguments quickly, give them four either/or combinations and five minutes in a breakout room to prepare. Bring everyone back and have a brainstorming play-off for points in teams. The last team to give an argument wins the point.
- Read the debates activity for tips before using this, and remember to avoid emotional topics.

Fill in drill

Category	Reading and speaking drill
Group size	One to one, any class size all together
Level	All levels
Age	All ages
Materials	Teacher uses screen share and annotation tools
Preparation	Choose or write a text or dialogue
Great for	Excellent memory drill for any language or grammar

Display a text or dialogue in screen share containing grammar and vocabulary you would like to review. Let the class read it out loud, then ask a few questions to check everyone understands it. Next, tell students to read the first sentence carefully. Now erase one word from that sentence and have everyone read it out again, filling in the blank from memory. Note-taking is not allowed. The missing word remains a gap from now to the end of the game.

Remove a second word from the sentence, so there are now two words missing. Students reread the passage. Keep going, and as time goes on, you gradually rub out more and more words until there are virtually none left, and the students know the whole passage by heart!

Here is an example of text using conditionals.

> What would you do if you won the lottery?
>
> I would first donate ten percent to charity, and then I would give some to my family. I expect my brother would buy a new car

right away. He'd get a Ferrari knowing him. Of course, that would depend on how much money I gave him, which would depend on how much I had won in the first place.

Start by deleting words such as 'would' and 'won' rather than 'lottery,' or delete verbs and little words rather than nouns first.

- To erase words, select a rectangle shape in the drawing tools and the colour white. Draw white rectangles over the words you want to hide.
- Start slowly and listen to see how students are doing. Delete more words when you hear that they are coping. Too few words being deleted will mean that the task is too easy; too many will make it too hard, so err on the side of caution.
- Too easy is better than too hard because at least students are drilling accurate English.
- To help students, delete part of a word and leave the first letter as a clue.
- When you have deleted most of the words, students can write them back in again. In the next lesson, see whether students can remember the vocabulary.
- This is an excellent game for grammar and language acquisition, but it does not have to be dry. Add an artistic dimension to your classes by using it with poetry, stories, inspiring speeches, or curious texts. For inspiring speeches, see the 'Movies — other movie ideas' in this book. I translated and modified this poem from French. The original author is anonymous:

Look at the light snow
flaying
Against the windowpane.
Who is up there is
playing;
Tearing the frosty clouds
Full of vapour
Into tiny pieces of paper?

Find a friend

Category	Speaking drill or conversation
Group size	4 to any number using breakout rooms
Level	Beginner to intermediate
Age	6 to adult
Materials	None. Breakout rooms with more than four students.
Preparation	None
Great for	Q and A, conversation, speaking fluency

Students are to find at least one other person who likes the same food/band/clothes/interests. To facilitate this:

1. Please put them in breakout rooms of four students each.
2. Shuffle the rooms after three minutes, so students have a fresh set of people to interview.
3. After three shuffles and a total of nine minutes, bring students back together, and ask who found a match.

This activity can be a speaking drill game for a specific Q and A format, like, 'I like coffee, do you?' And it can be a conversational activity where students find someone else who has five things in common:

We are both boys, we both live in Seattle, we both like Handel, pasta, and football.

Fizz buzz

Category	Speaking
Group size	One to one, and small groups of up to six in breakout rooms
Level	Beginner to intermediate
Age	6 to adult
Materials	None
Preparation	None
Great for	Counting, vocabulary brainstorming game

How to play

After a demonstration game, put students into breakout rooms to play in groups of 3 to 6. Playing one on one is fine too. It is better to have more groups with fewer students.

The first player says '1,' the next says '2,' the next says '3,' and so on. Go round the circle once so that students understand. A demonstration is worth a thousand words! Next, add a new element; any time a '2' comes up, including all numbers with 2 in them, like 12, 20, 21, and 22, the player says 'fizz.' For example, 1 fizz 3 4 5 6 7 8 9 10 11 fizz 13 14 15 16 17 18 19 fizz fizz fizz, etc. to 30, then 31, fizz, 33, etc.

Once the group has mastered this to some degree, throw in another element; any number with a 5 becomes 'buzz.' This would give 1 fizz 3 4 buzz 6 7 8 9 10 11 fizz 13 14 buzz 16, etc.

To complexify the game further, but not the first time you play, say that any number that divides by 2 or 5 is a fizz buzz. This addition is very much for older children and adults, or it will be too slow to be fun.

Language

Use this game in its original version to revise counting. Once students have mastered counting, but not before, use it for vocabulary revision. For example, every time the number 2 comes up, students name any word in English, or, for higher-level students, any word in a given vocabulary theme. Every time 5, or a number divisible by 5, comes up, students 'woof!' like a dog.

- Helena Murrer wrote to me with this excellent idea. 'I used Fizz Buzz as a warm-up but made it into a Halloween game. The witch would steal number 2, so instead of saying 2, or a number with 2 in it, students laughed like a witch. Then a ghost stole number 5 and replaced it with a howl. A cat stole number 4, which we replaced with a meow. Additional replacements could be made. The students loved it.'
- An alternative to Helena's idea is to use sounds for the weather like blowing for wind, clapping for thunder, and drumming fingers for rain. Using sounds can help students who are too shy to speak in public. The sounds become a stepping stone between silence and speaking English.

Flip a card

Category	Speaking
Group size	One to one and small groups
Level	All levels
Age	6 to adult
Materials	Online or real deck of cards
Preparation	None
Great for	Vocabulary revision, sentence construction

Preparation

Assign letters of the alphabet to each playing card and display them. The chart below is suitable for English:

Playing Card	Letter	Playing Card	Letter	Playing Card	Letter
Ace	A	Six	H-I-J-K-L	Jack	S
Two	B	Seven	M	Queen	T
Three	C	Eight	N-O	King	U-V-W-X-Y-Z
Four	D	Nine	P		
Five	E-F-G	Ten	Q-R		

You could allocate two letters to each card, but the W-X and the Y-Z cards would be difficult since only about 300 words start with the letter x in English and only about 2200 with either y or z. Therefore, I created the chart above to give students a better chance of finding a word each time.

A shuffled online deck of cards is handy. At the time of writing, 'random-cards.com' has a shuffled deck, but things change fast online, so type 'online deck of cards' into your browser, and you will find one. Otherwise, use real cards and hold each one up to the camera.

Each small group has a deck of playing cards shuffled and placed face down. The first player clicks on the top card to reveal it and says a word that starts with one of the two letters matched with that card. So, if students turn up a 10 of spades, hearts, clubs, or diamonds, they think of any word starting with Q or R. If successful, they earn a point. Students continue playing until there are no cards left in the deck. See who has the most points at the end.

- Play with a time limit to add excitement.
- Play in teams with students collaborating to be the first group to get through the deck of cards. For this variant, tweak your settings so that learners may rejoin the main room of their own accord. When a team returns to the main room, stop play, and see who has the most words.
- Optionally, revise vocabulary and prevent cheating with this extension: Teams copy their words into an Excel spreadsheet column. Highlight the column and click A-Z to put the words in alphabetical order. Rival teammates check the lists. There should be four words starting with 'A,' representing the four aces in the pack, four starting with 'B,' for the four twos. Four words should begin with either E, F, or G, representing the fives.

Apple }
Arm }
Ankle }
Ape }
Banana}
Beauty}
Bed }
Boat }
Car }
Cup }
Coat }
Colour }

Aces

Twos

Three

Dog }
Duck }
Doll }
Dinner }
Egg }
Eat }
Fish }
Goat }
Hat }
House }
Icecream}
Light }

Fours

Fives

Sixes

Intermediate variant

Students collaborate in groups, turning up four cards and writing a sentence using four words that start with the given letters. The phrases may follow a given grammatical structure or use any language for general revision.

For example, a student turns up an ace, a four, and a king, which correspond to the letters A, D and U, V, W, X, Y or Z. If required to use the simple past tense with these letter options, examples are 'Adam did walk' or 'Adam's dog was wet' or 'Anna drank on the yacht.'

For variations, allow extra words to be added to encourage creativity. You may also permit any word order.

Forfeits

Category	Versatile
Group size	One to one, any class size
Level	All levels
Age	All ages, perfect for kids
Materials	Usually none
Preparation	None
Great for	Fun, vocabulary revision, sentence construction

Forfeits are not punishments for bad behaviour. Giving a forfeit is a useful way to 'penalize' a student for an error without excluding them from the game. They are supposed to be fun and enjoyable and can spice up a game. They can be done individually or as a group, which is reassuring for shy students. Be aware that some students may feel uncomfortable or embarrassed, depending on the forfeit. If so, propose a different one to that student. Don't rule out daft forfeits with adults. Sometimes a bit of silliness makes students laugh, relaxes them, and allows them to concentrate better afterwards.

The best way to obtain forfeits that appeal to your students is to ask each pupil to think of three ideas for homework. Collect them and add them to your list for future games. Below are examples of forfeits that could be used in a multitude of games.

Some of these forfeits involve movement, and this is possible online if you step back from the computer so more of your body is visible.

- Name a picture flashcard.
- Think of a sentence or a question using the target language.

- Ask a friend anything in English.
- Name three things you like.
- Answer any question, such as 'Do you have a sister?'
- Walk with a pen between your knees.
- Balance an item on your head for three seconds.
- Count down from 10 to 0 and pull a face on 0.
- Say your name backwards.
- Write your name in the air with a body part, like your head or elbow.
- Do a silly dance or sing a song.
- Pretend to be a fly, chicken, pig, cat, lion, or snake.
- Yawn until someone else yawns too.
- Do a sum, such as 70 minus 62.
- Pretend to be a robot.
- Mime something for the class to guess.
- Say a tongue twister (see Tongue Twisters for ideas).
- Make anyone laugh.
- Stand on one leg and do not smile for 10 seconds.
- Pull a funny face.
- Dance for twenty seconds.
- Have students buzz like bees, trying to last the longest without taking a breath.
- Look at someone and do not smile for a full minute.
- Say a sentence about kangaroos or elephants or any other topic.
- Intermediates say two or three sentences about a topic.
- Advanced students give a one-minute talk about a topic.

Gap-fill game

Category	Reading and writing
Group size	One to one, all class sizes, in pairs or small groups
Level	All levels
Age	All ages
Materials	Pairs of gap-fills with different words missing.
Preparation	Gap-fills from your textbook, literature, or poetry
Great for	Grammar drill or general language

Here is an easy reading and writing activity. It is perfect for drilling specific grammar but is also useful for general language.

How to play

Divide the class into pairs or small groups. Share two documents, 1 and 2. Student A views document 1 and student B document 2. Both have the same reading passage, and both have missing words, but not the same ones. By comparing texts, students will together complete the document.

This task isn't very inspiring in pairs. It's better in threes or small groups. To liven it up, create teams and make it a race; the first three groups to finish win. Alternatively, if you are anti-competition, use a tight time-limit to add momentum. Don't wait until everyone has finished.

- Use short passages with big groups, so you don't abandon everyone in breakout rooms for longer than five minutes.
- With a small group, you might provide each student with a different version of the reading so that the whole group works together to fill in all the missing words.
- Have students prepare texts with missing words for homework for use in the next class.
- As a variation, have everyone fill in their gap-fill first and then compare with the original in pairs.

Language ideas

Use to drill grammar or vocabulary. For beginners, stick to short sentences and use only known words when dealing with a new grammar point. Use only one grammatical form when presenting new grammar but mix it up for a revision exercise. Here is an example for beginners to practise question formation.

Hello, __ my brother here?	Hello, is my ______ here?
I don't know. Is he tall?	I don't know. __ he tall?
____ medium height.	He's medium height.
What colour is ___ hair?	____ colour is his hair?
______.	Brown
_____ colour are his eyes?	What colour ____ his eyes?

Brown.	______.
What is he _______?	What is ___ wearing?
I don't know.	I don't know.
Why don't ___ phone him?	Why don't you phone him?
My phone has no battery and	___ phone has no battery and
__ don't ____ his number.	I don't know ___ number.

For advanced students, try poetry. Here is an anonymous poem called 'Men' from public-domain-poetry.com. Students will have to be attentive since there are so many repeated words.

Men are four:
He who knows and knows not that he knows, -
He is asleep - wake him;
He who knows not and knows not that he knows not, -
He is a fool - shun him;
He who knows not and knows that he knows not, -
He is a child - teach him;
He who knows and knows that He knows, -
He is a king - follow him.

Getting to know you

Category	Speaking fluency or speaking drill
Level	Beginner to intermediate
Group size	Two students minimum up to any class size
Age	8 to adult
Materials	None
Preparation	None
Great for	Question drill or general fluency conversation

This game is a good way for students to get to know each other and develop fluency. Divide the students into groups and give everyone 3 minutes to find out as much as possible about each other, preferably in English. Bring everyone back together and make two random teams. A student from team A makes a statement about someone else, such as 'Salim, you like tea.' Salim answers with true or false; if Salim answers 'correct,' team A wins a point. Now it is a student from team B's turn to make a statement about someone, such as 'Marta, you play tennis.' Marta answers with true or false, and so on. Tell the students that they must be honest, or the game is no fun.

- With a small group, use a free-for-all approach, where students contribute as soon as they think of a statement. Alternatively, let the students take turns in a more structured way. You'll need to make teams with a large group and have two separate games by making two breakout rooms, which would work once students know the game and are autonomous.
- You may like to award points for correctly formed statements since that often motivates students to take more care. Or, you may prefer to play at a faster pace and let some errors go. You can always share corrections and review them later.
- Use as a drill game for a series of specific questions; or for general conversation, where students ask anything they like and find out as much as they can about others.

Grammar auction

Category	Reading
Group size	Two students to any class size
Level	All levels
Age	8 to adult
Materials	Sentences
Preparation	Sentences to share one by one with screen share
Great for	Grammar drill, grammar revision, general language

This game is based on a public auction, but students aren't buying antiques – they are bidding on sentences. The object is to buy the sentences that are grammatically correct and avoid the ones that have errors in them. This exercise has several functions: to review previously taught grammar, to develop editing skills, and allow for a review of currency units.

Preparation

Either type all the sentences into a PowerPoint document one per slide, then reveal each one as you move through the game, or type them in the screen share document. With the second method, it's easy to write the amount of money bid and the buyer by each sentence as you go along.

There should be about three sentences per student, and forty percent or so should contain errors. Vary the level of difficulty and the number of mistakes but be sure to stick to grammar points that have been previously taught.

How to play

Students are in teams. Give students a budget, enough to potentially buy three sentences. If the starting bid for a sentence is $100, each student starts with $300 to spend.

Type or reveal the first sentence. If buyers think the sentence is correct, then they bid on it. Increase bids by $10 increments and if students keep bidding, go as high as $150, the maximum price for any sentence. If there are no bids at the opening price, lower the amount, and keep dropping it by $50 until you reach zero. Be swift; keep momentum to make the game more exciting; each sentence should not take more than thirty seconds.

When a sentence is purchased, the teacher notes the buyer's name under the team and the amount paid. At $150, a buyer can only buy two sentences, leaving a chance for teammates to participate.

At the end of the auction, the teacher goes through the sentences. If a sentence is correct, the team get the same points as dollars paid. If a sentence has one or more errors, then the class correct it together, and the team who bought it lose the same number of points as money paid. If a sentence is correct, but no one bought it, then all teams lose 100 points. The team with the most points at the end is the winner.

- To check that your students are not bidding more money than they have, tally up the winning team's points and check they do not exceed the sum of money given out at the beginning. If so, that team is disqualified.

- For inaccurate sentences, use the typical errors your students make all the time. Sneak in subtle errors for more advanced students, like omitting the capital letter for a proper name or month.

Grammar drill

Category	Collaborative speaking and writing drill
Group size	Two students to any class size in small groups
Level	All levels
Age	All ages
Materials	Pictures or words and an example sentence
Preparation	None
Great for	Grammar, sentence, or question drill, collaborative group game

How to play

Students work together to create sentences in this collaborative activity. Do a demonstration before splitting students into small groups. Provide an example sentence along with a list of words to each group. Every student in the group has to make a sentence using a word on the list and the target structure. Others in the group assess and decide together whether the sentence is correct. When a consensus is reached, all students write out the sentence. Each correct sentence is worth a point for the group.

Advanced example:

Noun	Sentence example
School	Hardly had we reached school when the bell rang.

Students are given the nouns and come up with an appropriate sentence:

Shoes	Hardly had she put her shoes on when it started to rain.
City	Hardly had the city lights come on when we had to go home.
Drink	Hardly had they finished their drinks when the bar closed.

Telephone	Hardly had his telephone conversation finished when his mum arrived.

Prefix and suffix example: Add pre or post to the word and make a sentence

Mortem	Doctors in Germany did a post-mortem.
Script	She made her most important point in the postscript!
Define	I need to predefine the steps we will take.
View	Would you please preview my work?

Example for beginners using pictures: I am wearing shoes. I am wearing a skirt.

Nouns	Sentence	Nouns
	I am wearing boots. I am wearing a shirt.	
	I am wearing a dress. I am wearing a hat.	

After five minutes:

1. Bring everyone back together and ask groups to share their sentences in turn.
2. Quickly scan these and ask everyone to try to spot any errors.
3. Note the number of points for that group and move to the next group.
4. Try and get all this collaborative marking done in five minutes. It should not be a drag.

- It is better to have two shorter rounds, with five words per group, than one long one with ten words; this gives you more contact with the class, so students don't feel the teacher isn't present. It can be lonely in a breakout room as a student, not to mention that the teacher has no idea what is going on.

- Aim to make four groups; otherwise, you will not have time to listen in and check students are on task. That said, make groups with no more than six students to maximise student participation. It does not matter if groups are not even. If logistically possible, include a more able student in each group.
- Circulate and monitor but do not get stuck with one group. If the first two groups you observe are stalling, bring everyone back, and reinforce the activity with more demonstrations; accuracy is essential with a drill activity.

Grammar knock out

Category	Listening grammar drill
Group size	One to one, any class size
Level	All levels
Age	All ages
Materials	Sentences
Preparation	Prepare the sentences you will use during the game
Great for	Drill game to introduce new grammar or revise

Use this game to introduce grammar. Students listen to a new grammar structure like 'Did you go to the cinema last night?' Explain the grammar in question, showing how the sentence is built.

Did = past simple of to do	Did
You = pronoun	He
Go = infinitive without the 'to'	Buy
+ rest of sentence	+ rest of sentence

Read a selection of similar sentences and have students assess whether they are right or wrong. Students do a thumbs-up for right and leave their hands down if wrong. Start by reading out grammatically correct questions. Gradually slip in some errors, such as 'Did you go to the shops tomorrow?' 'Did you went to the shops?' 'Did you bought some tomatoes yesterday?' If students do a thumbs up for these sentences, they are out. Keep going until there only a few students are left in the game, who are the winners. You can also play this by having everyone start the game standing up. When people make a mistake, they are out and sit down. Move swiftly, so each round is only a few minutes long. People who are out will soon be standing up and participating afresh in a new contest.

- You might put students in teams and let them track their points. Each group has a turn at a question, and if they get it wrong, opposing teams earn a point. Or, with kids, students who do a thumbs-up for an inaccurate question could do a forfeit; see Forfeits for ideas.
- Review a broader range of tenses and grammatical structures for more advanced students and stick to a limited amount of basic phrases for beginners.
- For one to one, give students three lives and say they should get through the list of twenty sentences without losing all three.

Guess the action

Category	Speaking
Group size	2 to 40
Level	Beginner to intermediate
Age	4 to 12
Materials	Ideas for action verbs to mime are included
Preparation	None
Great for	Great for present and past continuous

Present continuous and vocabulary

Divide the class into two teams. Show team one a verb. Team one mime that action and team two guess what they are doing. Group one continue acting while the teacher asks, 'What are they doing?' Students from group two call out their guesses, 'They are reading.' 'They are studying.'

Past continuous and vocabulary

Divide the class into two groups. Team one face the wall. Show team two a verb, which they mime until you say 'Freeze!'

Team two freeze and hold their positions; team one turn around and guess what they were doing before freezing.

Common verbs suitable for this game

Break, buy, catch, choose, come, cut, draw, drink, drive, eat, fall over, find, fly, forget, give, go out, go shopping, grow, hear, hide, hit, hold, hurt, learn, leave, lie down, lose, meet, put, read, ride, run, say, see, sell, send, sing, sit, sleep, smell, speak, spend, stand, steal, swim, take a photo, take off, teach, think, throw, understand, wake up, wear, win, and write.

- Guess the action is perfect for revising verbs and tenses. Pre-teach some verbs, or play a quick round of 'Brainstorm' with verbs before you play
- Demonstrate the game and put the students into breakout rooms to work in groups.
- Share documents with lists of actions, one list for team A and one for team B. Lists are provided in the Appendix.
- Students in the same team will not always mime in the same way. The verb 'work' may be interpreted differently depending on the person's imagination and experience. When several students mime, a bigger picture is created for the other team. Sometimes this makes it easier to guess the word, and sometimes harder, but it definitely adds to the fun!

Guess the meaning of dates and numbers

Category	Speaking fluency
Group size	One to one to any number in groups
Level	Lower intermediate and up
Age	10 to adult
Materials	None
Preparation	Can be done on the spur of the moment
Great for	Dates, questions, conversation, speaking fluency

Use one on one or put students in groups and have them guess the meaning of numbers by asking questions. For example:

1982, 3, 74

1982 is the student's year of birth, 3 is how many children he has, and 74 is the bus number he usually takes to class.

Dates could be historically significant, such as the end of a war, the election of a famous president, or the year of a revolution. Numbers could relate to general knowledge, such as how many countries there are in South America, Europe, and Africa. Numbers could also be funky stats or world records. The Guinness Book of Records would be useful. Try 147. It's the number of skips on roller skates performed in under thirty seconds by the world record holder skipping champion! Try 41. That's the age of the world's oldest living penguin, which lives in a zoo in Denmark.

Guess the question

Category	Speaking
Group size	One to one, any size in groups
Level	All levels
Age	All ages
Materials	None
Preparation	Decide on the questions for the exercise
Great for	Speaking drill, grammar review, questions

Use this to review language rather than for new structures. In screen share, write the first letter of every word in a question or sentence, such as W___ i_ y___ n___? Divide students into two teams. Team A has a go at guessing the first word. If correct, they can take a crack at the second word and so on; if they are wrong, team B has a turn. A team keeps guessing words until they make an error, and then the other team takes over. Only the team that gets the last word – in this case, starting with 'n' - wins the point!

W___ i_ y___ n___? could be any of these and more:

What is your name? Where is your niece? Who is your nephew? Why is Yann nodding?

Use questions or sentences that contain grammatical structures and vocabulary that you want to review.

Guess the word

Category	Speaking with optional writing
Group size	2 to 30
Level	Beginner to intermediate
Age	6 to adult
Materials	Pen and paper or the class board
Preparation	None
Great for	Vocabulary brainstorming game

How to play

Divide the class into two or three teams. Have a word in mind, like 'chocolate.' Say the first letter and write it down. Pause while students call out words starting with c, like cat, car, cold, call, come. Every word wins a point, but if someone guesses the word 'chocolate,' the team earns five points. Move on to the second letter, so now students must think of words starting with 'ch,' like child, chair, chicken, and chocolate – bingo, 5 points for whichever team guessed it first.

This game is perfect for highlighting bizarre spelling, silent letters, and words with two pronunciations. For example, light or through have silent letters, and 'bow' is pronounced in two different ways, depending on the meaning; a bow and arrow and 'to bow.'

- Make one student referee in charge of counting words suggested by each team; the fast way is to draw a dash for each point.
- An alternative way to score is to give a penalty for each wrong guess, and the team with the lowest score wins.
- Have the referee write the letters and the final word, so learners hear and see it, which further helps remember it.
- When the guesses slow down, move right on to another letter, don't wait until there is total silence and students look like they

have given up. By keeping the game moving, before students have run dry of ideas, you create a sense of urgency and excitement, or at the very least, you prevent the game from being a drag with a bunch of lethargic students.

- Play this game often because your students will get better at it with practise. Don't be demoralised if it's a bit flat the first time you play. Brainstorming games allow you to revise vast amounts of vocabulary in a short time. Use the vocabulary index of your syllabus for inspiration.
- Give your class a homework assignment where each person prepares a list of three words they find difficult to spell. Put learners into teams and have them play with their selection in the next lesson.

Guess who listening

Category	Listening
Level	Beginner to advanced
Group size	One to one and all class sizes
Age	All ages
Materials	Descriptions of people your students know
Preparation	Copy descriptions of famous people from Wikipedia; students can do this for homework. For beginners, describe students in class.
Great for	General language fluency

Talk about someone all your students know, such as the school director, one of the other students, or a celebrity. Start with oblique facts and gradually give more details until someone guesses who it is. To prepare quickly, copy a biography from Wikipedia or an appropriate source. Students can also choose someone for homework and read the biographical summary of one of their heroes or idols in the next class.

With a big class, distribute the summaries and let students work in small groups to guess the famous person. Here is an idea:

Who is the person in this story? The person is with her sister beside a lake. Suddenly, an animal runs by. *(The reader asks, any guesses? If none, continue reading.)* The person runs after it and falls down the animal's burrow into a fantastical world. The person grows larger or smaller by eating different things like cakes and mushrooms. Towards the end of the story, the person enters a lovely garden. The Knave of Hearts is charged with stealing some tarts. A trial is held, which the person thinks is ridiculous. She says so. Everyone is offended. There is a great commotion. Suddenly the person wakes up and is back where she started, sitting with her sister beside the lake.

If no one identifies the person, reread the passage, and say that the animal that runs by is a white rabbit with a watch in a hurry. Yes, you guessed it, it's Alice from 'Alice in Wonderland' by Charles Lutwidge Dodgson, better known by his pen name as Lewis Carroll.

This game is also perfect for general knowledge acquisition. Here is a copy and paste from Wikipedia on Stalin:

He was born in a small one-room house in Gori, Georgia. His father made and repaired shoes. His father was often drunk and violent; he used to hit his wife and son and died in a fight in 1890. Joseph had smallpox when he was young, which left his face scarred. Old photographs of Joseph were often changed later in his life to hide the scars. His left arm was also shorter because of an accident. He was educated at a church school and then studied to be a priest. He was an active student reading many books, especially by authors that were not allowed by the priests, like Karl Marx.

Continue with Stalin's life using the Wikipedia UK description until someone guesses who it is. Once you talk about how he executed or starved millions of Russians, students will probably recognize your man. Edit the text if it is too long or detailed for your student age group.

- This activity will be a flop if your students do not know or relate to the famous people you choose. Avoid this issue by asking students to tell you their favourite celebrities.

Type their name and 'biography' into your browser or see if they are entered in Wikipedia. Copy the description and read it out to the class, inserting 'this person' instead of the name.

- To have everyone participating actively, have students send you the identity via private message as soon as they guessed. Read till the end. No one knows whether anyone else has named the person, so those who don't know keep listening till the end. The first ten students to identify the mystery person win a point.

Hand sign stories

Category	Listening
Group size	One to one, any class size, whole-class activity
Level	All levels
Age	All ages
Materials	Cameras on
Preparation	Choose six words in a short text
Great for	New vocabulary, revising vocabulary, listening skills

This activity is an excellent way to learn vocabulary. Students will love it who show a preference for tactile learning (always moving, touching things, and having difficulty retaining material they have heard or read about). Tell students that this game will improve their listening skills and vocabulary recall.

How to play

First, introduce six vocabulary words and their meanings. Next, decide with the class on a gesture or sign to represent each word; these could be serious or silly, but they should be meaningful. For example, if the term were 'nurse,' you could stick your finger, or a pen, in your mouth like it was a thermometer, which would be a memorable sign (although some people might fret over germs.) Represent a doctor's stethoscope by putting your forefingers by your ears with the thumbs hanging down and touching under the chin. A teacher could be represented by miming writing on the board.

Optionally, help your students come up with signs for abstract concepts. For example, in the United States, raising your right hand could signify 'honesty,' as if swearing to tell the truth in court. In other countries, concepts are going to be different. Let students come up with hand signs rather than imposing your ideas. Your job is to facilitate a consensus on which signal to use for each term. Once you have all six gestures, run through the six words a few times while students mime so that everyone is familiar with them.

Next, instruct the students to listen to a story and make the correct hand sign every time they hear one of the vocabulary words. If the gesture is meaningful and if the text is context-rich, then students will learn the vocabulary with little trouble. The object is to complete the reading with everyone making the correct hand signs.

- There is no need to spend any time preparing hand signs because your students will have plenty of ideas. If necessary, put them in groups to brainstorm.
- Choose one gesture from the options for everyone to make together.
- Pause after each keyword to allow listeners time to make the gesture. There will be some lag, which is normal, especially the first time through the story.
- Students may not understand the story fully the first time since they will be focusing on listening for the six words and making the gestures. Always read it at least twice. The second time through, students will find it more comfortable and focus more on the story.
- In the next lesson, test the students' vocabulary; tell the story, but when you come to one of the six terms, use the gesture, and students name the word based on the hand sign they see. It is common to have a 100% recall.
- Instead of a story, use hand signs incorporated into a role-play. Students create a short dialogue where they use one or two terms with hand signs. They drill the role-play using an expressive gesture for each keyword.

Finding stories for this activity

The first time I used this activity, I spent ages looking for suitable texts for lower-level students. Simple stories were boring.

Interesting ones were either too long, did not repeat words, or the language was far too complicated.

For **beginners to intermediates**, anecdotes, short news articles, and jokes are a good source. The texts are short, the English modern, and metaphors do not abound. Here is a trivial news anecdote that could work for an adult student. The keywords for hand signs are:

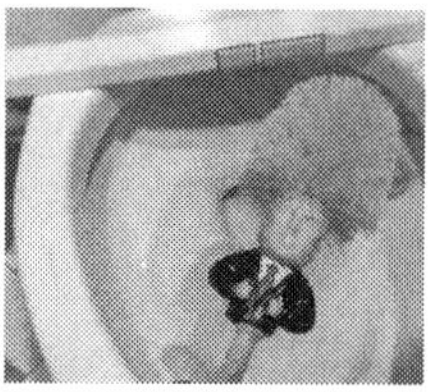

Prime Minister	manufacturing	toilet brush
Increasingly	business	skyrocketed

British humour has done it again: A manufacturing company is selling a toilet brush with Prime Minister Boris Johnson's face on it. Its creator said that it was nothing personal against the Prime Minister. He saw people had made a toilet brush with Donald Trump's face on it, and it was successful, so he thought, why don't I do some for Boris? Johnson has been increasingly unpopular in the UK since the beginning of the pandemic, a fact which may be good for business, as sales of the brush have skyrocketed during the past few weeks.

Jokes can be a great source of short stories and are often repetitive, which means plenty of participation with hand signs. As with all materials, be careful not to offend anyone with vulgarity or bad taste. Here is a neutral joke that should be inoffensive and is suitable for all ages.

Keywords: intellectual, robot*, question, answer, pay, paw

*The original joke has an imbecile, not a robot.

An intellectual proposes a game to a robot:

- If I ask you a question you can't answer, you give me £1. But, if you ask me a question and I don't know the answer, I give you £100.
- OK, replied the robot.

The intellectual starts with:

- What has four paws and goes 'miaou.'

- I don't know, says the robot, and pays £1.
- What has four paws and goes 'woof.'
- I don't know, says the robot, and pays £1.

When it's its turn, the robot asks:

- What has eight paws at midday and four in the evening?

Surprised, the intellectual thinks for ten minutes and eventually gives up, saying he doesn't know, and pays the robot £100. Then he asks:

- So, what's the answer to your question?
- I don't know, replies the robot, and it pays £1.

For **Intermediate levels** and up, Roald Dahl's stories are super for kids, and the 1001 tales of Arabian nights will keep you going for a long time. Rudyard Kipling's The Jungle Book must be one of the most famous stories of all time, but again, this is for intermediate learners and up. Hans Christian Andersen wrote great short stories. Jean de La Fontaine wrote famous poetic fables that would need summarizing with regular English.

Advanced students can work with poetry and classic texts, of which there is no shortage, and an extract will suffice. There is plenty of action and vocabulary to mime in this challenging extract from Charles Dicken's Oliver Twist, which my editing software classified as hard to read for a knowledgeable audience!

Oliver had not been within the walls of the workhouse a quarter of an hour, and had scarcely completed the demolition of a second slice of bread, when Mr. Bumble, who had handed him over to the care of an old woman, returned, and, telling him it was a board night, informed him that the board had said he was to appear before it forthwith. Not having a very clearly defined notion of what a live board was, Oliver was rather astounded by this intelligence, and was not quite certain whether he ought to laugh or cry. He had no time to think about the matter, however; for Mr. Bumble gave him a tap on the head to wake him up, and another on the back to make him lively, and bidding him follow, conducted him into a large whitewashed room where eight or ten fat gentlemen were sitting round a table, at the top of which, seated in an armchair rather higher than the rest, was a particularly fat gentleman with a very round, red face.

Classics often contain some outdated language; it's not often that an ESL learner will refer to a workhouse or bid someone to do something forthwith. Yet Dicken's syntax is sophisticated, which makes quite a change from many four-words-per-sentence novels of our times. This short paragraph is rich with interesting words like scarcely, clearly defined, notion, astounded, conducted, and whitewashed.

Hangman (or Snowman)

Category	Spelling and speaking
Group size	One to one, any class in pairs
Level	Beginner
Age	6 to adult
Materials	Pen and paper or a document in screen share and annotation tools
Preparation	None
Great for	Alphabet, spelling, vocabulary

How to play

The classic hangman game of old is perfect for learning the alphabet and for spelling. Decide on a word and draw a dash for each letter, so if it were 'dinosaur,' you would write _ _ _ _ _ _ _ _. The other player guesses what the word is, and they do this by naming the letters of the alphabet. When they say any of the letters in 'dinosaur,' fill it into the blank. If they say any other letter, start to draw the snowman.

The original hangman drawing represents a man being hung from a noose, which is a gruesome anachronism. Invent a sketch such as a house, the door being the last thing, or try a snowman as a non-violent alternative. Draw the snowman from the ground up in nine strokes or start with the complete snowman and erase something for each incorrect guess. Players may guess up to nine wrong letters before melting completely, as follows: the top half of the hat, hat rim, head, body, eyes, mouth, buttons, left arm, right arm. For eleven guesses, erase the buttons one by one.

As a technically simpler alternative, nine beautiful snowmen are included in the downloadable Appendix. Erase one for every incorrect guess.

Best in pairs in breakout rooms. One student has the annotation tool, chooses a word from a list you provide, writes out the dashes, fills in the letters as the other student guesses them, and gradually draws or erases the snowman when an incorrect letter is suggested. Learners may use pen and paper if annotation tools are not accessible.

- Use a time limit via an online stopwatch to add a touch of excitement.
- Work with guessing short sentences, not just single words.
- Play hangman with multiple words at a time to make it more interesting.

Hangman variant (also known as Rivet)

Category	Speaking drill
Group size	One to one, class in pairs or groups
Level	Beginner
Age	6 to adult
Materials	Pen and paper or a document in screen share and annotation tools
Preparation	None
Great for	Question & answer drill, grammar drill, vocabulary

Hangman may also be exploited to drill vocabulary. Here is an example for clothing. Put students in breakout rooms in pairs and give student A a picture of a person in clothes. The other students guess what the person is wearing before student A finishes the hangman. First, tell the players if the person is a man or a woman. If it's a picture of a man, students ask questions like:

Is he wearing a shirt?

If he is wearing a shirt, student A draws it or writes that item down. If he is not wearing a shirt, start the hangman.

Guess what is behind the blue box.

Answer: a wheel

Turn this into a general guessing game using multiple question forms; students could guess an object, something missing from a picture, or a sport or activity. The item or activity depicted must be identified before the hangman is completed. In the photo of the mechanic, the missing object is a wheel.

Hide and seek prepositions

Category	Speaking
Group size	One to one, class in groups in breakout rooms
Level	Beginner
Age	4 to adult
Materials	Things students have at home near their computer
Preparation	None
Great for	Prepositions revision

How to play

Students place a pen lid, eraser, or small item somewhere in their personal belongings. Other students ask questions to guess where it is. Start by going through some possible hiding places; in a pocket, under a book, inside a pencil case, under the table, on a chair, next to a book, in a bag, on a shelf, in a drawer, in your hand, etc.

Get each student to write a list of ten things they could use as hiding places, which will be different for each student. If I were to write a list right now for this game, it would have these items: mug, plate, telephone, computer stand, computer, mouse, table, tablecloth, notebook, chair, and pocket. I could hide something between the table and the tablecloth, under the plate, in the mug, and so on.

Play a round by way of demonstration. Display your list of ten hiding places and hide something. The class ask you questions, trying to be the one to guess correctly:

Is it under the computer stand?	Is it next to the mug?
Is it behind the computer?	Is it under the table?

Is it in between the table and the tablecloth?

Have everyone switch off their cameras and take 30 seconds to hide something. Have everyone switch their cameras back on while you put students into breakout rooms. Students then find all the hidden items by asking each other questions such as, 'Is it in your pocket?'

- Display a list of prepositions as prompts if necessary: in, on, under, next to, above, below, on top of, inside, in between, in front of, and near.
- Students share their list of ten possible hiding places in the breakout room to help the others ask relevant questions.
- If playing in pairs, students could count the number of questions they ask, and the one who guesses the hiding place with the fewest questions wins. That said, this idea might not work with kids since they often cheat!
- Use this game every few weeks for revision. The second time it will be much easier since students will know the game.

Higher or lower and comparatives

Category	Speaking
Group size	One to one, class in pairs in breakout rooms
Level	Beginner
Age	4 to adult
Materials	For higher and lower, an online deck of cards For other comparatives, pictures, or words
Preparation	None if using a deck of cards Vocabulary flashcards for other comparatives.
Great for	Comparatives

How to play

Use an online shuffled pack of cards (random cards.com) or search for 'shuffled deck of cards online.' Alternatively, use a real deck or the PowerPoint file with a shuffled deck included in the Appendix.

Demonstrate the game to the whole class. Turn over a playing card and read the number out loud. Those who think the next card will be higher point upwards and say 'Higher!' All those who believe it will be lower point downwards and say 'Lower!' Turn over the next card and read it out. Those who were wrong are out. Continue for three more cards and then count how many are still in the game. When most but not all students are out, stop the game; those still in are the winners. Please don't go on to the bitter end since it will be tedious for those out early. If you have a big class, put learners into groups to play together once they have seen the demo, put them in groups to play together. Students may count a point for every guess they get right. In pairs, players take it in turns to say whether the next card will be higher or lower. If student A opts for higher, then student B must say lower to avoid a tie.

Variant with pictures or words

A variant of this game is to use pictures or words. Players guess whether the next item or animal will be bigger or smaller, or perhaps heavier or lighter. People could be taller or shorter, buildings bigger or smaller, things more expensive or cheaper, cars and other transport faster or slower, and so on. Students can score points for correct guesses if they like.

If playing in threes or fours, and student A opts for faster, students B, C, and D must find different comparatives: slower, bigger, and smaller.

Homework

Category	Writing
Group size	One to one, all class sizes
Level	All levels
Age	All ages
Materials	None
Preparation	Prepare clear instructions for the students
Great for	Preparing work for use in games before class, marking work after class

Save time and have your students prepare material for future classes through homework. For example, have them write something that you mark. The students then bring the corrected version into class, and you use the rewritten material in an activity.

Examples of games where this is a helpful strategy are:

A day in the life	Anagrams	Battleships	Bingo
Describe the picture	Boggle	Call my bluff	Quizzes
Cryptic clues	Jokes	Gap-fill game	Interviews
Guess the word	Pairs	Memory Challenge	
Describe the word	Storytelling	Persuasion	Questionnaires
Guess who listening	Miming game	Truth or consequence	
Spelling game	Call my bluff definitions		

Hot seat

Category	Speaking fluency
Group size	One to one, any class size in groups
Level	High beginner to advanced
Age	10 to adult
Materials	None, breakout rooms for groups
Preparation	Make lists of five words for each team
Great for	General language, descriptions, vocabulary

Put students into four teams and give each one a unique list of five words. Put the teams into breakout rooms and allow three minutes to practise describing their terms without naming the word itself. Bring everyone back together when the time is up. Select a strong student from team A to go in the hot seat. This student has two minutes to describe all five words, while team B try to guess as many as possible. If all five are named, both teams A earn five points, which motivates all players to do their best at describing and guessing.

Repeat with teams C and D, or if you only have three groups, then rotate.

Team A describing words	Team B guessing meanings
Team B describing words	Team C guessing meanings
Team C describing words	Team A guessing meanings

If working one on one, swap roles with your student, or, if describing words is too difficult for your student, set a goal to win at least ten points over three rounds.

- Some students will hate the hot seat, being anxious at appearing a dunce in front of others, so don't force anyone to be there. It's best to have one person in the hot seat describing words and a team guessing. Putting a team in the hot seat is a great way to play in a real classroom, sharing the pressure and actively involving more students. Online communication is different; students are shyer to jump in, and the internet connection may cause lag, so it's best to have one student doing the main talking while a team call single words. If you have a slow connection, students could type their guesses into chat to not interrupt the person's flow in the hot seat.

Hot seat how

Category	Speaking fluency
Group size	One to one, any class size in groups
Level	High beginner to advanced
Age	10 to adult
Materials	None, breakout rooms for groups
Preparation	Make lists of five words for each team
Great for	General language, descriptions, vocabulary

Play as for Hot seat, but students explain how they make something without naming the thing itself, and others guess what they are making. For example, if the hot seat student is describing how to make a cup of tea, they cannot mention the words make, tea, or cup. It's surprising how much vocabulary you need. Try these for size:

Cup of coffee	Drive a car	Park a car
Sit down	Buy an avocado	Sew on a button
Open the fridge	Pick up a tissue	Look for your keys
Answer the phone	Wash clothes	Switch on a light
Fold a shirt	Plant a seed	Climb a ladder

Hang a picture	Make an omelette	Make a sandwich
Slice bread	Pluck a chicken	Wash the floor
Paint a wall	Empty a cupboard	Stack plates
Shuffle cards	Get dressed	Buy shoes
Write a letter		

Once you have done a demonstration game, ask students to brainstorm in groups and think of things to describe. Students will explain and guess actions relevant to their lives, such as; download an app, listen to music, text a friend, go to a party, etc.

Interviews

Category	Speaking fluency
Level	Lower intermediate to advanced
Group size	One to one, any size in pairs or groups
Age	10 to adult
Materials	Interview questions
Preparation	Famous people: no preparation Qualities: students prepare for this with homework
Great for	Conversation, Q&A, fluency, general language

1. Famous people – learning about them, talking about them
2. Qualities – types of jobs and qualities needed
3. Technicalities of job interviews
4. Interview ideas for children

1. Famous people Relevant and interesting for all kinds of students. No preparation is required. Use this activity with any interview. The example given here is suitable for beginners to lower intermediates and concerns describing and talking about people.

First, students think about a famous person they would like to meet. Put large classes into small groups of about four to ask each other questions about their choice of famous people and make notes. To motivate students, let them know there will be a class quiz after the activity. Bring everyone back together. Have students send all their facts to the teacher via chat, email, or however is most practical. The teacher can now use these facts in a quiz game.

2. Qualities This speaking activity deals with personal qualities, talents, skills, strengths, and weaknesses. Take a selection of jobs, such as sales manager, typist, conservationist, shop owner, physical education teacher, university professor, banker, stockbroker, and part-time help at a school canteen. Use various professions, including indoor and outdoor, physical, cerebral, social, and solitary occupations. Personalize the activity with your students' or their parents' job. You need half as many jobs as you have students, so if you have 30 students, you need 15 different employment vacancies. In pairs, students think of the qualities required to perform one of these well, and personal attributes that would clash. Have students write two lists, one for pros and one for cons.

Shuffle the pairs so that those who worked together are split up. One person is an employer, and the other is a candidate. The candidate has a list of qualities appropriate for one job; the employer tries to find a suitable candidate for his or her job. NB; employers and candidates do not tell each other what their job is – they interview each other and see if there is a match. After two minutes, shuffle the pairs to allow the employers to interview several candidates, after which they select a candidate from those interviewed.

- When you shuffle the pairs, some employers may end up opposite an employer; if so, the one whose surname is closer to A is the employer, and the other is the candidate.

One to one variant for qualities

I asked my student for a list of qualities needed for employment, and he came up with about twelve. Qualities included punctuality, reliability, likeable, good communicator, trustworthiness, fitness, creativity, attention to detail, leadership skills, following rules, intelligence, working as a team, etc. I then asked him to allocate three of these attributes to himself, three to each of his two daughters and one to his ex-wife. Students can work with anyone they know well, like a best friend, family member, or a work colleague. Next, I produced four jobs; a swimming instructor, a lawyer, an estate agent, and a chef. Next, my student had to allocate the jobs to himself, his daughters, and his ex-wife. He enjoyed doing this and thinking about his family. (I had checked that he didn't mind thinking about his ex.)

We used screen share to write in the qualities and the people, then add the jobs. My student had control of the mouse and dragged the attributes and occupations over to the relevant people.

We repeated the task with four more jobs: a gardener, a psychiatrist, a painter, and a school teacher. And again, with a market gardener, a stripper, a plumber, and an analyst.

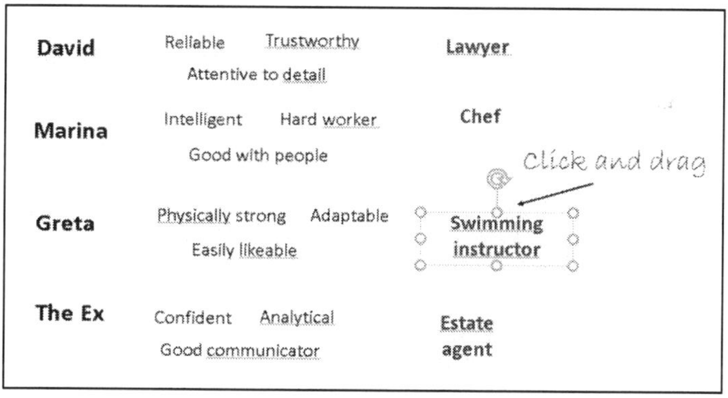

3. Technicalities of job interviews

- This activity is for students who are soon to be job seekers or interested in human resources. For other learners, play with one interview question to see if it sparks interest.

Give learners the task of preparing interview questions for homework. Mark these questions before class if you wish. Share appropriate questions and have students take turns interviewing each other. Students can question several candidates and select one for the job. Students can work in groups of four, with a panel of three interviewers and one student. Put weak students into panels as interviewers so that the activity does not grind to a halt.

Job interviews require a wide variety of language and tenses since candidates will be talking about themselves, their experience, and what they hope to contribute to the company and gain for themselves. Some types of interview questions are:

Behavioural interview questions These discuss how the candidate has coped in various job situations in the past. The idea is that past behaviour predicts how a candidate will act in a new job. Questions usually need a lengthy answer with anecdotes of about experience:

How did you solve a dispute in your former office?

Case interview questions The interviewer gives the candidate a scenario and asks the candidate to analyse it, manage it, and troubleshoot problems. The hypothetical situation could be the interviewer pretending to be a demanding customer to see how the candidate handles the issue.

Competency-based questions These questions ascertain if the candidate has the skills, knowledge, and expertise to handle a job. Requirements could be typing speed and accuracy, accounting skills, people management experience, competency in a foreign language, etc.

Panel job interview Several people interview the candidate simultaneously to allow recruiters to observe the candidate more closely. There is likely to be a broad mix of questions such as:

Tell me about yourself.
Where do you see yourself in five years?
What are your qualities?
What are your main weaknesses?
Why do you want to work for our company?
How would a friend describe you? And a colleague?
How would you handle a deadline that you are late for?
How would you handle opposition to a new policy or task?
How have you handled conflict in a working group in the past?
How have you handled a difficult client in the past?

What mistakes did you make in your previous position? Did you fix them?
Describe a successful moment in your previous job.

Interviews do not need to be about getting a job. They can be about anything:

Selecting a nutritionist to design meals for a hospital
Choosing one type of environmentally sound building over another
Evaluating one kind of energy over another
Selecting one uniform over another, and so on.

If you are teaching professional groups, give a technical interview relevant to your students' needs; if you teach engineers, ask questions about a construction project. Students will be more motivated if they recognise the activity is relevant to their language needs.

4. Interview ideas for children

What is something funny that you have done?
What is something naughty that you have done?
What do you like doing in your free time?
Ask about a pet.
What's your favourite food?
What do you like about yourself?
What can you do well?
What do you think your parents do at work all day?
What's the most important rule to follow at home?
What's the most important rule to follow at school?
What's the most important thing about friends?
Why do you think kids go to school?
What is your favourite outfit to wear?
What makes you annoyed?
What do you think is the best thing that could happen?
What makes you feel proud?
Do you have any nicknames that you like?

I spy

Category	Speaking
Group size	Small groups
Level	Beginners
Age	4 to 12
Materials	Pictures on the walls are useful
Preparation	None obligatorily or find pictures of scenes
Great for	Vocabulary revision, alphabet revision

How to play

Teach the game by showing an apple or object starting with an A. Teach all students to chant together:

I spy with my little eye, something beginning with A - A for apple.

Continue by showing something starting with a B, like a bag, and have the kids chant:

I spy with my little eye, something beginning with B - B for bag.

Now show a picture. It might be a scene, like people at the beach, or shopping, or at home. Or it might just be a list of vocabulary pictures. Say to the class:

I spy with my little eye, something beginning with B. What is it?

Tell students to guess what you have in mind. The item must be in the picture you show. Repeat for about five objects. Then switch to a different game.

For kids who have more vocabulary and autonomy, have them rehearse the chant a few more times and put them in breakout rooms to play in pairs or threes. Display the 'I spy' sentence in chat for reference.

I Spy can quickly become tedious if played as a large class – children can too easily drift off and stop participating.

I took a trip

Category	Speaking drill
Level	Beginner
Age	Children
Group size	One to one, any class size in groups
Materials	None
Preparation	None
Great for	Past tense question forms, vocabulary, other tenses

Start by saying :

I took a trip. What did I take with me?

The group members each name an item such as a t-shirt, a suitcase, a book, your dog, etc. Next, ask :

What did I wear around my neck?

Students always give the same answer, regardless of the question, which leads to incongruities. If anyone laughs or smiles at an answer, he or she does a forfeit.

Continue asking questions such as :

What did I eat? What did I photograph? What did I take swimming?

Play another round and let the students think up questions to ask. The game also works with other verb tenses.

Jigsaw listening

Category	Listening
Group size	One on one to any class size
Level	All levels
Age	8 to adult
Materials	An audio recording or a text or dialogue to read
Preparation	The dialogue or text jumbled in a PowerPoint
Great for	General listening skills, specific grammar or vocabulary in context

Give students the jumbled sentences of a reading passage. Chop the text into sentences for beginners. Split sentences in the middle for advanced students, for example;

> and then he opened the door and went in.
> Inside it was warm and

One strip may include the end of one sentence and the start of another. Tell students they will only hear the passage twice, after which they should try to put it in order. Allow a few minutes for this task before dividing students into groups to compare notes and finalize their version. Hear a few versions and rate for accuracy.

Experiment. First, let students hear the passage twice, then give them the sentences. Secondly, give students the text before the reading so they can look at it while listening. In my experience, students do better when they do not have the text in advance.

Finding texts

Ideal for lower levels are jokes, paragraphs from news articles, anecdotal science, or news items. For more advanced students, try an extract from a novel, a dialogue from a play, or a poem. The more you break down a text, the harder it is to unravel. This one lists nouns, verbs, and miscellaneous words. Punctuation marks provide a clue. Anything with a question mark or full stop is obviously at the end of a sentence. Words starting with a capital letter usually begin a sentence unless they are proper nouns.

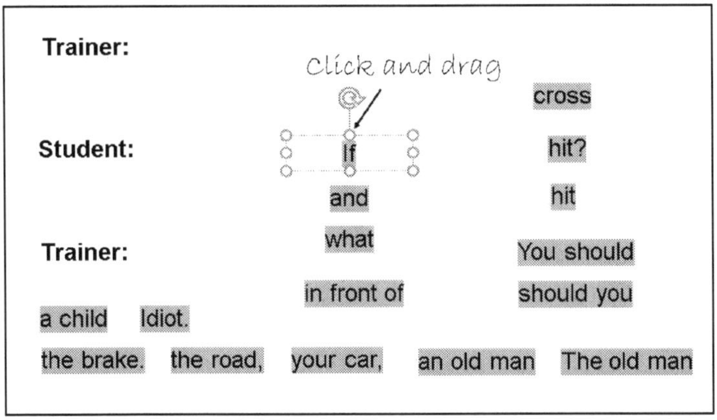

The solution is:

Trainer: If an old man and a child cross the road in front of your car, what should you hit?

Student: The old man.

Trainer: Idiot. You should hit the brake.

Here is a fun poem of higher levels; 'Cat,' written in 1938 by Eleonor Farjeon. This poem is now in the public domain in the US and countries where the copyright term is the author's life plus fifty years. The poem is narrated by a dog, which is chasing a cat up a tree. The vocabulary is onomatopoeic, with the cat spitting and the dog barking.

Cat!
Scat!
After her, after her,
Sleeky flatterer
Spitfire chatterer,
Scatter her, scatter her
Off her mat!
Wuff!
Wuff!
Treat her rough!
Git her, git her,
Whiskery spitter!
Catch her, catch her,
Green-eyed scratcher!
Slathery
Slithery
Hisser,
Don't miss her!
Run till you're dithery,
Hithery
Thithery
Pffst! pffst!
How she spits!
Spitch! Spatch!
Can't she scratch!
Scritching the bark

Of the sycamore-tree,
She's reached her ark
And hissing at me
Psftts psftt!
Wuff! Wuff!
Scat,
Cat!
That's
That!

Variation for small groups

Before reading the dialogue, give each student one sentence to place. Read the passage twice; students have their text and are listen for where it occurs. It may be a text that is repeated often, such as 'he said.' Allow a few minutes for students to cogitate in groups. The teacher now rereads the passage, pausing each time a sentence needs to be inserted.

Jigsaw reading find the odd one out

Category	Reading
Group size	One to one, any class size in groups
Level	Beginner to intermediate
Age	10 to adult
Materials	A reading passage
Preparation	Chop a text into sentences in a PowerPoint
Great for	Reading fluency, reading grammar drill

Give a chopped-up reading passage to students with one sentence that does not belong. They then work in breakout rooms with a three-minute time limit to discover the odd one out. Use a shorter passage and shorter time for beginners.

For beginners, use this activity as a grammar drill, with sentences split into two, all in the same tense, except for one. Students re-build all the sentences and identify the part that does not fit. It helps if students manipulate and re-order the sentences physically, and they can do that using PowerPoint and Zoom annotation tools. Here is an example below using an extract of '*From a Railway Carriage*,' by Robert Louis Stevenson. The odd one out is 'Three feet of snow and two of grit.' It doesn't rhyme or fit into the poem.

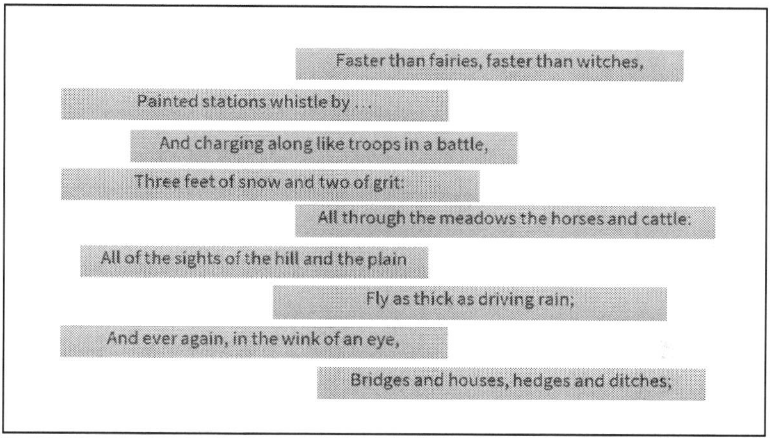

Jokes

Category	Speaking fluency
Group size	One to one, all class sizes
Level	Lower intermediate to advanced
Age	All ages
Materials	Appropriate jokes your students give you.
Preparation	Ask each student to give you jokes for homework
Great for	Speaking fluency, intonation, pronunciation, general language, and vocabulary

Have students find one or two jokes and send them to you before class. Check the jokes are not offensive and veto any that are. Make sure there are no duplicates since each student needs a different one. Save this collection for future classes.

Students are to practise telling their jokes fluently. Start by putting them in pairs in breakout rooms for 2-3 minutes to rehearse. Shuffle the rooms so students have a new audience. They should aim to tell their joke from memory.

Bring all students back together and have everyone perform for the class. It might be fun to vote on which jokes were funny.

You may have a problem if some people have long jokes while others have a one-liner. You can't leave everyone to practise for five minutes if most people have a joke that takes five seconds to tell. Specify, therefore, that the joke must not take more than a minute to tell; this way, everyone has time to finish their joke at least once in the two to three-minute practise session.

Jump the line

Category	Listening
Group size	One to one, any class size, whole-class activity
Level	Beginner
Age	4 to adult
Materials	Pictures
Preparation	Display pictures in two lines
Great for	Introducing new vocabulary or grammar

This game is for presenting new vocabulary or grammar. Kids jump from side to side, which they can do if they stand back from their computers. Otherwise, students may point right or left in front of the camera.

How to play

Display flashcards on either side of a line. Call out the items; players point to the right or the left depending on the picture's location in relation to the line. To teach professions vocabulary, call out single nouns like actress, singer, and businessman.

To work on grammar, use this game to familiarize players with a grammatical structure by repeating the same sentence but with a different noun each time. To revise professions and introduce the conditional, call out sentences like 'I'd like to be an actress' and 'I'd like to be a singer.' Do not introduce new vocabulary and a new structure in the same game.

Keep a straight face

Category	Speaking
Group size	One to one, up to 30 as a whole class activity
Level	Beginner to intermediate
Age	4 to 12
Materials	None
Preparation	None
Great for	Questions

How to play

Choose one student to be on the spot. The other students think up questions to ask that student, and the first person to have a question ready asks it—the student on the spot replies. All questions must now be answered with this same reply without the student on the spot smiling. The first question might be: 'Where do you live?' The response will be something like: 'Hong Kong.' The next question might be: 'What's your name?' The reply must be 'Hong Kong.' The following questions might be:

Where do you work?
What time do you leave for work?
What do you wear for work?
What do you have for lunch?
What's your boss called?

The answer is always 'Hong Kong.' If the student on the spot smiles or has any expression other than a dead-pan straight face, then he or she is off the spot, and another student takes over.

With a big class, once you have done a demo, put students in breakout rooms to play together; otherwise, there will be long delays in taking turns asking questions. Encourage students to ask different questions but allow beginners to repeat questions that have been asked already.

Low-level students may be prompted by a list of question words such as these:

What, when, where, who, how, which, whose, how many, how old, how much, how often, how long, and why.

Last word

Category	Speaking drill
Group size	One to one, all class sizes in groups with screen share
Level	Beginner to lower intermediate
Age	All ages
Materials	Pictures or words, screen share
Preparation	Charts with vocabulary flashcards or words
Great for	Vocabulary revision, grammar game

1	**shirt**	**lipstick**	**pillow**	**dog**
2	**forest**	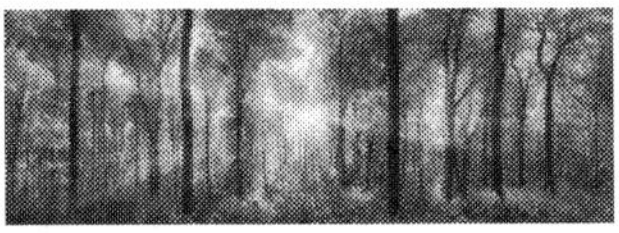	**bottle**	**telephone**
3	**cinema**	**TV**	**hours**	**plate**
4	**life saver**	**tea**	**sharks**	
	cup	**duck**		
5	**run**	**chase**	**money**	**boot**
6	**socks**	**plane**	**late**	
	vodka	**pilots**		

Each group has a chart with about 15 pictures or words laid out in a grid. Rows can be uneven and contain any number of items. Include a few colour pictures for visual interest. Students may remove any number of words from a given row per turn.

1. To remove a word, the student names the vocabulary picture or uses the term in a sentence.

2. To delete two words, students use two in a sentence.
3. The player who is left with the last image or word loses.

To prepare, paste pictures into a document. Save a master copy for future use. The teacher can delete images if playing with one student or a small group. If putting students into breakout rooms, they can delete the pictures using white-over or draw a line through them with the annotation tools.

For complete beginners, play this game with the alphabet – the player who takes the z loses. Equally, play with numbers; whoever is left with the last number loses.

Listen and draw

Category	Listening
Group size	One to one, up to 30 as a whole-class activity
Level	Beginner
Age	4 to adult
Materials	Pen and paper and cameras on
Preparation	None obligatory - pictures are beneficial
Great for	Alphabet, nouns

Listen and draw works beautifully with children and is also suitable for teen and adult beginners. Doodling and drawing aid learning, regardless of age.

Ideal for teaching the alphabet or nouns, the teacher says a word and asks students to draw and maybe colour it. While students are drawing, the teacher repeats and talks about the topic. For example, T for tree. Show pictures of beautiful trees to stimulate students visually, saying, 'Here is a tree. And look at this beautiful tree. This one is big. This one is huge. Now you draw a tree. A big tree, with branches and leaves. A beautiful tree. Colour your tree. What colour is it? Please show me your tree.'

Students may hold up their tree pictures to the camera so that you can admire them. Be sure to ask students to repeat the word 'tree' several times. The disadvantage of this game is that the teacher does all the talking, so use it for five minutes before switching to something else.

Lucky number

Category	Easy speaking
Group size	Any class size divided into groups of 3 to 6.
Level	Beginner
Age	4 to 12
Materials	None, pictures, or a list of words
Preparation	None with numbers and the alphabet For vocabulary, you need a list of words or pictures
Great for	Counting, alphabet, vocabulary drill

How to play

The teacher chooses six students to practise vocabulary, like numbers from 1 to 20 or the alphabet. The teacher displays a 'lucky number' on the whiteboard or in the chat, let's say 20. The first child says '1, 2, 3', the next one '4, 5, 6', the third says '7, 8, 9' and the fourth 10, 11, 12'. The children's excitement increases as they approach the lucky number! Whichever student says the lucky number earns a point for the team. Once students know how to play, split the class into groups to play again.

To work on vocabulary, share a list of vocabulary pictures or words and highlight the lucky word.

Mad gabs

Category	Speaking
Group size	One to one, any class size.
Level	All levels
Age	8 to adult
Materials	Words written the way they sound
Preparation	Explain concept - students prepare for homework
Great for	Fun, pronunciation, speaking

Students race to decipher misspelled words or phrases. Mad Gabs is a noisy, vocal game because it's exciting and requires reading out loud. Silent reading doesn't help much. To decipher successfully, students repeat the phrase in different ways until they hit on the correct pronunciation and stress. Throw in silent letters like 'h' to disguise the word.

Wair ah yu?	Where are you?
Wai rahy u?	Where are you?
Doooyoool iykh ymn?	Do you like him?
I zeny wunth air?	Is anyone there?
R Uf eely ng OK?	Are you feeling OK?
Hao war yu?	How are you?
Bana nna sand creehm	bananas and cream
il ike eetng pie napp uls	I like eating pineapples.
weerg owing tooth eb eech	We are going to the beach.
I zzth ahtm eyeb ook?	Is that my book?
T earnon thl ite.	Turn on the light.
Wo tryur eedng?	What are you reading?
You hess scend her prize	US Enterprise
Kay belt ella vission	cable television
Amma sun dhot com	amazon.com

Students can play in breakout rooms or in teams as a class. If playing with teams, each team gets two minutes to guess as many phrases as possible. If playing in breakout rooms, give each group the same 'Mad gabs' to race to decipher before the time is up.

Mad libs

Category	Listening for fluency
Group size	One to one, any class in groups of up to ten
Level	Intermediate to advanced
Age	10 to adult
Materials	A sheet of paper with a passage with blanks to fill in
Preparation	A text with blanks labelled with the part of speech
Great for	Parts of speech review, vocabulary, listening skills

Mad Libs is a madcap word game where you add crazy new words to existing sentences. Invented by Leonard Stern and Roger Price in 1953, while Stern was working on a script for 'The Honeymooners,' the pair developed the game into a full-fledged phenomenon. Mad Libs' books have stretched to every corner of pop culture, from 'Star Wars' to 'Adventure Time.'

There is only one rule to follow in Mad Libs: Fill in each of the blank spaces with the appropriate type of word. Label each space with the part of speech to be inserted, e.g., noun, verb, or adjective. Outside of that, the choice of word is entirely up to you, no matter how ridiculous. The more ridiculous it is, the more hilarious the outcome. Find or write a short story summary like the one below. It is helpful to highlight nouns, verbs, and adjectives in different colours. Original text:

A young (noun 1) **girl**, Little Red Riding Hood, (verb 1) **sets off** through the woods to visit her (adjective 1) **sick** (noun 2) **grandmother**. Along the way, she meets a (adjective 2) **hungry** (noun 3) **wolf**. The (noun 3) **wolf** rushes ahead of Red to her (noun 2) **grandmother**'s (noun 4) **house**, where he (verb 2) **impersonates** Little Red Riding Hood to gain access. The (noun 3) **wolf** (verb 3) **eats** the (noun 2) **grandmother**. When Red (verb 4) **arrives**, the (noun 3) **wolf** pretends to be her (noun 2) **grandmother,** and (verb 3) **eats** her too.

To make a gap-fill:

1. Copy and paste the original text and increase the spaces between lines.
2. Decide what parts of speech you want to review and delete these from the passage.
3. Make the blanks big enough to write in.

In the example below, if a word is repeated, like 'wolf,' then the new noun replaces 'wolf' for the entire reading, not just the first time it occurs.

A young (noun 1)_____, Little Red Riding Hood, (verb 1)______ through the woods to visit her (adjective 1)______ (noun 2)________. Along the way, she meets a (adjective 2) ______ (noun 3) _____. The (noun 3) _____ rushes ahead of Red to her (noun 2) ________'s (noun 4)______, where he (verb 2)________ Little Red Riding Hood to gain access. The (noun 3) _______ (verb 3) _______ the (noun 2) ________. When Red (verb 4) ________, the (noun 3) _______ pretends to be her (noun 2)_________ and (verb 3) ________ her too.

It can be more amusing if teachers display a list of weird or interesting words to choose from to spice up the text.

NOUNS	VERBS	ADJECTIVES	ADVERB
Eyeball	to vomit on	sticky	ravenously
Bath	to dream	scary	jealously
Kangaroo	to sprint	gross	suspiciously
Toenail	to dribble on	terrible	cleverly

This text and word list combination could give rise to the example below. Have fun adding the adverbs yourself.

A young (noun 1) kangaroo, Little Red Riding Hood, (verb 1) sprinted through the woods to visit her (adjective 1) scary (noun 2) eyeball. Along the way, she meets a (adjective 2) gross (noun 3) toenail. The (noun 3) toenail rushes ahead of Red to her (noun 2) eyeball's (noun 4) bath, where he (verb 2) vomits on Little Red Riding Hood to gain access. The (noun 3) toenail (verb 3) dribbles on the (noun 2) eyeball. When Red (verb 4) dreams, the (noun 3) toenail pretends to be her (noun 2) eyeball, and (verb 3) dribbles on her too.

How to play

Show students the original text and word list and let them take turns choosing words to add to the version with blanks.

Variation

Do not let the students see the text. Ask them for different parts of speech by saying, 'Give me an example of a noun/verb/adjective/adverb' etc. Write down the student's response in the relevant blank, but don't read anything yet. Continue around the room until all the blanks in the story are filled. Now read the story out loud, and generally, there will be some laughter, especially with kids.

- Write summaries of famous films relevant to your target audience. Simple dialogues work too.
- When you create your version with blanks, use colour coding because it is easy to get into a muddle!
- My adult students enjoy the challenge of trying to fit appropriate words in the blanks to make as much sense as possible of the story.

Here is Hans Christian Andersen's 'The Emperor's new clothes.'

There once was a vain emperor who only cared about new clothes. A group of clever (noun 1) designers came to town saying they would (verb 1) make a magical (noun 2) cloth that would be invisible to stupid people.

The emperor (verb 2) ordered a new (noun 3) dress made from the (noun 2) cloth, planning to use it to see who in his court was stupid. He (verb 3) sent his most trusted minister to look at the cloth. The minister found the (noun 1) designers working at empty tables. Not willing to look stupid, he said the (noun 2) cloth was beautiful. The emperor (verb 3) sent someone else from his court, and the same thing happened. Nobody was willing (verb 4) to say that they could not see the (noun 2) cloth.

Finally, the emperor himself went to see it, and again nobody was willing (verb 4) to say that they could not see a thing. So, the emperor (verb 2) ordered a beautiful (noun 3) dress to be made from the (noun 2) cloth that did not exist.

A big parade was planned, and the naked emperor strutted through his town with everyone admiring the beauty of his new (noun 3) dress. No one in the city would (verb 4) say they could not see it. Suddenly a child laughed, screaming that the emperor was naked. The emperor looked down and had (verb 4) to say that he was; however, the parade had to continue as if nothing had happened!

Using the nouns radiator, onion, donkey, and pen, and the verbs, eat, buy, cook, and run, this story becomes:

Here is another story, The Emperor's new clothes by Hans Christian Andersen.

There once was a vain emperor who only cared about new clothes. A group of clever (noun 1) radiators came to town saying they would (verb 1) eat a magical (noun 2) onion that would be invisible to stupid people.

The emperor (verb 2) bought a new (noun 3) donkey made from the (noun 2) onion, planning to use it to see who in his court was stupid. He (verb 3) cooked his most trusted minister to look at the onion. The minister found the (noun 1) radiators working at empty tables. Not willing to look stupid, he said the (noun 2) onion was beautiful. The emperor (verb 3) cooked someone else from his court, and the same thing happened. Nobody was willing (verb 4) to run that they could not see the (noun 2) onion.

Finally, the emperor himself went to see it, and again nobody was willing (verb 4) to run that they could not see a thing. So, the emperor (verb 2) bought a beautiful (noun 3) donkey to be made from the (noun 2) onion that did not exist.

A big parade was planned, and the naked emperor strutted through his town with everyone admiring the beauty of his new (noun 3) donkey. No one in the city would (verb 4) run they could not see it. Suddenly a child laughed, screaming that the emperor was naked. The emperor looked down and had (verb 4) to run that he was; however, the parade had to continue as if nothing had happened!

Make a match

Category	Writing, speaking drill
Group size	One to one, pairwork for all class sizes
Level	All levels
Age	All ages
Materials	Pen and paper, optionally use an online timer
Preparation	None
Great for	Vocabulary, short grammar drills, parts of speech, comparatives

Demonstrate the game and put students into pairs to play in breakout rooms. Students each write a different sport on seven cards or pieces of paper and a different place on seven other cards.

No writing is allowed from this point on.

Player A names a place from his selection of locations. Player B chooses a sport from his seven that can realistically be played at that place. Say player A chooses the beach as the spot, player B can say:

I play football on the beach.

B wins a point because it is possible to play football on the beach. It would not be possible to swim, because swimming is in the sea, not on the beach. The beach card and the football card are now discarded from the game and cannot be re-used. B now names a place, and A chooses a sport that could be done there. Now A and B only have six cards left. Once players have run through all seven places, they see which player has the most points.

Students may need vocabulary lists to serve as prompts for sports and places. Places could be the sky, the sea, the beach, a mountain, a wood, a field, a tennis court, a football pitch, and a park.

Adapt to any theme. Examples are:

- Food ingredients and recipes: flour goes with cake, sauce, biscuits
- Body parts and clothing items: head – hat, cap, beret, sun hat, feet – socks, shoes, legs – trousers, shorts, skirt, leggings, chest – shirt, dress, t-shirt, hands - gloves, arms – shirt, blouse, dress, bottom – shorts, pants, underwear, neck – scarf, tie, eyes – glasses, sunglasses)
- Describing people: Famous people or classmates and descriptions like brown hair, blue eyes, slim, pretty, tall
- Places and where you buy things: bookshop, café, chemist, cinema, farm, market, museum, post office, shop, shopping center, supermarket
- Places, towns, countries, and transport to get there
- Professions and professional objects: plumber and spanner, leak, pipes, electrician and wire, plug, screwdriver, actor and stage, film, cinema, singer and microphone, stage, concert hall, chef and oven, knife, food, computer geek, computer, director

and office, carpenter and wood, secretary and phone, salesman and briefcase, phone and office

- House and furniture: Kitchen and oven, table, chair, bedroom and bed, lamp, bookcase
- Animals and what they eat and drink
- Weather and sentences describing the weather: sun and it's sunny, it's warm, it's hot, rain and it's wet, it's raining, it's cold, wind, snow, ice, cloud, storm, blue sky, thunder, lightening
- An item and a hobby: guitar and playing music, baseball and sport, flower and gardening, flour and cooking, a picture and painting, a pool and swimming, a book and reading, a cinema and watching movies, a pen and writing, a classroom and learning, an airport and travelling
- Countries and capitals, cities, sites, geographical features
- Months of the year and special days in those months: Thanksgiving, Halloween, Christmas, Groundhog Day or Valentine's Day (Feb), Easter, April Fools, Mother's or Father's Day, May Day, or national holidays relevant to your students
- Comparatives: Any theme and bigger/smaller than, the same size as, faster/slower than, taller/shorter than, safer, more dangerous than, weaker, stronger than

Make a match parts of speech

Player A says 'conjunction,' and player B, if he has one in his seven parts of speech, makes a sentence with it and earns a point. The nine parts of speech are verb, noun, pronoun, adverb, adjective, conjunction, preposition, interjection, and article. Drilling down is possible using seven different verb tenses, seven sentences with one of three tenses, pronouns, subject pronouns, object pronouns, possessive pronouns, reflexive pronouns, and maybe possessive adjectives.

Make a match with comparatives

Players each write a list of seven comparatives and a list of seven nouns. Let's say player B has chosen these seven comparatives:

Faster than, smaller than, as big as, as pretty as, better, more beautiful than, worse

Player A has chosen these nouns:

Teapot, bike, poster, movie, book, friend, and chocolate.

Player A chooses 'bike.' Player B picks from one of his comparatives to make a sentence using 'bike,' like 'My bike is better than your 'bike.' Those two words are now out of the game. Player A chooses 'teapot.' Player B says, 'My teapot is smaller than yours.' Player A says 'poster,' player B says, 'That poster is more beautiful than this poster.' Etc. If player B gets 'chocolate' and 'faster' at the end, a sentence like 'I eat chocolate faster than you' would work, whereas 'My chocolate is faster than yours would not.

Make a sentence or a question

Category	Speaking, writing variant
Group size	2 to 30
Level	All levels
Age	6 to adult
Materials	None – optional bells or buzzers
Preparation	None
Great for	Questions, sentences, grammar drill

How to play

Divide your group into teams and say a word or phrase. Team A has 10 seconds to include it in any sentence or question. After 10 seconds, students on other teams can jump in with a suggestion.

- With bigger groups, make the best students judges, who validate the proposed sentences from an opposing team. Your most talented students will thus have an important role while being prevented from giving all the answers.
- There can also be a rule that whoever got the last answer correct waits one turn before answering again. You cannot expect your bright students to sit there and do nothing because they are better than everyone else, but you can ask them to share the airtime a little.

Language ideas

This game is adaptable for general English or specific grammar. To focus on a particular linguistic structure, specify the tense or have students include a particular phrase.

A simple example for beginners with food could be for students to think of sentences or questions about whether they like or dislike them.

Hold up a picture of some potatoes and say 'question.' Students think of a question including the word potatoes: 'Do you like potatoes?' 'May I have some potatoes, please?' 'Are there any potatoes?' 'How much are the potatoes?' 'How many kilos of potatoes would you like?' 'Where are the potatoes?' 'Are the potatoes cooked?' 'Do you want mayonnaise with your potatoes?' 'Why aren't we having potatoes for lunch today?'

Pictures are not essential though visual stimuli enhance learning and participation.

Here is a complex example for higher levels to work on if + past perfect + the perfect conditional. The teacher says the phrase, 'If I had wanted' and the word 'mother.' An appropriate sentence could be 'If I had wanted my mother to be here, I would have asked her.' With 'tiger,' a sentence could be 'If I had wanted to see a tiger, I would have gone to India.' And so on.

To keep everyone working hard and participating, have every team member create a sentence, but only one person is chosen to read theirs out for a chance to earn a point for the team.

Have students play in breakout rooms once they know the game.

Making up stories

Category	Speaking and writing
Group size	Individual, class in small groups in breakout rooms
Level	Intermediate to advanced
Age	All ages
Materials	Random words
Preparation	Write six words to be included in a story
Great for	General language, storytelling, grammar

How to play

Supply six words to students via a group message or read them out while students write them down. Give everyone the same vocabulary. Pupils invent and write a story in small groups. The story may be plausible or far-fetched, as long as the six words are included. The important thing is that the grammar is correct. Students will enjoy the challenge of making up a story and using their imagination rather than following the often dull and obvious storylines of picture compositions in textbooks.

Once they have written the stories, bring students back together and listen to all the story creations because it's no fun for students to work with no feedback. Therefore, if you have 30 students in your class, make groups of five, that way, you only have six stories to listen to, whereas, if you made pairs, you would have to listen to fifteen stories or leave some students out in the cold.

- To make the activity more exciting, give a time limit for the story creation, and stick to it. Experiment with 5 minutes and see what results you get. If every group has had time to include all the words, you know it was too long.
- If your students like competitions, award a point for each word used.
- Use words that appeal to your students, or atmospheric or picturesque ones that stimulate the creative juices, like strange, gloomy, exhilarating, or lurid.

Optional correction of grammar

Now that you have had fun hearing all the stories have groups swap their story with another group. Put students back into their breakout rooms. If it is too lengthy to make the same groups as before, use the random group creation tool. The groups attempt to correct any language mistakes, using a marker to highlight any errors. As far as the corrections go, there may be several versions offered. After five minutes, bring everyone back together and go through one of the stories' grammar corrections. It would be a drag to do this for every story, so instead, spend a few minutes answering specific queries. You can offer to mark students' work, and they can email you their story. Participating in marking forces students to focus on details such as verb endings and those little prepositions that are so often wrong. It is a valuable exercise in awareness.

Grammar

For grammar, specify what structure must be included in the story along with the vocabulary words. For tenses, define if the action was yesterday, is happening now, or is in the future.

- Encourage students to write short, simple sentences, as the temptation is to try to create an incredible story when the language and grammar are not yet there to do so.
- Play again and give the story's opening or final line, plus six words or phrases to include. Use vague openers to stimulate the imagination:

He should never have gone there.

I peered into the dark hole.

Today is the most important day of my life.

Examples of closing lines:

There was nothing for me to do but cry.

Luckily, I still had the coin in my pocket.

For lower intermediates, provide simpler sentences:

It's a fish.

Today I am taking the train to London.

Making up stories 2

Put students into groups and have them write a list of twenty-four curious words. Shuffle the groups. Each group makes up a story with a set of twenty-four words, with about six words per student. Suggest appropriate words to inspire your learners. Castle, fairy, witch, horse, magic, and giant might be exciting for children. Meeting, executive, sales manager, sales targets, clipboard, overhead projector, and PowerPoint presentation would make serious business students feel like their class was relevant to their needs.

Use this game one on one as well, with teacher and student alternating.

Students do not have to contribute complete sentences, as long as their word is included.

Student A: Today I went to the castle
Student B: to meet my fairy friend
Student C: and the witch.
Student A: I rode my horse.
Student B: The fairy waved her magic wand.
Student C: And a giant appeared.

Mastermind with words

Category	Spelling, writing
Group size	One on one, any class size in pairs
Level	All levels
Age	8 to adult
Materials	Mastermind template from the Appendix Play using screen share and annotation tools Students could draw or print templates at home
Preparation	Choose six words
Great for	Spelling drill, grammar

How to play

One player is the *code maker*, the other the *codebreaker*. The code maker chooses a pattern of four words. Duplicates are allowed, so the player could even choose the same four words, but this tends to be easy to guess. Blanks are allowed in the classic mastermind game, but not in my spelling version. The code maker writes down the four words in a specific order.

The codebreaker tries to guess the pattern, of both the word and the order, within thirteen turns. Each guess is made by writing the words on the decoding board. Once a row is done, the code maker provides feedback by copying and pasting coloured circles over the white ones. A red circle indicates a correct word in the right place, but it does not reveal which word or position is right. A yellow circle indicates a correct word in the wrong place.

Once feedback is provided, another guess is made; guesses and feedback continue to alternate until the codebreaker guesses correctly or all rows are full.

Use Mastermind for words that are interesting to spell and for grammar, like irregular verbs; he drank, she ate, we went, they saw, you had, I slept.

Classic Mastermind with colours

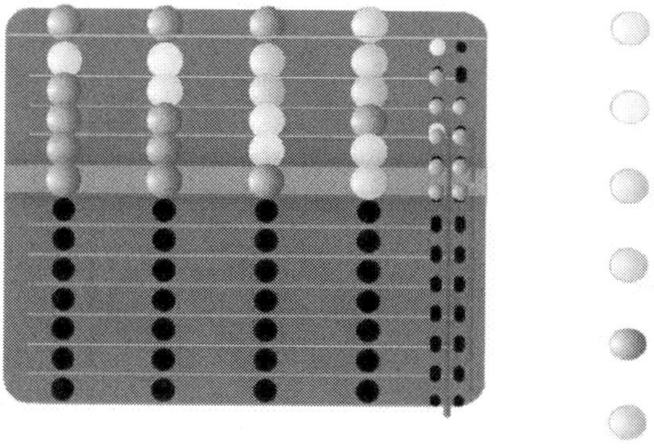

Mastermind spelling example

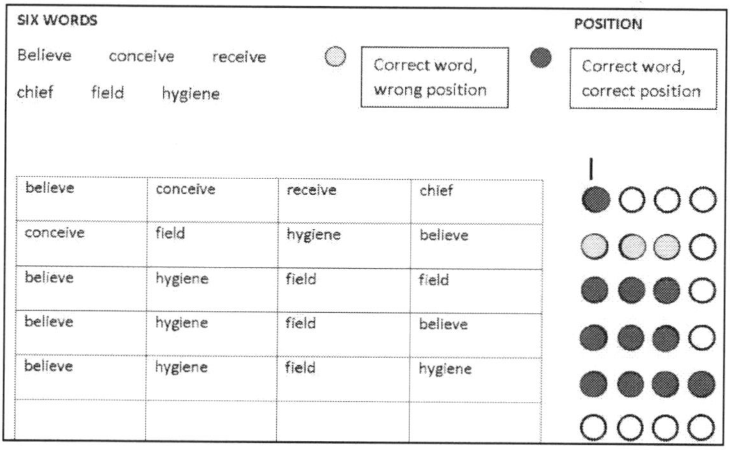

Miming game

Category	Speaking, writing, vocabulary revision
Group size	One to one, any class size in small groups or teams
Level	Beginner to Intermediate
Age	All ages, relaxing and fun for adults
Materials	Chart with things to mime and optionally points
Preparation	Think of things to mime or have students do this
Great for	Vocabulary, grammar, Q&A

Preparation

Prepare, or have students prepare items to mime, with a points scale. More points are awarded for more challenging words.

How to play

Put students into pairs or teams. Player A or Team A chooses a topic to be mimed and selects 1, 2, or 3 points.

TOPIC	A	B	C
EMOTIONS	1 point	2 points	3 points
ANIMALS	1 point	2 points	3 points
JOBS	1 point	2 points	3 points
PLACES	1 point	2 points	3 points

Player B or Team B has the answers and mimes the relevant word.

EMOTIONS	Happy	Tearful	Confused
ANIMALS	Cat	Lion	Seal
JOBS	Singer	Secretary	Salesman
PLACES	Restaurant	Cinema	Supermarket

Tweak and configure to suit your student numbers. If your online platform allows, have all team members mime so those guessing have plenty of ideas and clues to help them and keep everyone participating.

Have students each prepare a chart for homework. Use some of these in the next lesson and keep them in your resources for future classes.

Use with grammar or Q&A

Aside from reviewing vocabulary, use this game with sentences and for grammar. For example, the different squares can contain verb tenses such as present simple, present continuous, and past simple. Students make up a sentence using the correct tense to win the point. Expand this idea for any grammar, sentence, or question. For example, fill in the chart with where, why, how, what, which, do, does. Students pick their square and make a question starting with that question word.

Miming vocabulary

Category	Listening
Group size	One to one, any class size in small groups or teams
Level	Beginner to Intermediate
Age	All ages, relaxing and fun for adults
Materials	A list of nouns to mime
Preparation	None
Great for	New vocabulary, vocabulary revision, alphabet

Prepare a list of nouns and have students invent a gesture for each one. Pick one of the students and watch the mime. Have all students copy. Move on to the following letter and word. Repeat the above, make a mime for U, 'umbrella,' and then for V, 'van.'

Switch from one word to the other. Students listen and do the appropriate action. Have a student call out the vocabulary for others to mime. Play with advanced language for higher levels.

By acting the words in a meaningful way, students will remember them better.

Movie activities

Short movies are perfect for online lessons, as long as the teacher does something with the material instead of plonking students in front of it with no purpose or related activity. After all, students can sit in front of movies on their phones all day long with no input. Movie material ideas are:

1. Advertisements
2. Film trailers and extracts
3. Extract from a documentary, news, and interviews
4. Other video ideas

- If your online connection is unreliable, download the movie to your computer to avoid live streaming.
- Keep the clip short; thirty seconds to three minutes is good. Long videos can turn a lesson into the equivalent of a lecture where students are passive recipients.

Movie activity 1 – advertisements (UK) / commercials (US)

Category	Listening, speaking
Group size	One to one, any class size
Level	High beginner to advanced
Age	10 to adult
Materials	Picture or movie ads (see YouTube or equivalent)
Preparation	Use my example as a demonstration, then have students prepare for the next class
Great for	General language, critical thinking

As a warm-up, ask students to describe ads they know to the others. Which ads do they like and which make them want to buy?

Show an ad to the class. Next, present a list of questions about the advertising techniques. With these in mind, take another look at the ad and elicit comments. Video ads are ideal, but picture ads work well too. Here is an example below, with the ad, questions, and possible answers.

- Question: Who created the message?
- Answer: XYZ Telecommunications. (I made this up but, it's better to use real ads.)
- Question: Why was this message sent?
- Answer: XYZ sent this message to advertise its brand.
- Question: What techniques did they use to attract attention?
- Answers:
  - Attractive young people of mixed ethnicity, smiling and relaxed
  - Harmonious soft colours and casual clothing
  - Concepts of friendship, companionship, and having a good time together
  - Short, catchy phrase, 'keep in touch with your friends'
- Question: What values or information are included?
- Answer: The idea communicated is that if you are on your phone with your friends, you will be happy, relaxed, laughing and having fun, and sharing the pleasure of friendship, who are also on their phone. It is normal and cool to be on your phone when with friends.
- Question: What information relating to the product is omitted?

- Possible Answers:

  - Numerous studies have shown that too much screen time causes depression and other problems.
  - Mobile phone radiation may be dangerous.
  - Screen time isolates you from those around you. The group shown are not chatting, two people are vaguely communicating but not even making eye contact, and everyone else is staring at their screen.
- Question: How truthful is the ad?
- Answer: This answer will be subjective, depending on how students interact with their phones. In my view, it is true as I often see groups of young people on their phones, not talking to each other or watching videos.
- Question: Which market does the ad target?
- Answer: This is aimed at all teens and young adults. The ad includes girls and boys of different ethnicities to be as all-inclusive as possible.

Small group activity - make a live photo

Now that you have perused those questions have students create a live snapshot of the ad. Make pairs or small groups and give each one an ad to think about and prepare a 'live photo' of the product. To do this, students create a mime or freeze-frame to communicate the ad's content and meaning. While the group mime or pose, a narrator presents the ad, as per the questions above. Finally, the narrator asks the class to guess the product. The group keep miming or holding their pose and facial expressions until someone succeeds. Play this with your individual students, taking turns to act and describe ads for the other to guess.

Here is another example with a crafts ad, which the teacher can narrate as a demo. (I found a perfect example using Lego and Star Wars but can't include it here in case there are copyright issues.)

Show the ad to two or three students who quickly make a freeze-frame or mime. They can mime the dad, the kid, and someone can even be the model plane. It would help viewers imagine a scene if you can enlarge their videos or place them in a line. The rest of the class watch the mime and listen to your narration to guess the product.

Describe the ad: The idea is that if you buy this product, you will have a privileged moment with your dad all to yourself while he lovingly watches you. What they leave out is that painstaking hours are needed before you finish it. The final piece is bound to be missing, lost under a sofa. The ad is relatively truthful in that the product is the proper size in relation to the humans, but there's no way Dad will sit and watch. Annoyingly he will probably butt in and make most of it himself! What is it? Answer: A model plane craft.

Invent ads

Next, have each group invent its own ad. Brainstorm for ideas of products students could choose. Students spend a couple of minutes in breakout rooms creating their ad and then show the others. Vote at the end to see which product most students want to buy.

Using video ads

Video commercials are great because the advertiser has time to tell a story. Human psychology is driven by avoiding pain and going towards pleasure. Advertisers play on this. You might have a desperate 'homemaker,' with stained or grey laundry, who, having polluted the environment with some powerful detergent, is ecstatically happy with the state of the washing. When their kids come home from rugby covered in mud, they think with delight of their washing powder. Life is perfect, thanks to laundry detergent.

That said, laundry ads won't be of much interest to kids or teens. Find ads for products they know and that are relevant to your students. There are always the classics, like the Andrex loo roll ad and the Labrador, which has been going for decades; soft, long, and very strong. (Type Andrex toilet paper advert on YouTube, and you will find a choice.)

Repeat the critical thinking work using the videos. Have students vote on the best ad. Have students find an ad they like for homework and prepare to act it out to the class. Have students make up their own ad and perform it as a short skit. Vote on best sketches.

- Put a strong leader in each group. Don't put all the talented ones together. Spread the talent around, so there is someone to lead the group, linguistically and otherwise.
- Let students work with others who also like their chosen product. If someone hates it, they may be unhelpful on the ad-creation team, and the task may even annoy them.
- How about vintage ads from the 1950s? Or ads from different cultures? Hindu Indians will be interested in powders for their colour festival, a product for the West to explore! The Chinese, alas, could be interested in rhino horn and other obscure animal parts. Actually, it is best to leave that kind of thing out because it could be divisive and emotional.

Movie activity 2 – Film trailers and extracts

Category	Listening, speaking
Group size	One to one, any class size
Level	High beginner to advanced
Age	10 to adult
Materials	Movie extracts or trailers
Preparation	Choose one or more film trailers and download them
Great for	Listening, discussion

Show three trailers

Put the class in groups to discuss which film to see and why. Each group chooses one of the three by voting. After three minutes, bring everyone back together and see which the most popular film was.

Have students discuss in groups what they think happens in the film for five minutes. Bring the class back together and hear the various versions of the movie. Students can vote on their favourite version.

Using one movie trailer

Groups discuss and predict what will happen in the full movie.

Students imagine what the moral of the story is and why.

Groups create an opening scene or a final scene for the movie.

Students imagine a dialogue that could occur in the movie and perform it for the others.

Extracts

Show an extract from a film with no sound and have students invent the dialogue or narration. A search online for the most iconic movie scenes will yield lists of options. That said, I do not spend any time selecting a memorable scene; I use the first trailer I find on my local cinema website that does not involve anyone getting hurt! There is no dialogue, so your students will bring it alive. Still, I suggest avoiding violent and psychologically disturbing scenes because some people are highly susceptible and cannot handle them. About 36% of the British public enjoy horror films; therefore, most people do not.

Movie activity 3 – Extract from a documentary, news, and interviews

Category	Listening, speaking
Group size	One to one, any class size
Level	High beginner to advanced

Age	12 to adult
Materials	Audio-visual clips
Preparation	I recommend students source these
Great for	Listening, discussion

Task students with finding appropriate content. Peruse their submissions without watching everything, and veto anything violent, emotionally fraught, or inappropriate. Once you have selected a suitable clip:

- Students watch once and write questions.
- Show the extract again.
- Students hold a quiz in teams. Questions could be based on content in the movie clip, but surprising questions about extraneous details can be thrown in, such as the weather, the colour of someone's raincoat, or identifying the music.

Regarding content, politics and wars are best avoided, especially if you teach refugees or different ethnicities. Look for regional or positive news items since these rarely cause any problems. See the Debates activity for tips on avoiding divisive, fraught content.

I want to include a plug for the nature documentary film ***The Serengeti Rules***, directed by Nicolas Brown, released in 2019. This extraordinary film shows the work of five scientists over sixty-years. The future of our planet depends on their discovery being applied.

Other movie ideas

Sales and business videos: Analysis of sales techniques, the video's structure, how the message is communicated, body language analysis; students analyse a video for a product of their choice.

Great moments by eloquent speakers: Students perform extracts from a speech using mythical speeches from history. A search online for 'world's most famous speeches' or 'most persuasive speakers' will give you plenty of live speeches and transcripts. Some famous examples are:

Winston Churchill – June 1940 World War II – We will fight them on the beaches
Martin Luther King – 1963 – Civil rights speech - I have a dream
John Fitzgerald Kennedy – 1963 Ich bin ein Berliner
Abraham Lincoln – 1863 – The Gettysburg address
Nelson Mandela – 1964 – I am prepared to die
Mother Teresa – 1979 – Nobel lecture
Mahatma Gandhi – 1942 – Quit India

Silly videos

Students watch a funny clip and then get together to describe the clip using vivid adjectives, adverbs, and descriptive language. If students can make their text amusing, so much the better. There are plenty of funny videos online, all free. The best source of those is to ask your students. Tik Tok is trending at the moment, but new platforms pop up regularly.

Beginners can choose a funny video to show the class but must describe it beforehand. Giving them a template will help.

What is the topic?
Where does it happen?
Who are the characters?
What do they do during the video?
What happens at the end?

Videos made by class members: A home project students can share in class. The topic should be chosen by each student and can be anything they enjoy. Ideas are:

Short cooking film showing a recipe
Presentation of posters, pictures, and objects in their bedroom
Presentation of a family member
Interview with another student
Students invent and narrate a story using props and random objects
Video of DIY, fixing something, painting, making something
Video of a car engine, explaining what all the parts do
Video of putting on makeup
Video of creating a painting
How to draw video

Vocal technique video that all students can try in class (work with vowels, for example)
How to look after a pet
How to clean an electric cooking hob without scratching it

Mystery Bag

Category	Speaking
Group size	One to one, any class size
Level	Beginner to intermediate
Age	All ages
Materials	Real items or pictures
Preparation	A bag and an object
Great for	Vocabulary

Hide an object in a soft bag, show the shape, and ask students to guess what it is. Give clues like it is in the kitchen. If no one can name it, reveal a part of the item, such as the saucepan's handle or shiny side or part of the apple skin. Move it closer to the camera and away again. Have your students prepare a mystery object for the next class for others to solve, so not only the teacher has all the fun! Kids will love this, and it gives them something hands-on to do. Students must know the name of their item in English, and preferably, it should be a word they are supposed to know. A guideline for beginners could be to pick any word from a list or textbook index. If you do not have any vocabulary lists, use the internet to search for the '200 most common English nouns.' You need plenty of words to choose from because many common English nouns are not the sort of thing you can hide in a bag!

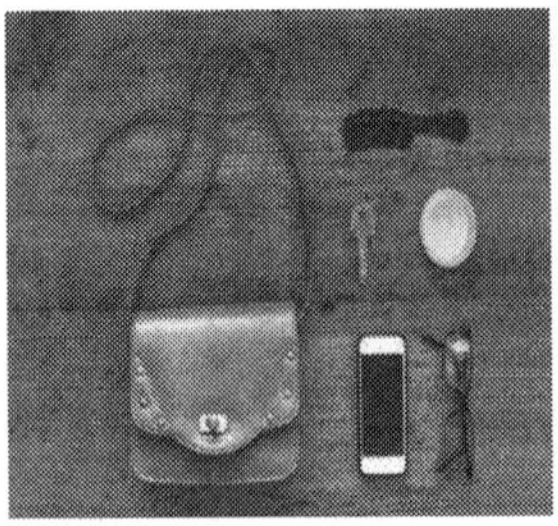
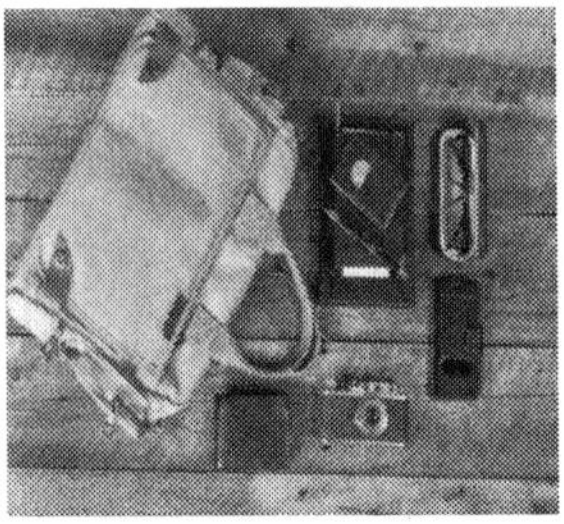

Play this game with pictures. Show a demonstration picture and ask students to create their own for a guessing game in the next lesson. Say half the students are to prepare a suitcase for a beach holiday and pack six items; the other half are to prepare a bag for a trip to the mountains. They either take a photo of their bag and contents or create a picture like those shown. In the next lesson, play bingo. The mountain students call out beach items until someone on the beach team has all six named. Swap and have the beach team guess the items in the mountain suitcases.

Another game could be to pack original but justifiable items and hope no one guesses them —the last person with things still to name wins.

A talented student can be tasked to write down all the items named so everyone can check off the photo or bag at the end to check the winner's contents.

Name the thing

Category	Speaking fluency
Group size	One to one, any class size in pairs or groups
Level	Lower intermediate to advanced
Age	All ages
Materials	Similar pictures, like 3 cars, or 3 similar but not identical people
Preparation	None
Great for	Conversation, questions, comparatives, descriptions

This game requires sets of similar pictures. Do a demonstration with the whole class first. Show the images and silently choose one. Students are to work out which one you have selected by asking questions that narrow down the choice. The more alike the pictures, the more language is required. Once students have completed this activity with you, they can repeat it in small groups of three or four. The more advanced students could do the questioning, as this is harder than answering.

Finding pictures easily and quickly for this game

Type what you are looking for into your internet browser, such as ‘pictures Asian women traditional silk,’ or ‘pictures vintage cars,’ and a selection will appear. Take a screenshot and copy and paste it into a document. I like to make a collage with twenty pictures. The snowmen pictures provided in the appendix for the game Hangman would be suitable for this activity.

At first glance, it may seem hard to distinguish between these cars or Asian ladies, but once you start looking at details, it’s easy. For example, only one lady is holding a bag. Clues can be found in their jewellery, dress details, hairstyles, and hand and eye positions.

Useful vocabulary for the vintage car activity would be shapes, curved roof, flat roof, square or round headlights, and the number of doors. It is easier to use bigger pictures in a PowerPoint, so the details are more apparent.

- It's good to have two students guessing, and two answering as this can avoid a weak student stalling the entire activity.
- Have students each collect a set of pictures for use in the next lesson and keep the best of those sets for future use.

No 'yes' or 'no'

Category	Speaking
Group size	One to one and small classes
Level	All levels
Age	All ages
Materials	None
Preparation	Topics for questions and examples
Great for	Short form answers, questions, general English, verb tense drill

One student is in the 'hot seat' at the front or in the middle of the room. The others ask a barrage of questions to this person, who must answer them without using 'yes' or 'no.' The minute the student in the hot seat accidentally lets slip a 'yes' or 'no,' he or she must give the place up to someone else. This game encourages the use of short-form answers such as 'I do' instead of 'yes' or 'I haven't' instead of 'no.' Review short-form answers before playing by brainstorming with the class. Point out that the correct short-form answer is contained in the question:

Past tense question and short-form answer drill:

Have you been to Paris?	I have. / I have not.
Did you see a movie?	I did. / I did not.
Could you eat the whole steak?	I could. / I could not.

This game is excellent for drilling questions with beginners. Students can stick to basic and repetitive questions.

Present tense drill:

Do you like jam?	I do.
Do you like apples?	I do.
Do you like sugar?	I do not.

Play in a freer way with more advanced students who have more language and vocabulary under their belts, or you may stick to playing with a specific question form to drill it thoroughly.

Students may score points for each question answered correctly. Equally, you may set a fixed time limit in the hot seat to ensure everyone has a turn and score points for all correct answers given during that time. Alternatively, you do not need to keep score, but give each student a chance to answer a set number of questions. If the hot seat person successfully answers six questions, they have won and can cede the spot to someone else. If you have too many students for everyone to have a turn, play again in another lesson with different people in the hot seat.

- Once the student has settled comfortably into the drill and is not likely to say yes or no, change your tone of voice as if really wanting to know the information. Switch into conversation mode. Shorten the question. Do you like sugar? Student: I do. Teacher: Really? Do you? Do you eat it a lot?

Noughts and crosses

Category	Speaking drill
Group size	One to one, any class size in pairs
Level	Beginner to lower intermediate
Age	4 to adult
Materials	Noughts and crosses sets - see below
Preparation	None
Great for	Vocabulary drill, sentences, questions drill

Set up

Share a grid with vocabulary pictures or words. A grid consists of nine squares in three rows of three. The players need access to the annotation tools.

How to play

The players first decide which marker they are using. One player starts by naming and drawing a cross on one of the pictures. The second player now has a turn, naming one of the remaining available images and drawing a nought. Continue until one of the players manages to form a line of three markers. Rows of three can be formed horizontally, vertically, and diagonally. Sometimes there is a winner, and sometimes it is a stalemate.

Language

For beginners, put a number in each square of the grid or a colour.

Intermediate players can say sentences about the picture rather than merely naming the object represented. Players cannot write their nought or cross unless they say the vocabulary in English or use the word in a sentence. If they cannot, they have to pick a different square, or the other player has another go.

Grammar example for pronouns, do and does.
Make a question using the word in the square.

do	you	it
he	she	does
we	they	I

Vocabulary translation using animals. Translate the word in the square.

cow	pig	cat
dog	lion	fish
bird	ant	duck

Vocabulary example using animals' body parts. To draw a nought of a cross, name a word in the square. (Flashcards from teachingenglishgames.com/eslflashcards)

Odd one out

Category	Speaking
Group size	One to one, any class size
Level	All levels
Age	All ages
Materials	None
Preparation	Prepare sets of five words
Great for	Conversation, speaking fluency, grammar, verb tenses, vocabulary

Write five words on the board. Students choose the 'odd one out' and say why. An easy example:

white green apple blue brown

The most obvious answer is that 'apple' is the only fruit, or possibly that apple is a noun, and white, green, blue, and brown are adjectives (non-golfers might not know that green can also be a noun). However, they could say apple is the only word containing the vowel 'a,' or starting with a vowel, that blue is the only four-letter-word, or that brown is the only word with one vowel. Often, there are many possible answers.

Example with verbs:

cooked flew bought saw made

'Cooked' is the odd one out because it is the only regular verb. 'Saw' could be the odd one out because you only need your eyes to see, whereas other body parts are required to accomplish the other verb actions. 'Cooked' could be the odd one out because it is the only action that needs heat.

Example with verbs for recognising tenses:

I drank, I ate, I wake up, I went, I saw

'I wake up' is the odd one out as it is in the present tense.

Example with nouns:

curtain, sofa, wardrobe, round table, telephone

The 'round table' is the odd one out because it is the only thing that is not rectangular. 'Telephone' is the odd one out because it is the only thing that is electronic.

Example for pronunciation:

toasted cooked wanted painted heated

'Cooked' is the odd one out because the 'ed' is pronounced 't' rather than 'id.'

Example for plurals:

church dress box wish woman

'Woman' is the odd one out because to make it plural, you change an internal letter; all the others require -es.

Students often enjoy compiling lists for other teams too.

One lemon

Category	Easy speaking
Group size	Divide class into groups of about 8 to 12 students Minimum of 3 pupils
Level	Beginner
Age	5 to adult
Materials	None
Preparation	None
Great for vocabulary	Warm-up, numbers, singular and plural nouns,

I love the absurdity of this game. Try it for numbers, as described below, or replace numbers with vocabulary words.

How to play

Do a demonstration with about ten students and then split the class into groups of about eight. Each player has a number. To allocate these, read each student's name and say the number. The student concerned repeats their number back to you and makes a note of it. This way, you are sure everyone has got their number and that they are participating. If anyone doesn't respond, give that number to someone else who is present. If you allocate a number to someone who has sloped off to the loo, it'll ruin the game. Start with:

'One lemon
Half a lemon
Calls three lemons.'

Immediately, student number three says:

'Three lemons
Half a lemon
Calls ten lemons.'

Try these variants

- Students must be on alert when they are called. If they don't react immediately, they get a penalty point, or they are out.
- If a player calls on a player who is out, they get a penalty too.
- Any time the numbers three, five, and nine are called, that person has to change the noun.

Combine with adjectives to practise word order, for example:

'One brown eye
Half a brown eye
Calls three brown eyes.'

Number three has to change the noun (or adjective), so number three says:

'One blue nose
Half a blue nose
Calls eleven blue noses.'

- The game is nonsense, but you can use it with any language and, since it is a drill, accuracy is essential. Despite the absurdity apparent, verify that all phrases and plurals are correct.

Persuasion

Category	Speaking fluency
Group size	Three students minimum to any class size
Level	High beginner to advanced
Age	12 to adult
Materials	Optional fact sheets
Preparation	Have students prepare for the game for homework
Great for	Conversation and general English, general and specialist topics

In groups, students try to persuade other students to buy a product, vote for a cause, or change their view on a topic. This persuasion technique can be used for any theme to generate a reason to communicate and stimulate the students. It is ideal for specialist subjects and general language.

Here are a few example topics:

• favourite holiday destination: travel agents and customers

• best product: sellers and customers

• favourite day out: tour guides and customers

• food to be served in school canteen: nutritionists and parents

• which school for your child: headmasters and parents

• which job: employers and job seekers

• which design: architects and buyers

• managers seeking to promote an employee

• which bank: bank managers and customers (ideal for business English). Give the bank managers the homework task of choosing a bank and reading up on the types of loans, rates, and terms available. The other students can prepare to choose a mortgage. In class, see which bank managers recruit the most clients and which mortgage brokers make the most sales.

• Which party: hosts describe what their party will be like, and guests decide which party they want to go to

• Which political party: party leaders present their policies, and voters choose whom to elect. Allow for some outrageous parties, such as the Monster Raving Loony Party in the UK. Be sure students know they can take on a role rather than express personal views. Have students each prepare a party manifesto for homework to use in class.

• Which city tour: tour guides try to recruit sightseers for their favourite city

• Which country? Ambassadors try to attract immigrants to their country. If you have refugees or feel that this is too sensitive a topic, play with imaginary countries that have fantasy ideas such as free food for children and so on

• Which pet is best

Here is a detailed example using the topic of dream homes. If you don't like this topic, go for a favourite sport, job, film, or expedition. First, brainstorm ideal features for a dream home. Jot down new vocabulary as students call out their ideas. Half the class prepare a property fact sheet, and the other half create a fact sheet on their ideal home. They might search online for a dream home for homework and download a few photos and the description. Give students a template as a starting point.

- Location: city center, town center, countryside, isolated
- Distance to nearest local shops: kilometers or miles
- Two keys services that are nearby: Golf courses, ski resorts, shopping centers, cinemas, public pools, tennis club, racetrack, beach, lake, sailing club, concert hall, gaming center, hospital, old age pensioner's home
- Property size: In feet or m2, the number of bedrooms, bathrooms, and types of room
- Size of grounds, if any: Square meters, feet, number of acres or hectares
- Nature of grounds: Garden, balcony, agricultural land, woods, river, beach, ski slopes
- Parking: on the street, closed garage, shared garage, adapted to electric cars
- Features: fireplace, pool, gym, tennis court, fishing, sports, helipad
- Architectural style: modern, historic, castle, mansion, bungalow, compact, apartment, portable home

Once you have your dream home fact sheets, split learners into groups. Each group will naturally contain a mix of home buyers and estate agents. Tell students they only have two minutes to sell and interview, after which they will be shuffled into a new group, four times over. Estate agents quickly present their homes and answer questions from the buyers. Shuffle the groups every two minutes until you have mixed them up four times. There should be plenty of conversation going on in all the breakout rooms. Visit a few to observe but try not to interrupt.

You could now check and see if everyone has made a sale and a purchase. Students who have not could have a fun forfeit as a consequence. See the forfeits section for ideas. Alternatively, here is a closing activity for a small group. Once students have finished browsing properties in groups, run an auction. Everyone decides how much they want to spend on their home and writes the amount down. It can be any amount, but if they do not spend at least 50% of the amount, they lose. The sellers price their property. It can be any price, but if they don't sell it for more than 50% of the amount, they lose.

Each estate agent shows their property via screen share or by holding it up to the camera. He or she gives the starting price and acts as the auctioneer for his or her house. The class bid until someone buys it; if no one wants it, the seller decreases the price until someone buys it.

Here's another idea, which might be too long-winded with a big class. Experiment. Have four estate agents show their property pictures to the class via screen share or their cameras. Ask buyers who have seen this property previously to vote and see which is the most popular. The most popular one stays in; the other three are out. To vote, do a thumbs-up count for each property; again, students can only vote if they have seen this property before in one of the breakout room sessions. Take another batch of four properties and repeat. You'll do this about four times with a class or 30. When you have four to five finalist properties, take a final vote and see which the winner is.

Photo activities

Category	Speaking
Group size	One to one, all class sizes in groups
Level	All levels
Age	8 to adult
Materials	Students need cameras; phone cameras will do
Preparation	Students take photos and upload them homework
Great for	Vocabulary, useful for shy students because participation is anonymous

Encourage students to be creative. How about running an art project? For example, ask students for tips and know-how on how to take creative photos using their phones. You might not want to get too technical because many people will glaze over fast, but some basics like picture composition, lighting, and focus points should be interesting to everyone. Everyone takes a photo for homework and submits it anonymously to the pool. Students take it specifically for this task, which saves some from showing off with exotic holidays; everyone attempts to be creative with an everyday object they have at home and then votes on their favourites. You can have different categories such as the most beautiful, mysterious, bizarre, and funny. At the end, the winners can be identified, if you like.

Creative pictures don't have to be exotic; they can be created with everyday objects. Who can take the most creative photo of a book? Taking close-ups can be fun because if you zoom in close to an item, it can be hard to tell what it is. Have a competition like that, a guessing game, using photos students take for homework. See these examples below for ideas. The first two are easy to guess. The answers are at the end of this game description.

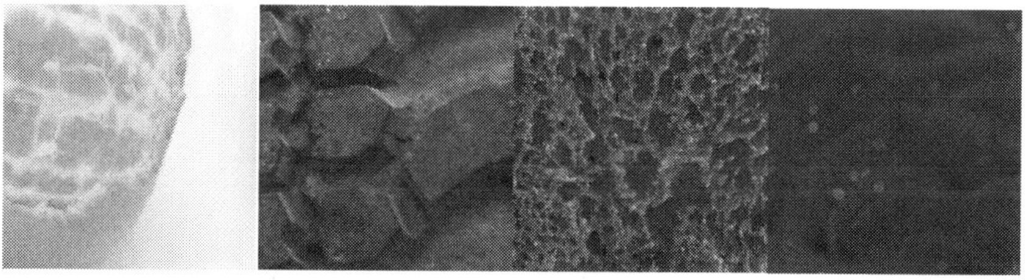

- Students submit their photos anonymously to avoid the 'social media we like sheep' phenomena, where you pick your mate's image, even if it's a load of rubbish because if you do not, he will never speak to you again!
- As a variant to submitting close-ups, students can display a picture they have zoomed in on. Teams can compete to guess the object or scene; if no one can, zoom out a little until someone identifies it.
- Answers for the close-ups; tangerine, tyre, bread, and rose.

Pictionary

Category	Speaking
Group size	One to one, any class size up to 40, in teams
Level	Beginner to intermediate
Age	5 to adult
Materials	Students use the annotation tools or pen and paper
Preparation	None
Great for	Vocabulary revision

How to play

Pictionary is a classic game where one player draws an object, and the other players try to be the first to guess what it is. The one who names it first has a turn at drawing. Ask all students to jot down a thing they will draw at the start of the game. The item can be anything, but it must be vocabulary that the class are supposed to know.

It's fun to put players into teams to spice up the activity. Make two pairs if you have four students. See the introduction for quick ways to make teams with big classes. When students name the object being drawn, they say their team number so the teacher can note the point, preferably on the shared whiteboard, where the drawing is taking place; this way, students can track their score compared to other teams.

- Some students might complain that they can't draw. Tell them to think of something easy like the sun, the moon, a picture, a table, a house, a book, or a hand.
- If a student cannot think of what to draw and everyone is waiting, pick someone else and come back to them later when they have thought of something. Do what you need to do to avoid long gaps of hesitation and inactivity because you will lose the class's interest.
- It may be necessary to stop the game before everyone has had a go at drawing. Remember, always stop games while the players are enjoying them, and well before they show signs of boredom.

Picture flashcards

Category	Speaking
Group size	One to one, any class size
Level	Beginner to intermediate
Age	4 to adult
Materials	Picture flashcards, cameras
Preparation	None if you have flashcards
Great for	Rapid vocabulary revision and learning vocabulary

Game one

For lightning-speed vocabulary revision, hold up pictures to the camera and have players name the item. Divide the class into teams and give each one a minute to identify as many images as possible while you show them flashcards rapidly. Ideally, have one pupil on a stopwatch while another two keep score, counting a point for each correct word.

One to one

Swipe flashcards across the screen or start from far away and zoom into the camera. The speed will depend on the internet connection. Sometimes the swiping does not work because the student only sees a blur. Test and adapt. Show the same pictures several times. Students will get faster and faster as they recognise the shape and colours. Show words that the student hesitates with repeatedly until they are learned.

- Show each picture for a maximum of three seconds and move on, even if no one named the word in time.
- Tell students that flashcards can appear more than once, so they should pay attention even if it is not their team's turn.
- To prevent the same person from answering everything, have a rule where a person cannot name pictures two in a row.

- Hundreds of downloadable flashcards for kids are available from the author's website: see the Other Resources section for details.
- Play for five minutes or so as a team game.

Game two

Display ten pictures in screen share or show them via the computer or your phone camera. Students race to name them all as fast as possible. If there is a picture they don't know, they say "pass" and get a five-second penalty. If you teach individually, the student can have several goes and try to be faster each time. For two to six pupils, take turns and see who is the quickest. When some students are much better than all the others, give them more words to say to keep them challenged in the same timeframe. If they say that it's not fair, tell them that, like in video games, they are on the next level, so of course, it's harder!

Pictures could be partially hidden for variety, as shown. This frieze is included in colour in the downloadable Appendix.

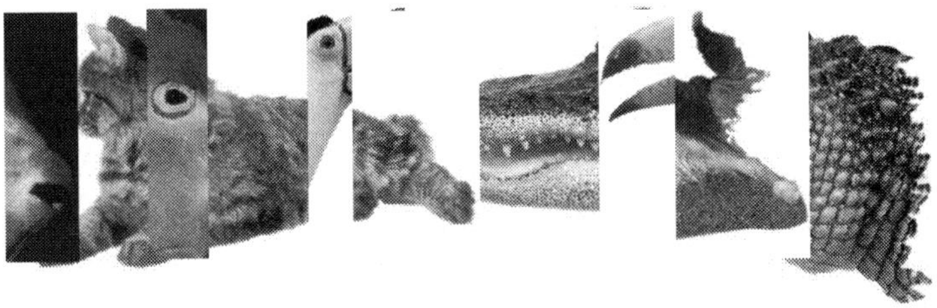

Picture memory challenge

Category	Speaking fluency
Group size	One to one, any class size in pairs or teams
Level	Beginner to intermediate
Age	6 to adult
Materials	Scenes and questions, examples in the Appendix
Preparation	None if you use those in the Appendix, otherwise 10 minutes to find images and write questions.
Great for	Prepositions, vocabulary, Q and A, verb drill

How to play

Play as a class or in teams. Tell students you are going to show them a picture for one minute and then ask ten questions. Students are to write their answers down. Those who get nine or more answers right are the winners.

Play in pairs, providing the picture and questions to Student A for student B to answer. To make the game easier for children, show the picture for ten seconds at a time. When child B is stuck, show it again for ten seconds, and so on. For example, display a drawing of a cat under a chair. Hide it and ask, 'Where is the cat?' Ask another question such as, 'What colour is the chair?' until child B cannot answer. At that point, child A holds up the picture for another five seconds before continuing through the questions. You might give child B three opportunities to look at the image and answer as many questions as possible. On the other hand, let very young children continue until they have answered everything because they can be sensitive to the idea of 'losing.'

Enlarge the images as much as you can without them being too blurred. The larger the picture, the easier it is to see details.

One to one

For an individual lesson, prepare ten questions in advance or make them up off the cuff. Display the picture for one minute. Ask all ten questions, noting the ones the student answers. Show it again, for a few seconds, and ask the remaining questions again. Try this again with a different picture. Let the student find a scene and ask you questions in the next lesson.

- Point-scoring is optional, though it does give an incentive to concentrate.
- Give lower levels a list of questions for each picture and put them in pairs in breakout rooms.
- Be sure to do a demo for the whole class, so students know what to expect and carefully study their picture.
- For a future lesson, have students find scenes and prepare questions.

Materials

This game requires scenes, such as places, views, or a room with people. Type 'picture of a park with children' into your browser, and you will find suitable scenes with plenty going on. Or try 'picture of a classroom with students.' You might give the people names to make talking about the picture easier; is Wayne wearing a striped shirt or a grey tracksuit?

It's easy to find pictures online, but to help you, I included some examples, with questions, in the Appendix: a goat scene, Horse beach, Sunglasses at Night, and Cabin Fever.

Questions suitable for beginners for the goat scene are:

1. How many goats are there in the picture?
2. Is the man wearing a hat?
3. Is the lady wearing gloves?
4. What colour are the lady's trousers? (Or pants for the US)
5. What is the man holding? / What is in the man's hand?
6. What is the lady holding?
7. What colour are the man's shoes?
8. How many trees are in the picture?
9. Is the lady wearing a necklace?
10. Is the lady wearing earrings? (A trick question because you cannot see her ears.)

There are four other pictures in the Appendix for this game, including three silly ones, Horse Beach, Sunglasses at Night, Cabin Fever, and the one below. Crop this one to show fewer men to make the game easier.

This girl with puppets is a nice example for kids:

Ping pang pong

Category	Speaking drill
Group size	6 to 30
Level	Beginner
Age	From 6 to adult
Materials	None
Preparation	None
Great for	Numbers, vocabulary drill for beginners

How to play

Give each student a number. The teacher starts by saying, 'Ping, pang, pong number 2.' Number 2 says ping, number 3 says pang, and number 4 says pong, followed by a different number, such as 10. Number 10 says ping, number 11 says pang, and number 12 says pong, plus a new number.

To drill vocabulary, replace numbers with words like pen, pencil, rubber, number 22. Now number 22 says pen, number 23 says pencil, and number 24 says rubber plus a different number.

- Try the game with five numbers (or words) for 20 students plus so more people are active during each turn.
- One way to allocate numbers quickly is to show a list of first names in alphabetical order. Students scan the list for their number and note it down. Students must write down their number!
    1. Claire
    2. Daniel
    3. Pierre
    4. Susie

Presentations

Category	Speaking fluency
Group size	One to one, any class size
Level	High beginner to advanced
Age	All ages
Materials	None
Preparation	Students prepare this for homework
Great for	General English, speaking, listening, skills for life

Students each prepare a presentation on a given subject for homework. For best results, allow them to choose their topics. Three minutes is long enough for intermediates, but you could go up to ten minutes with advanced learners. If you have a small group, presentations can be longer, but with a large class, you will have to keep them short, or you will not have time to listen to them all. Students should not read out their talks but must do them from memory, using notes or bullet-points. Therefore, students will have to rehearse delivering their content to achieve a degree of fluency and confidence.

When commenting on presentations, first point out what went well and what you liked. Have other students comment on what they enjoyed. It is judicious to encourage students rather than rip them apart and potentially make others nervous about delivering their talk.

Pointers for giving good presentations:

- Know your topic well
- Tell the audience what you are going to tell them, then tell them, and then tell them what you told them – i.e., have an introduction, content, and summary
- Vary your tone and speed of speech
- Make eye contact with the audience and seem confident
- Check the audience can hear you and speak clearly
- Use an anecdote, story, or metaphor to illustrate a point
- Keep any visuals simple and colourful
- Rehearse repeatedly in sections until you are confident

Giving presentations is popular with business English students, especially if the topics are business-related.

Pronunciation hands up

Category	Listening for phonemes and pronunciation
Group size	One to one, any class size
Level	All levels for pronunciation
Age	5 to adult
Materials	None
Preparation	Note words students have difficulty pronouncing
Great for	Phonemes, pronunciation

How to play

This listening game works with phonemes and pronunciation. The teacher repeats a word continuously and then unexpectedly changes a letter or phoneme. For example, say 'lorry, lorry, lorry, lorry, lolly, lolly, lolly, lolly, lorry, lorry, lorry.' When the students hear the change, they raise their hands. When the word reverts to lorry, students lower their hands.

With a small group, put students in pairs and award points to the first one who holds up a hand. Deduct points for hands going up before the change! Split larger classes into teams.

- A challenge is to let the students take the speaking role, which certainly encourages them to focus on how they pronounce words.
- Try ship and sheep with Spanish students, pass and path with French pupils and lorry or lolly with Japanese learners, blueberry and brewery for Germans.
- Have fun with any words that sound similar, like accept / except, affect / effect, complementary / complimentary, choose / chose, loose / lose, of / off, personal / personnel, quiet / quite, there / they're, hall / hole, horse / hose, ball / bowl, ball / bull, role / rule, walk / work, sport / support, soap / soup

Question and answer

Category	Speaking and writing drill
Group size	Smaller class sizes divided into teams
Level	Beginner to intermediate
Age	4 to 12
Materials	None
Preparation	None
Great for	Q & A drill

With students in teams, tell everyone to write a question using a target structure or tense. Randomly select a student from group one who asks their question from memory, looking straight at the camera without glancing down at notes. Team one score a point if their question is grammatically correct. Choose someone from each group in turn, so all teams have a chance to win a point from round one. Repeat for round two, choosing other students.

Although students do not all speak, everyone works hard since no one knows who will be picked to read the sentence or question. If a student does not have a question ready, that team forfeits the chance to earn a point.

- Continue until the question-and-answer structures are well ingrained, but do not play for more than ten minutes at most. If students need additional work, switch to a different game, but continue with the same language.
- For intermediates, allow your pupils to come up with the actual question form by telling them to ask for the time or find out someone's age or birthday, and so on.

Question and answer memory game

Category	Speaking drill or fluency, writing drill
Group size	One to one, any class size in pairs or small groups
Level	Beginner to intermediate
Age	4 to 12 Great for kids and fun-loving adults
Materials	None
Preparation	None
Great for	Q & A drill or fluency

Children form pairs and have one minute to observe each other. One student then switches off his or her video and asks the other, 'What colour are my eyes?' The other student endeavours to reply correctly. Other questions might be: 'What am I wearing?' 'What colour is my shirt?' 'Am I wearing earrings?'

Tell students they will play again in the next class and to prepare some extra clothes or props. They might show three photographs and have three questions ready for each. They could also ask each other about family, friends, and pets, and then ask things like 'Do I like dogs?' 'Do I have a cat?' 'Do I have any sisters?'

- Weak students would benefit from being in a small group rather than a pair, learning from others, instead of sitting there incapable of participating and frustrating their partner.

Question and answer lottery match

Category	Writing and speaking
Group size	All group sizes, including large classes
Level	All levels
Age	6 to 12
Materials	Questions
Preparation	None
Great for	Q&A revision, fluency

Set up

Before playing, ask your class to brainstorm questions to refresh their memories. If necessary, draw prompts on the board to elicit them, like a clock face for 'What time is it?' Or, sketch a suitcase for 'Where are you going?' If you are at a loss for drawing prompts, write 'what, when, where, how, which, who, and why.' Other question prompts are; does he, have you, were they, did she, and so on.

How to play

First, every student works alone, writing down one question and one answer. Allow a minute for this. Next, split students into two breakout rooms to form team one and team two. Group one compare and make sure they have different types of question and not three people with, 'What time is it?' Team two do the same, but for answers. 'I'm going to London,' and 'We are going to New York' are the same, because they both reply to 'Where are you going?' Group two need to write a replacement answer. Allow five minutes for this task and bring everyone back together regardless of whether they have finished.

A student from team A asks a question, preferably from memory. If it is 100% correct, that group score two points. If there is a small error, give one point for encouragement, but not with higher levels. If team B has an answer that fits this question, then they win a point. For example, a member of team A asks, 'How old are you?' That grammatically correct question earns one point for A. Now anyone from another team can call out a matching answer, like 'I'm seven.' If correct, they win a point for their team.

Pupils must have the answer on their paper to call it out to make the game a form of lottery and not just a test to answer questions.

Questionnaires market research project

Category	Writing and speaking
Group size	Minimum of 4 students, with no upper limit. For one on one, students interview friends and family outside of class
Level	All levels
Age	8 to adult
Materials	Questionnaires
Preparation	Prepare a questionnaire or have students do this
Great for	General language, multi-skilled activity

Carrying out market research is a great way for students to gain confidence speaking English with a safe structure. Lower-level students can take the role of the researcher since the questions are fixed. Start with brainstorming, as a class or in teams, where students invent new products. Each student, or group, should have one or two new products that need to be tested, i.e., do people want them, will they buy them, and how much will they pay? New items or services could be brand new inventions, a new food item, style of furniture, topical magazine, car model, or anything really!

Once students have some new products, they must establish their market research objectives and create a questionnaire. Students should work in pairs or groups.

Researchers interview and note responses. Results are analyzed, and finally, everyone discovers what products were successful.

Give students some guidelines to create the basis of a questionnaire.

- How much should the product cost?
- What is the level of interest in the product?
- Find out who is likely to buy it—gender, age, nationality, people who like cats, etc.
- Ask what brand they think it is.
- Have a multiple-choice question where they check off similar products they already buy.
- Use scales, not yes or no. How likely are they to buy on a scale of one to ten?
- Have an open-ended question such as suggestions for improvement.
- What do they like about it?
- Have interviewees choose the colour of the product from a choice of three. When an electronics company asked young people what colour their new music player should be, most said yellow. But when told to pick up a player on their way out, everybody took black!

Students enter their results into a spreadsheet and calculate the percentages. If that is too much work, have them assess the answers approximately and identify any patterns, grouping similar responses together. Finally, each group prepares a presentation of the product's likely success, what people like, whether they will buy it, and for how much. Group members could each present on one of the questions to share the task around.

Beginners can research simple things, such as how many brothers and sisters everyone has, what pets everyone has at home, or in what country everyone was born. Work out the percentages and show them in a bar or pie chart. Younger children can skip the maths and do the questions. There are videos and instructions online, in English, for constructing a pie chart, which could be a fun challenge for students. Otherwise, have them search for ‘free pie chart maker online.’ I did find one that required no login and was easy to use. A bar chart is much simpler to create.

UK Pet Owners

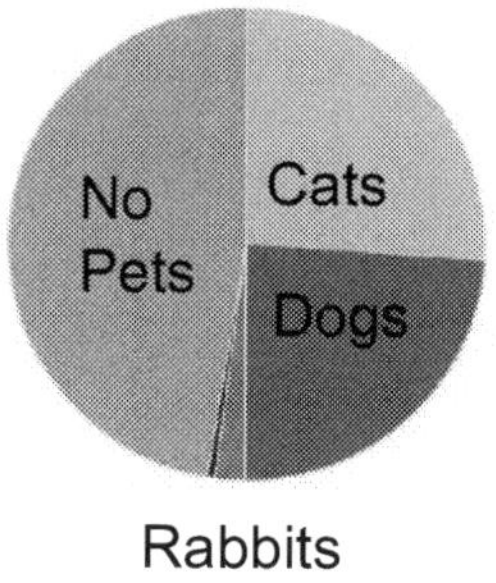

Cats	26%
Dogs	24%
Rabbits	2%
No pets	48%

South Korea Pet Owners

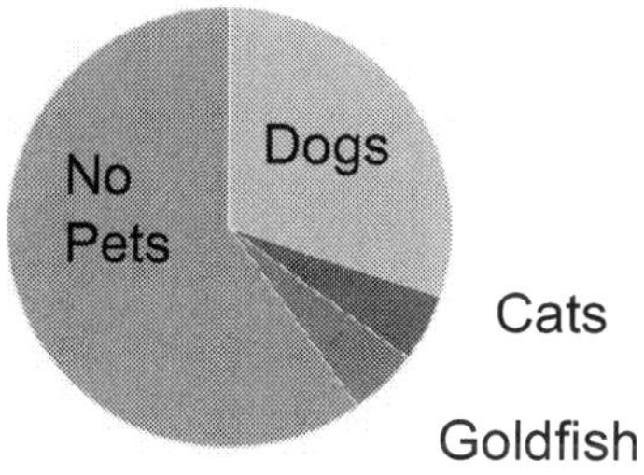

Dogs	30%
Cats	5%
Goldfish	5%
No pets	60%

Other topics

Have students prepare questionnaires on topics, such as beard trimming techniques, regulations on office attire or wearing a uniform at school, what new service the community needs most, what should be done about a specific local problem, etc. Each group prepares a questionnaire together. Then split everyone into pairs for interviews. Shuffle them as necessary. Tweak this according to your class size but aim for as many students to be interviewed as possible.

Quiz or Forfeit

Category	Speaking fluency, reading questions
Group size	One to one and up to maybe 30 students
Level	Beginner to intermediate
Age	All ages but excellent for kids
Materials	Questions
Preparation	None, or optionally questions, or students prepare for homework
Great for	Grammar or vocabulary drill, speaking fluency, general knowledge, Q & A

Prepare a list of grammar, vocabulary, or trivia questions, or have each student write some and send them to you. See 'Blow your house down' for ideas.

How to play

Ask questions, and if the student cannot answer, the whole team gets a forfeit. See 'Forfeits' for ideas. Having the entire team do the forfeit encourages active participation from more students at once. Make teams and invite students to send you questions via private chat, which you share after making any necessary corrections. Teams earn points for asking questions as well as answering them.

Language ideas

Adapt the difficulty of the questions and topics to the age and level of your students. For example: What is one plus two? What is the naughtiest thing you ever did? Name a yellow fruit. What is the opposite of hot? Have you eaten octopus? What is the capital of South Africa? What is the past participle of 'to buy?' What fruit is round and can be green or red? What fruit is oval and hairy? What animal has a pouch? Convert a question or sentence to a different tense. And so on. Have the class write trivia questions for homework and play again with those in the next lesson. That way, you will get topics relevant to your students.

Quizzes

Category	Speaking and optionally writing
Group size	One to one, all class sizes
Level	All levels
Age	All ages
Materials	Questions
Preparation	The class prepare questions for homework
Great for	Language drills, Q&A, grammar, fluency, general knowledge

The popularity of TV quiz shows and general knowledge games like Trivial Pursuit is testimony to how much people love quizzes. Quizzes are ideal for a language class because questions can be tailored to students, even with complete beginners.

Quiz ideas are:

- For complete beginners, questions can be translating vocabulary, answering questions about yourself, or saying what colour an item is.

- For a quiz with no preparation, students could:
    - turn sentences into questions and vice versa
    - change the tense of a sentence or question
    - provide a synonym or antonym
    - describe the meaning of a word
    - add an adjective to a sentence
    - add a word to a sentence
    - translate something
    - explain a metaphor

In short, whatever you are covering in your classes can be converted into a quiz question.

- General knowledge or specialist knowledge questions are also excellent for practising general English and are fun for the class.

For a quiz to work well, it is crucial the topics interest your students, regardless of whether they do you. With teens, I use a 'guess who'-style quiz about a pop icon they like, and they are chuffed (pleased!) when they guess the answer – the person in question means something to them, whereas a grey-haired politician may receive a different reaction.

Divide the class into groups and tell them to prepare a quiz. Each team chooses its topic, such as pop music, books, films, sport, capital cities, art, history, etc. Each team member comes up with one or two questions about that topic. Teams must know the answers without looking them up online! Allow five minutes or so for students to write their questions. If necessary, display some question word prompts like when, what, where, why, how, who, and which. Put the teams into panels, collect the questions, and have a TV show-type quiz.

During the lesson, divide students into small teams. You, or a student, hold all the questions and ask each group a question from the list, awarding points for correct answers and triple points for correct answers that are grammatically correct.

To involve more students and avoid them sitting passively, waiting for a turn, ask team A a question. All team members write their answers in the chat. As long as one correct answer is given, the team win the point.

- It's best to check questions in advance for errors so students formulate questions correctly during the class.
- A star student can be given the job of deciding if questions are accurate, awarding single or triple points. Being given a responsible role should keep more advanced students challenged and save them from getting bored.
- Since quizzes are excellent for reviewing grammar and vocabulary, it's worth holding them regularly. There is no issue with using the same questions as long as new ones are added. Students' general knowledge will improve as an additional benefit.
- The best way to have a successful quiz is to ask the students to choose topics and prepare questions for homework. Thus, the

teacher uses no free time to obtain fun, relevant questions without being an expert.

- In addition to the students' categories, suggest adding a traditional general knowledge one, like geography, history, science, grammar, literature, or the arts, for students to research and broaden their minds.

Reading comprehension

Category	Reading, writing, speaking
Group size	One to one, any class size
Level	All levels
Age	6 to adult
Materials	Reading passages
Preparation	Choose a text
Great for	Reading, writing, grammar, Q & A

How to play

Display a text for students to study carefully for three minutes. Hide the text and ask students to write some questions relevant to the content. Allow a couple of minutes for this. Divide the class into two teams. Team one asks team two a question, for one point, and team two scores a point for answering. Continue but if everyone grinds to a halt, show the text again for another minute to allow students to find facts they missed the first time. Repeat the Q & A format and see which team does best.

- Inevitably, with a game like this, the brightest students will be tempted to do all the work. Solve this by making them scorekeepers, deciding if questions are grammatically correct or not.
- A time limit adds zest to the activity.
- Creating questions for colleagues involves all students directly in the task.

- Using memory alone to answer questions adds to the challenge and fun. It's not just a question of looking through the text but trying to remember it.

Reading race

Category	Reading, scanning, writing
Group size	All group sizes
Level	All levels
Age	All ages
Materials	Reading passage with questions
Preparation	Choose a reading passage and write questions
Great for	Reading, scanning for information, writing answers

Explain the purpose of the activity, which is to improve general language skills and vocabulary through reading and see how quickly students can scan written material for information.

Give students a text to read, preferably a topic that is of interest to them. Relevant material could be something from an online magazine, a news item, song lyrics, a poem, an extract from a play, or a passage from your textbook if you have one. Start writing questions in screen-share. As soon as you start writing, students race to answer your questions by scanning the written material. Your first questions may not concern the first paragraph but could relate to the information given in the middle of the passage. Students can write their answers in note form or as complete sentences, as you wish. When you have finished writing out the last question, allow another 30 seconds and stop the activity. Students see how many questions they have answered. Repeat this with a different passage.

As an option, once students have completed this activity, you may like to ask them to think of an additional question about the passage, which they ask a class member.

- The trick to this traditional reading comprehension activity is to give a tight time limit to add excitement and use topics that interest students.

Reading race variant

Play in teams. Display a poem, dialogue, reading passage, or a list of words. The teacher says a word, phrase, or sentence. Students skim through the material, and if it's there, they race to write it down. Deduct a penalty from the team if the word is not there!

Advanced vocabulary variant - Predict words, then scan for them

Pick a topic, such as deforestation. Put students in breakout rooms, in teams, to discuss and write down ten words they think are highly relevant to the topic. Bring everyone back together and display the first few paragraphs of a description of deforestation, for example, the Wikipedia page. Everyone silently scans the text looking for the ten words. After two minutes, stop the clock, compare notes, and see which team had the most. Try again with a different theme.

Here is an example using the theme 'Shopping.' My ten words were:

shop	boutique	supermarket	high street
sale	discount	shopping center	merchandise
open	customer		

Only two of these words were in the Wikipedia extract; shop and customer. I would have done better if I had chosen:

customer	goods	purchase	shopper	online
consumer	money	services	product	retail

Here is a second example using the theme 'Architecture,' and my ten words were:

architect	planning	innovative	materials	size
budget	building	timeframe	design	purpose

The Wikipedia text had four of my words; architect, designing, planning, and building.

- Allow derivatives. For the word retail, allow retailer and retailing. For shop allow shopper and shopping, etc.

Recognising tenses

Category	Listening
Group size	One to about ten, the teacher needs to see everyone via the cameras
Level	Beginner to intermediate
Age	All ages
Materials	Computer camera on
Preparation	None
Great for	Verb tenses

This game helps review tenses or revise two tenses while introducing a new one.

How to play

- When students hear a sentence in the present tense, they indicate the present moment with a suitable gesture, like pointing downwards as if indicating here and now.
- When they hear a sentence in the past tense, everyone points behind their shoulder.
- When they hear a sentence in the future, everyone points forward.

An alternative for kids with energy to burn is to have them stand up, run around their chair, and sit down again. Play with any mixture of tenses. Add extra movements such as clapping for the present continuous, and so on. Ask the class for their suggestions for actions that best represent a given tense and use those.

This game can use many tenses but should not be so complex that students are permanently confused!

Remember and write

Category	Writing
Group size	One to one, any class size, whole-class activity
Level	Beginner to high intermediate
Age	6 to adult
Materials	Pictures of objects
Preparation	None if students prepare for homework 1 minute with words, 10 minutes with pictures
Great for	Vocabulary revision, grammar drill

How to play

Display 12 objects via the screen share. Give the class a limited time to look at and memorize all the items. Then cover them over and allow a couple of minutes for everyone to write down all the objects from memory. For beginners, label the items to help pupils learn and remember the spelling. To practise grammar with this vocabulary revision game, ask the pupils to write a sentence containing each of the words using the target structure or tense.

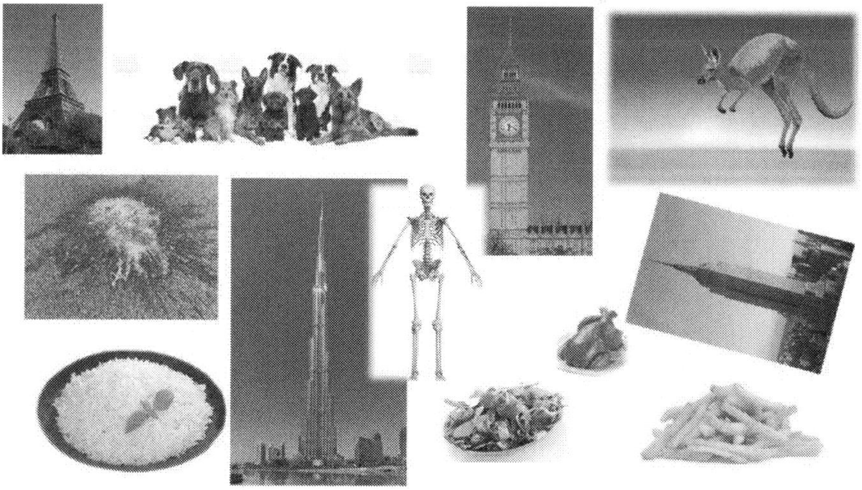

The above example is included in the Appendix with four simple past statements to fill in from memory; I went to Paris,

London, New York, and Dubai. I saw some dogs, a kangaroo, some vomit, and a skeleton. I ate some rice, some chicken, some chips, and a salad.

- Potentially award points for correct items and extra points for the correct spelling.
- If you are not teaching writing, use this game and have pupils draw the objects instead.
- Use vocabulary themes, as in the office example below, and for random words that pupils should know for an upcoming exam.

Round-robin

Category	Speaking
Group size	One to one, any class size
Level	Beginner to intermediate
Age	All ages
Materials	None
Preparation	None
Great for	Speaking fluency, short conversations, small talk, giving advice

Round-robin is good for conversation and small talk. There's no out-of-class preparation, and you can play Round-Robin at any time.

Preparation

The example that follows is for giving advice. Each student writes down or keeps in mind a mild complaint or problem, such as 'I'm cold.' Elicit some possible solutions for the problem, such as 'I'll turn up the heating' or 'close the window.'

Before you start the activity, elicit ways of giving advice and write them in screen-share. Ideas are; you should, why don't you, you ought, if I were you I would, it would be best if, you could try, you had better, and so on. With lower levels, give three options and rehearse a few short conversations chorally. As the activity goes on, gradually remove the written prompts, so students are forced to speak from memory.

How to play

The teacher starts by calling out a student's name, who states his or her problem: 'I'm cold.' The student names someone else who responds to the complaint with simple advice like 'Would you like a jacket?' or 'Shall I close the window.' Having offered advice, this student now states a complaint, names someone else, and so it goes on.

This co-operative game has no winners or losers, so add some peps and encourage fluency by making teams. See how quickly each team completes one turn. Play again and try to beat the time.

It's best to keep this game light rather than get into real problems. Use fictional characters to avoid being personal and offending people. For example, avoid 'I am getting divorced.' Instead, use 'My friend is getting divorced.'

Other topics

Instead of complaints, discuss personal history, which resembles a common type of small talk. Allow students to pretend to be someone else if they prefer; you never know, someone's personal life may be distressing. Of course, they don't have to tell the truth – what matters is to speak correct English. Use Round-robin to drill any question and answer:

Where are you from?

Which is your favourite social media platform?

I'm having a party. How can I make it the best party ever?

How can I persuade my parents to give me some money?

What do you do in your free time?

Scissors paper stone

Category	Speaking
Group size	One to one, any class size in pairs or threes
Level	Beginner to intermediate
Age	6 to adult
Materials	Pictures, students need their camera
Preparation	None
Great for	Vocabulary revision game

How to play

Holding the hand flat symbolizes paper; making a fist symbolizes stone; opening the first two fingers into a V forms scissors.

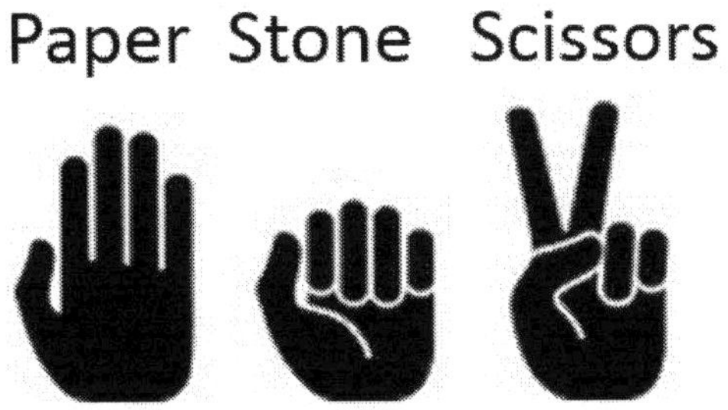

Players make a fist with one hand. On the count of three, players change one fist into either scissors, paper, or stone. The scissors cut the paper, which wraps the stone, which blunts the scissors. In other words, the scissors win over the paper, which defeats over the stone, which prevails over the scissors.

Try this at any time to decide who goes first. Use it for a vocabulary game where each pair has five items as a set of pictures, e.g., a pen, an eraser, a pencil, a ruler, and a book —play scissors paper stone. The winner names any item and, if successful, takes that item as a point. Continue until all five pictures are claimed.

Explain the game, do a demo, check students understand, and put them in pairs in breakout rooms to play with a list of vocabulary pictures.

Sentence playoff

Category	Speaking fluency or writing
Group size	One to one, any class size in teams
Level	Intermediate to advanced
Age	All ages
Materials	None
Preparation	Prepare a few examples for demonstration
Great for	General English

See how many sentences your students invent that all contain a particular word. For example, ‘paint’ would be a good choice because it has more than one function; it can be a verb or a noun. Allow two minutes for all the students – in groups or individually – to write down as many sentences as possible containing the word. Then have a playoff between teams, ping-pong style, and see which team has the most sentences that are grammatically correct. Examples include:

I can paint. Can you paint? I love painting.
He paints every week. I need some paint.
Please buy me some paint.

With advanced students bypass the writing stage and play directly as a speaking game.

- Correcting the sentences during play would ruin the game. Let the activity flow and pick up on a few blunders afterwards, asking students to correct the errors as a group.
- Play several times in a row for best results.

Shopping list memory game

Category	Speaking drill
Group size	One to one, any class size in pairs or small groups
Level	Beginner to intermediate
Age	6 to adult
Materials	Optional pictures
Preparation	None, pictures for beginners
Great for	Vocabulary revision, grammar drill

How to play

Demonstrate how to play, then play individually or put students into breakout rooms to play in groups of 3 or 4. Player 1 names a vocabulary item or makes a sentence about it, as required. Player 2 repeats whatever player 1 said and adds an item to the list. And so it continues, with the list growing longer and longer. For example:

Player 1: In my trolley, I have some milk.

Player 2: In my trolley, I have some milk and some chocolate.

Player 3: In my trolley, I have some milk, some chocolate, and some oranges.

For younger players, use pictures as prompts; for older or intermediate players, rely on memory alone.

Language ideas

This game is adaptable to a multitude of language uses, for example:

There is/there are

In my wardrobe, there are socks, there are shoes, there are shirts, and there is a scarf.

Her name is/his name is

Her name is Samia, his name is Oskar, her name is Hiram, and his name is Paolo.

She's a/he's a

She's a doctor, he's a student, she's a waitress, and he's a train driver.

She/he likes; she/he does not like

She likes coffee, he likes milk, she does not like fish, and he does not like tomatoes.

He plays/she plays

He plays golf, she plays tennis, he plays football, and she plays basketball.

Past tense with ate and drank

Yesterday I drank milk, I ate chocolate, and I ate pizza.

Pronunciation ideas to adapt to the phonemes of your choice

To help my advanced-level French student, who consistently uses a 'z' sound in place of 'th,' we played with objects starting with 'th.' He is competitive, so we used a points system; he lost a life whenever he said the wrong sound. His pronunciation came on leaps and bounds because he had to concentrate on it. There aren't many nouns starting with 'th' in English, and those that do are mostly advanced vocabulary terms. Therefore, I created a word list with picture prompts for more obscure items. I circled each word as it was added to the list. We could see the written words as prompts, but we had to remember the order, and my student had to focus on pronunciation.

On Thursday, I thought I saw a thing, three pigs, thirty cows, three hundred ducks, a thigh, a three-cornered pizza, a thunderstorm, a three-dimensional picture, a theatre, a thick book, a thief, a thistle, a thorn, a thorn bird, a thong, a thread, a threadbare T-shirt, and a thimble.

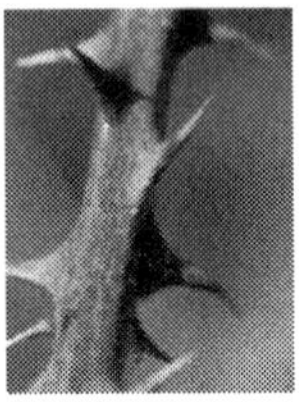

A simpler shopping list for 'th' pronunciation would be; this book, that flower, their house, those bottles, these plates, and so on.

Another way to play would be to start each time with a sentence full of the target sound or phoneme, such as:

The thirsty thief thrust through the thorny thicket with the stolen TV.

The thirsty thief thrust through the thorny thicket with the stolen TV and computer.

Show me

Category	Listening
Group size	One to one, pairwork, whole class option
Level	Beginners
Age	All ages
Materials	Pictures or items to hand Variant where players access the annotation tools
Preparation	None
Great for	Introducing new vocabulary

How to play

This simple game introduces new vocabulary and revises it before a speaking activity. It allows you to observe how pupils are doing, which words they need more work on, and when they are ready for more.

With real items

Ask players to show you an item. For example, say, 'Show me a pen.' Everyone holds up a pen. 'Show me a blue pen' – students hold up a blue pen. Here are other ideas: show me the floor, ceiling, wall, left wall, right wall, a rubber, ruler, hand, leg, foot, skirt, sock, door, a pen in a pencil case, a rubber under a pencil case, and so on.

To get kids moving, have them bring things to the camera. Tell them to find something blue, flat, thin, or round, an item the same size as their hand, something you can't eat, and something you can.

With pictures onscreen

Display vocabulary flashcards or a scene and have pupils circle or tick the picture you name. This activity is appropriate for individual or small group lessons. For larger classes, use it for revision in breakout rooms. Find suitable pictures online by typing things like this into your browser 'busy summer holiday beach scene picture' or 'busy football stadium image.' Have pupils

highlight objects you name in the picture. This collage picture with a travel theme is included in the Appendix.

Silly dialogues

Category	Writing, reading out loud
Group size	One on one, any class size in groups of about 10.
Level	All levels
Age	6 to adult
Materials	None
Preparation	None
Great for	Writing skills, speaking fluency, general language

How to play

The class write a story or dialogue collectively. Here is a well-known example using a 'romance.' Everyone writes chunks of the story as per your instructions. Start the story with everyone writing a girl's name and a description of her. Label that part 'section one.' Each player now writes a boy's (or other sex) name and a description, which becomes section two. Next, the students write about how they met, the first words the boy said to the girl (or vice-versa), how the girl replied to the boy, what happened next, where they went, what other people said, the consequences, what the newspapers said, and what happened in their future. Students must label each section of the story with a number. When everyone has finished, read some of the stories aloud, asking for section one from one student, section two from another, section three from a third, and so on.

In summary, the story and dialogue snippets are as follows:

1. Name and description of a girl
2. Name and description of a boy or partner
3. How they met
4. First words girl said
5. Reply from the other person
6. What happened next
7. Where did they go
8. What other people said

9. What were the consequences
10. What the papers said
11. What happened in the future

Other scenarios

Experiment with a variety of different scenarios for this game. For example:

- Someone came to your door to sell an item. Parts of the story could include what he was selling, what you bought, what the thing is used for, where you put it in the house, how much it cost, what you purchased next, why, and what you did with it.
- A patient goes to the doctor. Parts of the story could include which body part hurt, how the patient was injured, what the doctor says/does/examines, what he or she needs to do to get better, what medicine he or she needs to take, and what will happen next.
- A customer orders food in a restaurant. The story could include what he or she orders, what kind of restaurant it is, who he or she is with, what is wrong when the food arrives, what you say to the waiter, followed by the waiter's reply, and what happens next.
- Two friends meet up to play. The story could include what the first friend said, what the second one replied, where they went, what they did, what went wrong, what the friends say to their parents, how the parents responded, and what happened next.

Silly songs

Category	Writing, reading or singing out loud
Group size	One on one, any class size in groups
Level	All levels
Age	6 to adult
Materials	None
Preparation	Learn the tune of a famous song students know
Great for	Creative writing, speaking fluency, general language

This song activity is fun, challenging, and creative. Students write new lyrics for a familiar tune. Take a well-known movie theme or classic song and put everyday language to it. For example, take

The Beatles 'All You Need is Love.' Students get together in groups and write new words based on describing their day.

Brush, brush, brush, wash, wash, wash, brush, brush, brush, it's easy!

Every day I brush my teeth.
Every day I wash my face.
Every day I put on my clothes, it's easy!
All you need is a sink, da da da da da.
All you need is some soap, da da da da da.
All you need are some clothes, yeah, that is all you need.

Here are simpler words for beginners. Brush brush brush, brush your teeth, etc.

All you need is toothpaste, da, da da da. All you need is toothpaste; toothpaste is all you need.

Alternatively, have students make up another verse or chorus for their own choice of song – if they are willing, they can even sing it to the others. Most adults are self-conscious when it comes to singing in front of others, but they might join in if singing in a group. Those reluctant to sing can always say their lyrics in the rhythm of the song.

1. Work on the song in sections. Complete it in chunks, taking ten minutes of several lessons to add variety.
2. Use the 'Chants' activity from this book to introduce the opening lyrics and have students say them in rhythm. Snapping fingers, tapping, and improvised percussion help stay in time. Achieving fluency usually takes some practise.
3. Listen to the first minute of the original song.
4. Have a keen student find a karaoke video that displays the lyrics as the song plays, including vocals. YouTube has plenty of these for free. Work on talking or singing along.
5. Give students a poem or lyrics from a different song to put to a melody.

- Once kids have mastered their new words, they can happily sing the song for weeks. Teens can be too cool to sing; it depends. Anyone fun-loving who likes singing will enjoy the challenge.

- Choose a song students already know because it will be enough of a challenge fitting new words to the melody without learning the tune.
- Select songs with predictable rhythm. I thought Kool and the Gang's Celebration would be easy, and I knew my student loved it. It turned out to be a nightmare knowing exactly when to come in!
- Don't spend time thinking of alternative lyrics yourself; let your students come up with ideas. It'll help if they work in groups to bounce off each other for inspiration.

Simon says

Category	Listening
Group size	One on one and small groups
Level	Beginners to lower intermediate
Age	All ages
Materials	Students need cameras on
Preparation	None
Great for	Body parts, commands, general vocabulary

How to play

Simon Says can be adapted to all ages, becoming increasingly sophisticated as the players get older or have a greater command of English. In the classic game, the teacher is Simon and gives players instructions they must follow, but only if Simon says so. For example:

- Simon says, touch your nose.

Simon touches his nose, and all players touch theirs.

- Simon says, touch your feet.

Simon touches his feet, and all players touch theirs.

- Touch your head.

Simon touches his head, but players must not touch their head since Simon didn't say so. Any players touching their head lose a life.

- Students can stand further away from their cameras to show more of their body.
- In the classic version, any players who touched their head would be out, but it's better to lose a life instead. The idea is to have everyone playing, not sitting around watching. Alternatively, as soon as three people are out, restart the game with everyone playing again.

Language ideas

Simon Says is the perfect game for body parts, and once your players have the hang of the vocabulary, they can be Simon. The language potential for Simon Says does not stop there. Here are some other examples of actions that Simon can say :

- Raise your left hand
- Touch your nose
- Touch something blue
- Touch an item of clothing
- Jump on the spot
- Run around your chair
- Stand up, sit down
- Look up, look down, look left, look right, look around
- Draw a cross on the bicycle. (Show pictures via screen share and give your pupil use of the annotation tools.)

A complex version of Simon Says

For players with a good command of the language, and once they have mastered Simon Says, complicate the game to keep them on their toes. In this version, Simon says two actions at once. There is no punctuation in the examples below since the teacher should run the instructions together.

- Simon says raise your hand and Simon says touch your leg.
- The players must raise their hand and touch their leg.
- Simon says eat ice-cream and touch your nose.

The players must eat ice cream but not touch their nose because Simon did not say so.

And here is a third even more complicated version – you might need to rehearse being Simon for this one! When Simon says to do something, the players keep doing it until Simon specifically asks them to stop. In the meantime, Simon continues with other requests. For example:

- Simon says touch your head.
- Simon says touch your shoulder and Simon says stick your tongue out.
- Simon says spin around and shout 'Jump!'

At this point, the players should be spinning around with one hand on their head and the other on their shoulder, sticking their tongue out, but they should not shout 'Jump!' as Simon did not say to do so. Simon then continues with:

- Simon says stop touching your head and rub your stomach instead.

Players must stop touching their heads but should not rub their stomachs, as Simon did not say so.

I'm sure you get the picture. This game is such fun. The trick for you, as Simon, is to keep the pace up, linking the commands rapidly, so your players' attention is riveted on listening to your every word!

There is nothing to prevent you from playing until there is a winner. The better you are as Simon, the sooner you will trick everyone into making a mistake and have a winner quickly, before those who are out become restless. To make it easy to see who is still in, those who are out sit down. I have seen this played with 8,000 adults at a seminar, and the game lasted less than 5 minutes before everyone was out!

Simon Says speaking variant

Allow your players to be Simon. There could be several Simons at once. While one Simon is giving a command, the other can be thinking of the next one – this ensures the pace is fast and furious, which it needs to be for this game to be fun.

Simon Says for grammar

Players listen to sentences and respond according to the tense. Define which tenses to act on or ignore, such as acting on the simple past and the present perfect. The teacher says, 'I went to the park. Touch your nose.' Students touch their nose because this sentence is past simple. The teacher says, 'I am eating a cake. Touch your leg.' Students don't move since the tense is neither the simple past nor the present perfect. Use this idea with any grammar. It's a good speaking drill too, but make small groups and give weaker students simpler grammar to work on, or the game will drag since the student won't be able to think up sentences quickly.

Solve it

Category	Speaking drill
Group size	Minimum four students, groups, whole-class activity
Level	Intermediate to advanced
Age	10 to adult
Materials	None
Preparation	None
Great for	Grammar or vocabulary drill

Play in small groups for greater engagement. The aim of the game is to find the link between objects. As students find this, they join in. Open with a statement like, 'I'm going away for the weekend; I'm packing a saucepan and a toothbrush.' Since this sentence will be repeated throughout the game, make sure it is correct and includes grammar relevant to whatever you are studying.

The second player continues with: 'I'm going away for the weekend; I'm packing a saucepan, a toothbrush, and a camera.' Reject this answer because it does not fit the criteria. The following student repeats the sentence so far and adds a different item. Keep rejecting the suggestions until someone says something starting with 'h.' For the item to be accepted, it must begin with the final letter of the last thing on the list, so here, a hat or a hairbrush would do. The game continues until the first three players work out why their answers are being rejected or accepted. When every student has had a turn, add another item, which will provide further clues if no one has guessed the link by this point. Play usually continues until everyone has caught on, but I recommend stopping well before this because it's humiliating to be the last one to be in the know.

Besides making links via letters, use other connections such as all items must be hard; a saucepan would be fine, but not a sleeping bag. Likewise, things could be soft, artificial, natural, alive, smelly, or small enough to fit into your pocket.

Spell and act

Category	Listening
Group size	One to one, class of up to approximately 15
Level	Beginner to high intermediate
Age	6 to 12
Materials	Cameras on
Preparation	None
Great for	Spelling, alphabet, vocabulary

How to play

Spell a word such as 's-a-d,' for players to mime. Say a sentence and spell one word, like, 'I play t-e-n-n-i-s.' Younger players may write down the letters since they may have trouble visualizing the word. Players may spell words for another team.

Spelling game

Category	Spelling
Group size	Pairwork, small groups in breakout rooms, teams
Level	All levels
Age	6 to adult
Materials	Words
Preparation	Write a list of words
Great for	Spelling, vocabulary

In pairs

Give each student a list of ten words. Player one reads the first word to player two, who writes it. Players can either use the annotation tools and share screens or write on paper and hold it up to the camera. Player one checks the spelling, and if correct, player two wins a point. Students go through the list, then swap over.

Collaborative variant

Play as a collaborative game too. Each group is a team competing against other groups. Give each team some pictures. Together the group decide how each word is spelled, and everyone writes it down. Bring everyone back together and have students check their work. Ask the groups to tell you how many words they got right.

Team variant

Students choose words for the other team to spell. The rule is that they must know how to spell them themselves! A follow-up activity is for students to note any misspelled words and learn them for homework. In the next lesson, play again and include all the terms that caused problems. The results will be better, which is encouraging for students.

Spot the Difference

Category	Speaking or writing
Group size	One on one and any class size in pairs or groups
Level	Beginner to intermediate
Age	All ages
Materials	Two similar but not identical pictures
Preparation	Find pictures. The Appendix has two.
Great for	Contrasting present and past tense, general language, and vocabulary

How to play

Prepare two identical pictures and either colour them differently or add some changes to one of them. Show the first picture for a minute, then cover it up and show the second picture. Your pupils spot the differences and possibly make a note of them.

Display a few fill-in-the-blanks-type sentences on the board as a prompt if necessary. For example, draw a picture of a cowboy. Draw a second picture of the same cowboy but with a pink hat, a feather, and some different coloured pointy boots. Write on the board: The cowboy _ _ _ wearing a _ _ _ _ _ _ / _ _ _, but now he _ _ / _ _ _ _ _ _ _ _ a _ _ _ _ _ / _ _ _. The pupils fill in: The cowboy was wearing a black hat, now he is wearing a pink hat.

If you search online for 'spot the difference pictures,' you will find plenty. A couple are included in the Appendix. Another way to obtain two similar pictures could be to use a live webcam, such as a tourist office website https://www.visitlondon.com/things-to-do/sightseeing/london-attraction/webcams-of-london. The webcam of Westminster Bridge is quite good because you can see the colours of cars and people on the bridge. Save the image in the morning and then again another day or at a different time. The background will be the same, but there will be differences in the people, the time of day, and what is happening.

Stop!

Category	Writing and speaking
Group size	One on one and any class size
Level	Beginner to intermediate
Age	8 to adult
Materials	Pen and paper
Preparation	None
Great for	Vocabulary revision, general knowledge

'Stop' is an excellent vocabulary revision game and an enjoyable, challenging game for general knowledge.

How to play

All players draw a chart with five or six columns. Each column has a heading, such as numbers, names, countries, animals, clothes, professions, TV shows, food, fruits, items they would like to have, etc. Use headings for which the players will know plenty of vocabulary. One of the players starts the game by calling out the letters of the alphabet. The next player randomly calls out 'Stop!' The person saying the alphabet stops on that letter. Everyone now writes down an item starting with that letter in each category. The first person to finish says 'Stop!' Everyone stops writing, whether finished or not.

If no one has said 'Stop' after one minute, perhaps because everyone is having difficulty thinking up words beginning with the chosen letter, say 'Stop' yourself. Otherwise, the game will drag. Continue for a few rounds and review the answers, awarding a point for each word written. If someone has something that no one else has, then award double points. Have all players call out their answers so that everyone hears the vocabulary repeatedly. Players tick off their words when they are called. Here is an example of a player's chart:

Letter	**Animals**	**Countries**	**Professions**	**Colours**
B	bee	Belgium	banker	black
R	rabbit	Rwanda	runner	ruby

- This game requires significant vocabulary knowledge, and beginners will have gaps in their charts; this doesn't matter if you move quickly on to a fresh letter, rather than agonizing over finding words when the vocabulary range isn't there. Overcome this limitation by using broader categories such as nouns, verbs, and names rather than countries, clothes, and furniture.
- Choose appropriate categories. Countries will be difficult for children. More challenging topics are educational in the broader sense and so are worth working on with older students. Themes

could be composers, painters, car manufacturers, fashion brands, food, pop bands, office items, household objects, musical instruments.

Summaries and expansions

Category	Writing
Group size	One to one, any class size
Level	Intermediate to advanced
Age	Teens and adults
Materials	Texts
Preparation	Teacher or students find a text
Great for	General English

In this task, students write a summary of a text. The text must be as short as possible while containing all key points. Here is an example.

> It is with great pleasure that I write to you concerning our forthcoming meeting on 15th June. I am thoroughly looking forward to discussing the lesser-spotted miniature penguin with you. I shall be bringing along my collection of over three thousand recordings taken during my honeymoon in Ecuador to identify and classify.

Students compete to write the most concise version of this without leaving out any critical points:

> I am happy to meet on 15th June to discuss Ecuadorian penguins and classify my recordings.

Alternatively, have fun reversing the activity and making a short sentence into one that is as long-winded as possible.

> Yesterday it was sunny, and I had a lovely walk in the park.

Expanded sample:

Earlier this week, yesterday, in fact, given the delightful sunny weather that drew me irresistibly outside, I took the time and the opportunity to stroll about the park enjoying a lovely walk.

Motivate students by having various awards, and hopefully, each group will win something. Awards could be for the shortest, the longest, the most eloquent, the most amusing, the fastest, and the perfectionists (the group that finishes last!).

Telling stories

Category	Writing and speaking
Group size	One on one, any class size
Level	High beginner to advanced
Age	8 to adult
Materials	None
Preparation	None obligatory
Great for fluency	Speaking and writing skills for general language

Storytelling is a skill for life. People of all ages love stories. Interesting people are often good storytellers and hold the attention of their listeners, whatever the topic. Stories are everywhere; even a conversation may contain anecdotes. Being a good storyteller is not just about the tale; intonation, speed, and delivery are just as important. Good speakers captivate their audience, so working on this fluency technique can positively impact your students' whole life.

Have students write a flash story of under 50 words using the guidelines below. Tell students they will be reading their stories to others and to write about things they feel happy to share. To help your students write a good story, give them ideas to incorporate:

Start with a hook A hook is an introductory line to put your story in context so listeners can more easily understand what follows and why you are talking about it.

That reminds me of the scariest thing I ever did.

I have come to suspect that my mother-in-law is a witch. You'll never guess what happened.

A hook is a way to test the water and see if your audience is interested in your topic. If no one seems interested, you might want to tell the short version or not tell it at all.

Know your audience Will your audience be interested in your story? What is in it for them?

Connect with the audience

Humour, transformation, suspense, surprise, and mystery will make your listeners curious to know more. Use informal speech, don't be distant and cold since you want listeners to feel included and part of the story. Use personal details.

Prefer Positivity People prefer to be uplifted. If you want to make everyone gloomy, tell a tragic, desperate story with no hopeful outcome, and where all is nothing but despair.

Keep it short and sweet If it's a funny story, get to the funny stuff asap, don't bog everyone down in uninteresting details, like whether it was a Tuesday or a Wednesday or whether you had whisky or beer at the bar, who cares? Leave out irrelevant information that may be true but is not on point; too many asides, and you will lose your listeners' interest. They will soon realise that you are focusing on the sound of your own voice and not them!

Choose the right time Don't interrupt someone else to tell your story, and never interrupt someone before they get to their punchline; you hate it when people do that to you! Make sure your tale fits the mood. If people are discussing a tragic crisis, they might not be interested in your crazy neighbour's dog at that moment. So, make sure your story has some connection to the conversation.

Describe Use adjectives! Be descriptive. Why was the dog frightening? Was it snarling with fangs showing? Use vivid details related to the story, not extraneous stuff about a vintage car with a gorgeous brunette that drove by while you were standing there frozen-stiff in front of the growling dog. Read what Dale Carnegie said in *The Art of Public Speaking*:

> Your purpose is to make your audience see what you saw, hear what you heard, feel what you felt. Relevant detail, couched in concrete, colourful language, is the best way to recreate the incident as it happened and to picture it for the audience.

Have characters The main character might be you if telling a personal story. Include dialogues to bring your characters to life.

Storytelling is a performance Use body gestures, vary your tone. Use the pace of the story to keep your audience engaged. For example, speak more quickly to show action or excitement during appropriate parts of the story. Pause to add drama to a specific section or to give your audience time to assimilate essential points. Silence at the right moment can have a powerful impact on an audience.

Have a structure

Nearly all stories have an intro, conflict, or event and resolution. When you get to the end, stop! Let someone else be in the limelight.

Let listeners think for themselves

You might want to skip the moralizing part of a story that one tends to get at the end of American films as if the audience were too stupid to figure out the message for themselves. It could be condescending to bang on about the moral if the story made it obvious.

Practise

Put students in pairs to practise telling their stories to each other. Shuffle the pairs and repeat. Do this several times. At the end, bring everyone back together and ask the class if there were any tales they particularly liked. If so, have some class members tell their story to everyone.

Thirty circles

Category	Speaking
Group size	One to one to all class sizes
Level	All levels
Age	All ages
Materials	Pen, paper, sharing results via screen share or cameras
Preparation	None
Great for	Exploring vocabulary, optional flash-fiction speaking or writing activity

Use Bob McKim's **30 Circles** idea to develop creativity. (McKim was a Standford University Researcher.) Students draw 30 circles and then take five minutes to turn those circles into anything they can imagine. Try this with triangles, rectangles, and squares too.

Students compare items drawn. Does anyone have a unique concept? Make it a co-operative or team game, with students working together to develop the most ideas. You can cover a lot of vocabulary like this, and if you want to get more English into it, have students do a **flash-fiction** activity by making up a short story with ten items drawn in their 30 circles.

Have an award for the funniest circle, the best drawn, the coolest, and the most original.

Time bomb

Category	Speaking drill, speaking fluency option
Group size	One to one, groups of up to approximately fifteen
Level	All levels
Age	All ages
Materials	Screen share a list of students' names
Preparation	None
Great for	Vocabulary, grammar drill, Q and A

How to play

Define which vocabulary items or grammar to drill, like, sentences in the simple past. Show a list of all your students' names. Share the screen, and using a highlighter from the annotation tools, move slowly from one first name to the next. The student highlighted says the target sentence as quickly as possible. Do a demo round, so everyone knows what to do.

Set a timer for 30 seconds and start the game. Whoever is speaking when the timer goes off does a forfeit. The forfeit can be answering a question or pretending to be a bunny. See Forfeits for ideas. While the student performs their forfeit, the teacher resets the timer and starts another round right away. Here is an example for the past tense of irregular verbs:

> I saw an old friend at the shop. He saw me. While we were standing in the queue, we noticed that we had both bought the same beer!

- If the timer goes off in the pause between players, the player about to speak does the forfeit. The person who has just finished speaking is cleared.

One to one

Teacher and student alternate lines in a dialogue or ask and answer questions. The one talking, or about to speak when the bomb goes off, does a forfeit. See forfeits for ideas.

Language

For speaking fluency, all students repeat the same sentence. For grammar, have students make up a sentence in the required tense. More advanced students might do a question-and-answer format. Student A asks a question. The next student highlighted answers. The third student asks a different question, and so on.

- Keep the highlighter moving slowly and inexorably towards another name, the highlighter can never stop, or the game will drag.
- You might not want to go round the names in order because that could be too predictable, and students at extremes of the list can switch off. Do be sure, though, to include everyone.
- Moving the highlighter slowly and steadily is better than jumping unpredictably about the list because there may be some delay with students who have a slower connection.
- Set the timer for a different number of seconds each round, never more than 45 seconds, always more than 15 seconds to give students time to start the game.
- This game would work well with tongue twisters. If the player fudges the tongue twister, he or she starts it again.

Tongue Twisters

Category	Speaking
Group size	One to one, any class size, practise in groups
Level	Intermediate to advanced
Age	6 to adult
Materials	None
Preparation	Choose one or more tongue twisters
Great for	Fluency in speaking, pronunciation focus

Tongue twisters are fun and usually make people smile. Difficult to pronounce, especially when say them quickly, they are ideal for working on pronunciation. Try these three tongue-twister activities.

1. Have students practise them, working on specific pronunciation issues, and improving fluency
2. Give out tongue twisters as anagrams for the class to untangle.
3. Dictate the tongue twister in a monotone with no punctuation. Students punctuate it and work out the meaning.

Stick to short phrases for beginners as longer tongue twisters may be demoralisingly tricky. Repeat these three times as fast as you can:

Six sticky skeletons
Red lorry, yellow lorry
Eleven benevolent elephants
Fresh fried fish
Daddy draws doors
Black bug blue bug
She sees cheese
If a dog chews shoes, whose shoes does he choose?
A hissing snake sought to sneak a snack.
I scream, you scream, we all scream for ice cream.
Round and round the rocks the rugged rascal ran.

Here are some classic tongue twisters to enjoy.

Peter Piper picked a peck of pickled peppers, a peck of pickled peppers Peter Piper picked.

She sells seashells on the seashore. The shells she sells are seashells.

I wish to wish the wish you wish to wish, but if you wish the wish the witch wishes, I won't wish the wish you wish to wish.

Betty bought butter but the butter was bitter, so Betty bought better butter to make the bitter butter better.

If a black bug bleeds black blood, what colour blood does a blue bug bleed?

I saw a saw that could out saw any saw I ever saw before.

Any noise annoys an oyster but a noisy noise annoys an oyster more.

How much wood would a woodchuck chuck if a woodchuck could chuck wood?

Fuzzy Wuzzy was a bear. Fuzzy Wuzzy had no hair. Fuzzy Wuzzy wasn't fuzzy, was he?

Advanced tongue twisters

If you must cross a course cross cow across a crowded cow crossing, cross the cross coarse cow across the crowded cow crossing carefully.

Mr. See owned a saw. And Mr. Soar owned a seesaw. Now See's saw sawed Soar's seesaw before Soar saw See, which made Soar sore. Had Soar seen See's saw before See sawed Soar's seesaw; See's saw would not have sawed Soar's seesaw.

I cannot bear to see a bear bear down upon a hare.
When bare of hair he strips the hare, right there I cry, 'Forbear!'

A tree toad loved a she-toad who lived up in a tree. He was a two-toed tree toad but a three-toed toad was she. The two-toed tree toad tried to win the three-toed she-toad's heart, for the two-toed tree toad loved the ground that the three-toed tree toad trod. But the two-toed tree toad tried in vain. He couldn't please her whim. From her tree toad bower with her three-toed power, the she-toad vetoed him.

TPR – Total physical response

Category	Listening, speaking
Group size	One to one, any class size
Level	All levels
Age	All ages but essential for children
Materials	None
Preparation	None
Great for	Concentration, immersion, participation, energy levels

Movement helps learners be immersed, improving energy levels and aiding concentration. Include TPR in every lesson, especially with children, to counter the constraints of being stuck at the computer. Have kids stretch up while saying months of the year, starting low for January and finishing as high as possible for December. Work out meaningful actions for song lyrics and perform to music. Have kids make up actions to poems, chants, and stories. The following games encourage TPR; Hand sign stories, Show me, Simon says, Miming games, Drawing games, Quiz or forfeit, Word flashcards, and Chants. Also, giving students control of the annotation tools involves them more in their learning process.

Triangles talking point

Category	Speaking fluency
Group size	Minimum 3 students, any class size in groups
Level	High beginner to advanced
Age	8 to adult
Materials	None
Preparation	Decide on the three points of each triangle
Great for	Small talk, conversation, comparatives

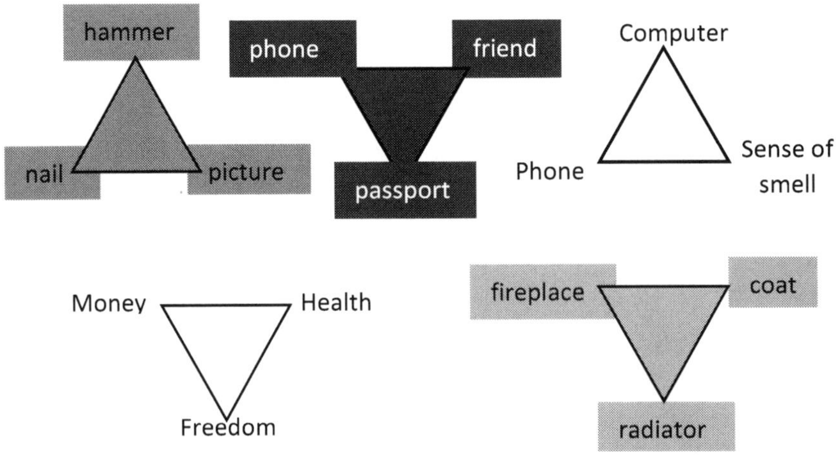

Draw a triangle in screen share and write one object in each corner, for example, lorry, bus, and car. Students debate in threes which is the best, and why? You'll get some interesting answers. Run contests for the most original, the longest, the most convincing, and the funniest responses. Give half the trios a different triangle to debate, so listening to feedback after group work is more varied. Have students make triangles for homework for debate in the next lesson.

Have students make triangles for homework for debate in the next lesson.

True or false vocabulary and grammar drill

Category	Listening
Group size	One to one, any class size
Level	Beginner to lower intermediate
Age	4 to adult
Materials	None, items optional
Preparation	None
Great for	Vocabulary or grammar drill, revision, prepositions, a/an/some, plurals

How to play

A student switches off the camera and puts on some clothes or props, like a hat, tie, or scarf. The class asks in unison, 'What are you wearing?' The person hidden from view replies, 'I'm wearing a red hat.'

Each student decides whether this is true or false, and whoever thinks it is true does thumbs up to the camera; whoever believes it is false keeps both hands out of sight. Now the person switches on the camera to reveal or not a red hat. (If real clothes are not available or are too time-consuming, use pictures.) If a red hat is correct, then all those who did a thumbs up are in, and the rest are out, or vice versa if there was no red hat. The player with the clothes or props switches the camera off again and has ten seconds to make a change. Continue until most people are out.

- Only allow that pupil a few seconds to dress up to ensure that the others do not get restless waiting. The class can count to 30 or say the alphabet while the other pupil puts on their prop. Of course, dressing up is only one idea for this game. It could be played with animals, with the question being 'Do you have any pets?' or hobbies and so on.
- Another way to play is for each class member to hold up a paper marked with a tick or a cross, or 'true' or 'false.' Everyone starts the game standing up. The hidden person chooses whether to wear the red hat, and students vote either true or false. Everyone wrong is eliminated, sits down, and stays seated until only a few students are standing.

Language ideas

Name an item or say a statement, and the class says whether it is true or false. For example, point to a carrot and say 'Potato.' Students respond with 'False.' Hold a pen under a chair and say, 'The pen is under the chair.' The class say, 'True.'

For a more challenging game, test students' knowledge of plurals – point to a picture of a mouse and say 'Mice.' That would be incorrect. Check 'a,' 'an,' and 'some;' if you pointed to bananas, 'some bananas' would be correct. 'An orange' would be right for one orange, but 'some orange' would be incorrect.

For beginners, or to revise vocabulary, show two pictures, for example, a picture of a plane and a truck. A pupil writes one of these words down or draws the object, and says 'plane,' or a sentence such as 'I'm going to Paris by plane.' The class must guess whether this is true or false. If the player wrote plane, it's true; if not, it's false.

If the class is big, there will be no time for everyone to have a go. So, have everyone call out the picture they think is correct. They may also call out the sentence you are drilling. This way, everyone has a chance to say the words. Students award themselves points if they are correct. Some will cheat and pretend they said the right word, but does it matter? After all, we want them to speak English and feel good about it!

For a question drill, show different transport pictures via screen share. One person writes one down or draws the item. The teacher points to the car. Each student, in turn, asks a question and hopes to be the one to guess correctly. For example, the first student asks, 'Do you have a car?' Answer: 'No, I haven't.' The second student asks, 'Do you have a plane?' and so on until the answer is 'Yes, I have.' The student with the word or picture shows it via the camera to prove it's true. With a big class, have everyone ask the question in unison and see how many guesses it takes. Divide the class into teams. Each team tries to guess with fewer questions than the others.

Adapt this game to ask any question. Choose a question form and then pick some vocabulary that goes well with that question form.

Twenty seconds

Category	Speaking
Group size	One to one, any class size in groups
Level	All levels
Age	All ages
Materials	A stopwatch or timer
Preparation	None
Great for	Grammar drill and fluency speaking exercise

Give a student a phrase or sentence to repeat as many times as possible in twenty seconds. Other students listen and track the number of repetitions. One person is on the stopwatch – most people have one on their phone. A phone or hand timer is quicker than fiddling with an online timer, though it can add to the excitement if people can see the time being used up. To keep kids watching in the game, have them call out, 'time's up!' and do a funky action when the timer hits zero.

A more challenging task would be to answer a question with as many different answers as possible in the given time, such as: Where do you live? I live in England. I live in London. I live in France. I live in Germany. I live in Berlin. And so on until the twenty seconds are up.

What's her name? Her name's Sally. Her name's Suzy. Her name's Mercedes. Her name's Tina.
What do you eat for breakfast? I eat eggs. I eat toast. I eat yoghurt. I eat fruit.

Very Large Class Choral Work

Category	Speaking drill
Group size	Large classes
Level	Beginner to lower intermediate
Age	4 to 12
Materials	None
Preparation	None
Great for	Drill Q&A, grammar drill

I observed this technique when I was teaching in Nepal. The teacher would ask, 'What are you wearing?' And the class would call out, 'What are you wearing?' The teacher repeated, 'What are you wearing,' and students called back, 'What are you wearing?' But louder. This went on until the kids were literally yelling at the teacher. It was hilarious. I would say that despite their unheated classrooms with no glass in the windows and their dog-eared textbooks, their level of English was better than their French counterparts. So, even if this is not the most imaginative way of getting students to participate in class, it is still better than the teacher doing all the talking and only a few students answering.

Unlike in Nepal, have students answer your question, not repeat it. So, if you ask, 'Do you play tennis?' Students respond together with either 'Yes I do' or 'No I don't.' If their answer is yes, they stand up or do a thumbs-up. If it is no, they sit or do a thumbs down.

Continue with another question like, 'Do you play football?' Then divide the class, half asking questions in unison while the other half answer. Use picture prompts to reinforce vocabulary.

Vocabulary circle game

Category	Speaking drill
Group size	One to one, any class size in groups of five max in breakout rooms
Level	Beginner to advanced
Age	5 to adult
Materials	Screen share and list of student names
Preparation	None
Great for	New vocabulary drill, new grammar drill, story invention

Easy version

This variant of the 'Shopping list memory game' is a perfect vocabulary or grammar drill. Display the students' names so they can see in which order they are to speak. If you have more than ten students, do a demonstration, then have students play independently in groups of four to five to play in breakout rooms.

Start the game by saying 'One hat.' Each person repeats this until it comes back to you. The first student on the list then adds one item – 'One hat, two gloves' – and this goes around the group until it comes back to that student. The next player on the list adds a third item, and so on. Use with any vocabulary or short phrase. The teacher can add the new words with younger players to keep the game moving forward more fluidly.

Intermediate version

Again, display the students' names so they can see in which order they are to speak. Play as above but give each student a line of a poem. Choose a poem with short sentences so that they are easier to remember. The 'Cat scat' poem in 'Jigsaw listening' would be a fun choice for this activity.

Accuracy is vital in a drill game such as this. And yet, since every student has one correctly written line of the poem, they can play in breakout rooms even without the teacher present. The student with line one is responsible for ensuring the others repeat it correctly each time. And so on for each line of the poem or text.

Advanced version

Play as above with advanced players but have them invent and recite a story. Make students weave a specific tense, grammatical structure, or vocabulary words into their tale. As the phrases are repeated, they should be correct to avoid inadvertently reinforcing errors. Extend the activity by asking players to write the story up from memory afterwards.

Vocabulary memory game

Category	Spelling, speaking
Group size	One to one, any class size in pairs or small groups
Level	Intermediate to advanced
Age	8 to 12
Materials	Display a document in screen share and edit it during the game
Preparation	Edit the word document template in the Appendix
Great for	Learning to spell or revising vocabulary

Vocabulary memory game is a shorter, faster variant of 'Concentration.'

Preparation

Make a chart or use the template provided in the Appendix. A chart should consist of words, or images, hidden by rectangles. Using words will practise spelling, while pictures will be for revising vocabulary. The 'Concentration' game PowerPoints also suitable for this activity.

Young children can play with three to six rectangles, while older learners can cope with many more. The more you have, the harder it is.

How to play

Display your Word document in the screen share.

Click to highlight a coloured box and delete it. Ask students, 'What's this?' They answer. Click 'Undo,' and the box reappears. Repeat for two more boxes. Return to the first box, hover over it, and ask, 'What's this?' Students try to remember what was under the box. Jump about as fast as you can, going back to words students are unsure of more often. Switch to a different game after a few minutes.

What am I?

Category	Speaking fluency
Group size	One to one, any class in pairs or small groups
Level	Intermediate to advanced
Age	10 to adult
Materials	None
Preparation	None
Great for	Questions, short-form answers

How to play

Ask students to think of a product they like or know and write it down. Put them in pairs in breakout rooms to guess what the other student's product is by asking questions. Give a time limit to add some peps and motivation. Students can ask anything that requires a yes or no answer. Alternatively, use famous people, sports players, artists, celebrities, musicians, or cartoon characters.

Encourage those answering the questions to use short-form answers rather than just yes or no. Before the time limit starts, brainstorm relevant questions to narrow down the options gradually. For example:

Is it alive or dead?
Is it big or small?
Is it found inside?
Do you find it in a park?

Can it walk?
Can you eat it?
Can you drink it?
Is it biodegradable?
Is it electronic?
Is it a game?
Is it bigger than a house?
Is it smaller than a mouse?
Is it square, round or triangular?
Is it hard?
Is it made of metal?
Is it natural?
Is it part of a human being?
Can you buy it in a shop?
Is it something you watch?
Is it invisible?
Could I pick it up?
Is it artistic?
Does it make a sound?
Is it in the sky?
Is it below ground?
Is it real?
Is it expensive?
Can it go more than 100 mph?

- It's best if students choose their products and famous people because you are sure they will pick something relevant to their age group. If you suggest Abraham Lincoln, thinking he is super famous, your Serbian teenagers might never have heard of him, but they will know who Nikola Tesla is.
- Put weak students in a small group with more competent English speakers rather than in pairs. They can join in if they think of a question, but at least they won't frustrate their partner by sitting sit tongue-tied for the duration.

What's that sound?

Category	Speaking
Group size	One to one and any class size
Level	Beginner to intermediate
Age	All ages
Materials	An app with sounds or music extracts
Preparation	Download an app with a library of sounds. Teens prepare the music version.
Great for	Vocabulary

For kids and beginners, download an app or find a website with a library of sounds. Make teams, play a sound, and take a guess from each group. If all teams think the sound is a sheep, and it is, that's a point for each one. If ever the sounds are less obvious, but all the groups give the same answer, switch to each team taking a turn at guessing a sound instead.

For teens, have them prepare ten-second extracts of their favourite songs for others to identify. Some students will enjoy doing that, whereas I prefer doing something else with my time! You could also include short snippets from great classics, like the first three notes of Beethoven's fifth symphony or the opening few bars of J.S. Bach's Toccata and Fugue in D Minor.

Which one has gone?

Category	Speaking drill
Group size	One to one, any class size in pairs or small groups
Level	Beginners
Age	All ages
Materials	Flashcards or pre-prepared PowerPoint with vocabulary pictures. The Appendix has an example.
Preparation	None if you have flashcards. Ten minutes for the PowerPoint version.
Great for	Vocabulary drill, Q&A grammar drill

No prep version with flashcards

Display six flashcards to the camera. You could spread these out like playing cards or connect your phone to the camera and film the cards on your desk.

Preparation

Prepare a PowerPoint with vocabulary pictures or words. To make this quick, copy and paste six to eight vocabulary pictures into a PowerPoint and make 20 duplicates of that slide. Leave the first slide intact. Next, delete one picture from the second slide, a different one from the third slide, and so on. See the example in the downloadable Appendix for an example.

How to play

Use screen share and open the PowerPoint in slide share. Students look at the first slide and attempt to memorize all the pictures there. Click through to the second slide and say, 'Which one has gone?' Students try to be the first to identify and name the missing picture.

- With four-year-olds, start with two pictures and gradually add to them. With kids, have everyone answer, with no emphasis on the pupil who answers first.
- Preferably have students play in teams; it's more fun than going it alone.
- If your students can screen share in breakout rooms, give them the PowerPoint and let them play in small groups, with one student as the leader asking the questions.
- If you have teens or adults, it's a killer if you change an item's position, so suddenly the motorbike isn't top left anymore. You can also surprise students by occasionally deleting two images.
- Nine pictures are tricky, even for adults; I would play with six pictures for kids and eight pictures with teens and adults.

Language

Use any question for this game, not just 'Which one has gone?' For example, with food pictures, use a question like 'What did I have for lunch today?' Students can answer with single vocabulary words or put the missing noun into a sentence for a grammar drill. E.g., I had pizza for lunch.

With transport flashcards, we used sentences about travel, which was helpful for little words like 'to,' 'by,' 'on,' and 'the,' as well as the transport vocabulary itself. If the missing transport item was a motorbike, I named a place my student could reach by motorbike, like Bourg Saint Maurice, a nearby town. The student identified the missing item and replied, 'I went to Bourg Saint Maurice by motorbike.' If the plane was missing, I named a foreign country, like Russia, and the student replied, 'I went to Russia by plane.' (The use of the article and countries came up, like 'the Caribbean' compared to 'Greece.') If the bicycle was missing, I said 'the supermarket,' or somewhere my student could realistically reach by bicycle.

Flashcards shown are from my flashcard set; see other resources.

Who said it?

Category	Speaking drill or fluency activity
Group size	Minimum five students, up to all class sizes
Level	Beginner to lower intermediate
Age	All ages
Materials	Students have pen and paper and turn off videos
Preparation	None
Great for	Telling the time, Q & A drill, general English

Telling the time example: Each class member draws a clock and chooses a time to draw on their clock face. A student, says 'It's half past five.' If no one has chosen half past five, the student tries another time until someone has it. Anyone who chose that time calls back, 'It's half past five.' The student identifies who replied by the sound of their voice. If they can't do it, ask the others if anyone knows who it is. Whatever the outcome, it's the mystery person's turn to say the time on their clock now.

Language drill: Use any Q and A drill for the game.

General English: Have students read a text or talk for ten seconds on a topic. Other students guess who is speaking. The teacher sends a private message to the next person who is to talk.

Who wants to be a millionaire? Adaptation

Category	Speaking fluency or drill, optional writing in chat
Group size	One to one to any class size
Level	All levels
Age	All ages
Materials	Screen share and ideally annotation tools
Preparation	Vocab, grammar, or general knowledge questions
Great for	General English for fluency, vocabulary drill, grammar drill, Q&A See also quizzes

How to play

Split the class into two teams. Screen share a document with two columns of five squares each. With smaller groups, add up to ten squares to the columns.

Ask team one any question. Any team member may answer, and if he or she is correct, draw a tick on the first box in the column. That student cannot answer any more questions in this round but can send answers via the chat to teammates – this keeps the bright students involved while helping out the weaker ones. Now ask the team if they want to continue or stop.

If the team elect to continue, the teacher asks another question, and one of the other students on the team answers. If correct, tick the second box; if incorrect, delete the ticks, and students are back at the starting line. Perhaps, if you include more questions, teams can slip to a certain point if they give a wrong answer, rather than losing all the 'money' won up to that point. Once the team has either elected to stop or given an incorrect answer, taking them back down the chart, it is the other team's turn.

Question suggestions

Vocabulary drill Students name picture flashcards.

Grammar drill Ask the same question each time, like 'What's your name?' or 'What colour is your hair?' Each student answers according to his or her hair colour. If you are in a country where everyone has black hair, use something else, like 'What are you wearing?' or 'How do you travel to school?' or 'What do you have for breakfast?' Drill any questions in any tense.

Grammar revision Use varied questions.

General knowledge	Fluency and general English.

- With a large class, keep the questions coming rapidly. Simplify the questions if the game is slow. Ask the team listening to write questions for the other team to answer during the next round. This keeps all students involved and actively participating rather than passively sitting, waiting for a turn.
- If appropriate to your students' level, have them send you question suggestions via the chat during the game.
- As mentioned above, but I think it worth repeating here in the tips, allow students to send messages to each other via their chat to help team members. This makes it a collaborative game, keeps the bright students involved while preventing them from doing all the talking, and saves weaker students from becoming unpopular because they keep losing all the team points!
- Ask less talented students questions early in the game so fewer points are lost if they cannot answer.
- Once students understand the game, they could play in breakout rooms, with the best students in the class asking the questions. You would need to provide questions and answers to the group leader to ensure accuracy. Either that or ask for questions in advance and correct any mistakes.

Why?

Category	Speaking
Level	All levels
Group size	One to one, any class size in groups
Age	All ages
Materials	None although creative pictures are a bonus
Preparation	None
Great for	Conversation, general language, imagination

Thanks to Olga Benedik in Ukraine for sending me this idea, which encourages creative thinking and general language.

This game is played with or without pictures. A student makes a statement such as 'He is hot. Why?' The others invent a plausible answer such as 'He is hot because the sun is shining.'

Pictures are a fun way in which to spark the imagination. For example, using a picture of a man, ask, 'Why is he wearing this shirt in particular?' Students use their creativity to invent something like it was the only clean one he had left!

Have students write questions for others. Artistic pictures can generate creative questions. To find online, type 'creative artistic images.'

Word association and word chain games

Category	Speaking or writing for vocabulary revision
Group size	One to one, any class size in groups of three to five
Level	High beginner to advanced
Age	8 to adult
Materials	None
Preparation	None
Great for	Vocabulary, pronunciation, spelling

One student says a word, such as 'elephant,' and the next student offers a related term, such as grey, leg, or big. Play this one on one, alternating teacher and student. With classes, divide students into teams in breakout rooms. Each group starts by writing down the same word. Groups now have two minutes to make the longest chain. A chain could be:

- words that relate in some way
- finding words that rhyme
- words that start with the same sound
- words that begin with the last letter of the previous word
- difficult - change one letter like coat, coal, foal, foil, soil, sail, nail, bail, ball, fall
- alternating nouns and adjectives that relate, like this:

Tall, house, clean, hospital, sad, funeral, black, tie.

Bring everyone back together, listen to the chains and see which team has the longest. If there are errors in the chain, that team is eliminated.

Word chain around the alphabet

Category	Speaking
Group size	One to one, any class size in groups of three to five
Level	High beginner to advanced
Age	8 to adult
Materials	None
Preparation	None
Great for	Vocabulary revision, general knowledge

This word chain game is a spoken version of 'Stop.'

Taking a theme such as countries, students go through the alphabet: Afghanistan, Belgium, Congo, Denmark, Ethiopia, etc. Play in pairs or small groups in breakout rooms to save students waiting forever between turns.

Another method is to play with one big group, but with students in threes, and any one of the three can answer when it's their turn. This makes the game more fluid and keeps more people actively involved. If a trio take longer than ten seconds to find an answer, they skip a turn, and the word moves on to the next three. Subject areas could include nouns, verbs, adjectives, adverbs, jobs, countries/independent states, cities, car brands, food items, names, famous people, sports, composers, writers, etc.

The game will move faster if you ask students to prepare for it for homework. Demonstrate how the game works, and then give students the theme or themes you will use in the next lesson. General trivia categories go down well, as students feel they are learning on two levels: as well as practising their English, they are improving their general knowledge.

This game can be played as a competition – players are 'out' if they cannot think of a word. Avoid this with individuals; put students into pairs or small groups to compete. This game also works well as a collaboration where each team's goal is to make it round the alphabet. Have two teams racing to complete the task, which is then performed in front of the others. Using the collaborative method also means more repetition as the team tries to make it from a to z.

If playing this with young children, provide them with picture prompts.

Word flashcards

Category	Reading and speaking
Group size	One to one to any class size
Level	Beginner
Age	All ages but excellent for kids
Materials	Word flashcards or picture flashcards.
Preparation	Have word flashcards or show words in screen share
Great for	Vocabulary revision, vocabulary drill game

How to play

Divide the class into teams. Get all students clapping a steady four-beat rhythm:

1. Slap the top of the thighs with both hands at the same time.
2. Clap hands together in front of the chest.
3. Click the left thumb and middle finger.
4. Then click the right thumb and middle finger.

If pupils are too young to click their fingers, give them a different action. Once students have this rhythm going, show a word flashcard during the thigh slap. Students have two beats to read it, and everyone says the word on the last click. Rehearse this a few times. Go slow; you can always speed up once students have mastered it. You can make teams, keep the rhythm going continuously, and have groups one and two alternate saying the words.

If you want to make it a competition, try this: To earn a point, at least half the team should say the word. If only one pupil says it, then no point is awarded. As you discard the used words, make three piles: one pile of points earned by team A, the second pile of points for team B and, the third pile of cards that did not score. This way, it is easy to count the points and revise those that didn't score a point.

Language options are;

- Show words in English that students read
- Show words in the native language that students translate.
- Show pictures that students name in the second language.

If using word cards for spelling, for fun at the end of a game, surprise the class by fishing out a giant or complicated word.

Word photographs

Category	Spelling
Group size	One to one, any class size
Level	All levels
Age	6 to adult
Materials	Words you draw a shape around, onscreen whiteboard
Preparation	None
Great for	Spelling, vocabulary revision

How to play

The essence of this game is to look at word shapes as pictures as well as letters. Here is the technique. Look at a word and take a mental picture of it. Zoom in, focus, and then close your eyes and visualize the word in your head. Now ask yourself what the first letter is, the last and the third, and so on. With some training, this technique will become automatic, and the brain learns to photograph words and hear them as sounds. These exercises help exponentially with spelling.

To play:

1. Show a word for five seconds via the camera or screen share.
2. Let children take a mental photograph.
3. Remove the word and ask, 'What is the third letter?'
4. Let the class call it out and write that letter on the whiteboard, which you have shared. Continue until the entire word is written.

Word stress chant and spell or draw

Category	Speaking and spelling
Group size	Any class size
Level	All levels
Age	All ages, variant without spelling for younger pupils
Materials	Students need access to the whiteboard
Preparation	None
Great for	Word stress, fluency, vocabulary revision, spelling

How to play

Here's a way to work on word stress. The teacher says a word with the correct emphasis. The class chant this in unison correctly ten times, clapping on the strong syllable each time. While this is happening, one student writes the word from memory on the whiteboard before the chanting is up. If you have enough students to make teams, give points where the word is spelled correctly within the timeframe. This game provides lots of speaking time to everyone and also works on spelling.

If your pupils are not learning to write, use the same idea, but have pupils draw the item instead.

Zip zap vocabulary revision

Category	Speaking
Group size	Small groups, large classes split into breakout rooms
Level	Beginner to intermediate
Age	5 to adult
Materials	Picture flashcards and cameras on
Preparation	Have flashcards
Great for	Vocabulary revision, short phrases

How to play

All students must be visible via the camera, and each draws a different vocabulary item. Players show their drawings to the camera and ask the others what they are, in case it is not apparent, which it might not be if a student can't draw! Now everyone can identify the pictures start by calling out one of the words, like this, 'zip zap bananas.' The student with the bananas immediately names another image in the group, e.g., 'zip zap apples.' The player with the apples in turn names another drawing, and so on. The 'zip zap' is cool to say and allows a second's thinking time, making the game more fluent.

Once students know how to play, let them try in breakout rooms for five minutes.

- If you notice the same word being repeated too often, have the student holding that card put it down for a minute. That student could draw a different picture and join back in when ready. Then everyone draws something else and plays again.

Language

Students can call out the vocabulary words or short phrases. So, for the fruit example above, students could drill, 'Zip zap I like bananas, I like apples, I like pears,' and so on. If using weather pictures, drill 'it's raining, it's sunny, it's windy' etc. Any phrases will do but keep them short, so the game is snappy.

Appendix

Please access the printable games that complement this book by filling in the form on the link below or by emailing Shelley Ann Vernon: info@teachingenglishgames.com. You will find blank templates as well as pre-filled examples for immediate use in class.

http://www.teachingenglishgames.com/receive-online

Printable extras are provided for:

A-Day-In-The Life-Teens-Online-Board
A-Day-In-The-Life-Adults-Online-Board
A-Day-In-The-Life-Online-Blank-Template
Adverb-cards
Alphabet-War-lower-case
Alphabet-War-upper-case
Battleships-Grid_Blank
Battleships-Grid_High-Beginner
Battleships-Grid-Low-Beginner
Bingo card template
Board-game-pirate-theme
Concentration-Pronunciation
Concentration-Transport
Connect-Four-Alphabet
Connect-Four-Blank
Hangman-Snowman
Jigsaw listening dialogue
Jigsaw-reading-Find-the-odd-one-out
Mastermind-Example
Various picture memory challenge options
Remember-and-Write-simple-past
Spot the difference options for kids
Vocabulary-memory-game-template
Which-one-has-gone-Transport

Please email me for help using any of the activities in this book or if you are stuck for ideas. Shelley Ann Vernon, at info@teachingenglishgames.com If you appreciate this book, I would be so grateful for a 5* review, wherever you bought it. I am always here to help and am looking forward to hearing from you.

Other Resources

Other books and resources by Shelley Ann Vernon include:

Ideal for teaching children online

1. **Song movies**

https://www.teachingenglishgames.com/teaching-english-songs-12-3

2. **Stories in MP4 with audio by native speakers.**

Forty stories in total. 1-10, 11-20, Special Days, About Me and Daily Life.

https://www.teachingenglishgames.com/learn-english-with-movies

3. **Worksheets and Funsheets to go with the stories**

Ideal for teaching in the classroom

Plays and skits for children

- Download teachingenglishgames.com/eslplays.htm
- Paperback http://getbook.at/SkitsForChildren

Skits for teens

- Download teachingenglishgames.com/ESL-plays-and-skits-for-teens
- Paperback http://getbook.at/SkitsForTeens

Story Kits for preschool and primary school with:

- Lesson plans with games
- Flashcards
- PowerPoints
- Worksheets and funsheets
- Songs

Games books for preschool, primary school, teens and adults and one to one teaching in the classroom.

Email Shelley for information or visit
www.teachingenglishgames.com or
https://www.amazon.com/Shelley-Ann-Vernon/e/B00LZT28DW

About the Author

Following her BA degree in languages at Durham University, England, in 1989, Shelley Vernon took a TEFL qualification and became a teacher. She taught in language schools in the UK and privately around the world for several years.

Having been largely bored herself while in school, Shelley was determined not to put her own students through the same desperate clock-watching. Hence she always strove to prepare fun, stimulating lessons that pupils would enjoy and remember. She taught using various methods, including the driest textbooks imaginable, which called for creativity to make lessons more interesting. However, it was only when she started to teach children, including pre-schoolers at Montessori, that she really discovered the joy of teaching through games.

She has shared her ideas and adaptations with tens of thousands of teachers around the world, bringing enthusiasm, a love of learning, and great results into the classroom. Shelley's approach concentrates on enhancing listening and speaking skills through language games which involve repetition and fluency activities with genuine communicative value rather than artificial conversation.

She has created games books for all ages, a curriculum of illustrated stories, three albums of songs, plays and skits, and a games book for teaching one to one.

In addition to her degree in foreign languages, Shelley holds a university degree in music (2000) from Canterbury Christchurch College. She loves classical music, dogs, and horses and enjoys keeping fit with sport, yoga and, in brief moments of keenness, agonizing fitness DVDs. She also writes songs and has three preschool songs CDs. She occasionally speaks at conferences such as IATEFL Cardiff 2009, YALS Belgrade 2011, UCN, Hjorring, Denmark 2014, Barcelona 'Exams Catalunya' 2015.

Shelley Ann Vernon's Author Central Page:
https://www.amazon.com/Shelley-Ann-Vernon/e/B00LZT28DW
See also KOBO, libraries and bookshops.

Printed in Great Britain
by Amazon

13232953R00167